Living The American Dream?

(Press button 2 to continue in English)

A book by
Nick Robson

ISBN 13: 978-0-615-17859-2

Limited First Edition
(December 2007)

This book is currently available on eBay
by searching under the following User IDs:

living*the*american*dream
(www.ebay.com)

living-the-american-dream
(www.ebay.co.uk)

or by mail order from:
www.livingtheamericandream.co.uk
www.amazon.com

Publisher - Nick Robson

Printed in the United States by Morris Publishing
3212 East Highway 30
Kearney, NE 68847
1-800-650-7888

'Living The American Dream?' is dedicated to the three wonderful girls in my life, Jayne, Lucy and Harriet. Without their encouragement, patience and endless love, this book would never have been completed.

Special thanks goes to the following for their advice, information, anecdotes, support and kindness:

Candice Beckham
Ian Camplin
Christine Clarke
George Crimarco
Diane Croll
Craig & Pam Dallas
Robert & Lori Desruisseaux
Mark Emberton
Kelly Flowers
Adam & Jennifer Kurtin
Steve & Julianne McGovern
Eilis McKay
Gene Nitti
Gabe Sanders
Gordon Smith
Lynn Stellman
Patrick Stracuzzi
Mark Thaxton
Dave Trott
Chris Twohey

I would also like to thank all the staff at Eagle Marsh Golf Club, Martin County Golf Club and The Saints Golf Club, many of whom indirectly assisted in the production of this book.

Cover design and internal layout by Nick Robson
'Lucy's Cats' by Lucy Robson
Photograph of 'Waving American Flag' by Philip Coblentz
(courtesy of Alamy Ltd. UK)
All other photography by Nick Robson

iii

Chapter Headings

Chapter 1

Introduction - Greener Grass

There is a common misconception that the grass is greener on the other side but in reality, the sad truth remains that it rarely is. It may taste a little creamier at the top of the bottle, but in the end it's the same milk, just a different cow.

Whenever we discover somewhere new or different, how many times do we ask ourselves what it might be like to live in our newly found and seemingly perfect oasis? I'm guessing it's a feeling that many of us have had at one time or another during the course of our travels around the world. Of course, moving to a new country is enormously different from trying a new holiday destination and like many others, I vividly remember the meticulous examination of new and exotic hotspots each time my wife and I grabbed feverishly at the travel brochures when Christmas was finally over in England. However, the rekindling of memories from a cherished fortnight may not be enough to conquer the reality of actually living a foreign lifestyle on a permanent basis. It's a huge decision to make and a potentially fruitless journey if we don't clearly establish what we're searching for and grasp the seriousness of the journey on which we're about to embark.

During my first visit to the United States, I was so entranced by everything I discovered there, that I immediately began to ponder the idea of emigrating. But visions of living a new life in a new world are often sanctified and sanitised by the temporary abandonment of our normal daily reality when taking a two week vacation. So although I instantly found a passion for all things American on my first trip across the Atlantic, I slowly realised that the reality of living in the USA would be somewhat different to the relaxed and carefree existence of a fortnight's holiday.

Therefore, this book has been written in an attempt to identify the differences between living in the USA and living in the UK and the difficulties faced by Britons who harbour a desire to live in America. I should confess now that although some aspects of America disturb and worry me, throughout my time living here I can honestly report that I have had the warmest, most welcoming and hospitable treatment that I could ever have wished for and should I ever return to the UK, I will always look back on my time in America with complete and utter affection. It is important to say this, as my aim in the production of this book, is not to disrespect, belittle or denigrate, merely to emphasise the differences between two countries that have long been and shall always remain allies, partners and actually, pretty good friends.

A number of people have asked me about the titling and sub-titling of this book. The main title, 'Living The American Dream?' is not a statement of course, but in fact a questionable statement and the subtitle is just my humble attempt at humour based on the bilingual message that greets you when calling any 1-800 number in corporate America. Given that English is the current primary language in the US, there is a degree of speculation amongst a number of educated commentators, that Spanish could become the main language by around 2020 and English relegated to a secondary form of communication. Whether there's any real truth in this theory is currently a moot point but I think it's worth drawing attention to the very real possibility that this may develop at some point down the line.

When writing anything that is a general or generic view of a subject, it is impossible to go into specifics, particularly when that particular subject is so immense. So although there are fifty states in the USA, all of them so incredibly different to each other, many of the examples and anecdotes in this book will more likely have been taken from California, Florida, New York or Texas. According to demographic and population records, these states would appear to be the most popular destinations for British immigrants, and seemingly in that order of preference. Chicago and Philadelphia have also seen historically high British settlement but somewhat less so in recent decades.

One of the most heartening things I've discovered since I first came to the USA is that Americans in general, are incredibly complimentary about Great Britain. The fondness that they display towards our people and country is utterly genuine. They have an absolute passion for British history and culture and often seem to ignore their own extraordinary background, in fact sometimes almost dismissively and apologetically. I will never understand this but conversely, I suppose I don't currently view my own country with the same wondrous feelings that Americans harbour towards the British Isles. Every time I had previously visited the USA, I found it more difficult to take in the enormity and intricacies of this incredible country and even now, the fact that this pioneering race did so much, so quickly and with relatively so few, still baffles me. From the Great Lakes to The Hoover Dam, from the Mississippi Delta to a small piece of granite called Manhattan, this country is more magical than even Disneyland could dream. Whatever is felt by others about Americans, the fact remains that I will always be more in awe of them than they will ever be of me.

So why did I write this book? Well, simply put, when I first started to investigate the possibility of living in the United States, I was unable to find an all-encompassing and published guide that illustrated the many cultural, social, legal and financial hurdles facing those British citizens who harboured a secret desire to live in America. And there certainly wasn't one available that was written in layman's terms or one that was easy to understand and to which I could make quick reference. Of course, there are countless websites that will answer individual questions on specific issues but even with today's broadband internet speeds, the task of finding all of the answers takes patience, time and devotion to each question. As I became more and more aware of the significant proportion of British migrants independently seeking a new life in the USA, and also of the increasing numbers of employees of Anglo-American businesses despatched there to work, I soon realised that a book of this type might prove immensely useful to that particular group of émigrés and may even provide pleasant fodder for a few others.

Although this book was originally written to target a primarily British audience, it was also hoped that it might provide a moderate degree of interest for Americans too. (The book is written in the UK version of the English language so for American readers, there may be some confusion on certain spellings. This will be covered in a later chapter where the UK/USA spelling anomalies are further examined and hopefully explained) The first half dozen or so chapters in this book deal primarily with the logistical hurdles that need to be overcome in the process of trying to move to America and also with the inherent problems that need to be addressed once there. The rest of the book is hopefully more light-hearted with the focus on some of the everyday differences between the English and the American way of life. But as with anything that is the product of one man's mind or that which is merely an individual comment or point of view, there are many who will read this small book of observations and radically disagree with the content. However, I didn't set out to write the book in such a politically correct manner that I might avoid all possible criticism, so if any offence is caused then it should be stated that none was ever intended. There may also be minor factual errors or omissions but this is equally unintentional, merely the way I have perceived the data or understood the situation. For this, I apologise at the outset and ask that any negative issues be taken with a pinch of salt, the original desire to shine a small light on the differences between two countries and never, ever with malice aforethought. To paraphrase Abraham Lincoln, you can't please all of the people, all of the time. Not usually, anyway.

That said, it would be my hope that this book is a mixture of the truly remarkable, the unique and the original and the lighter and darker sides of all that would be American. It is written to entertain and to provoke thought but never with prejudicial intent. It is an irreverent but hopefully not irrelevant insight into the American way of life. If there is any reason to suggest that the USA has more internal problems than any other First World country, it is more to do with the speed that this extraordinary country has emerged as a leading world power than with anything else. Other countries, particularly some of the Western European nations, have had thousands of years to work things out and not just a few hundred.

My first memory that the USA even existed was on July 20th, 1969 when the US spaceship, Apollo 11, finally landed on the moon and Neil Armstrong became the first man to step foot on a terrain that wasn't Earth. I was eight years old at that time and as I watched this moment in history, I was mesmerised by the grainy black and white pictures that flickered on our small television set. I wasn't sure then if what I was seeing was real, and in many ways I found it hard to absorb the enormity of what was being accomplished. You have to remember that in 1969, the microwave oven hadn't yet been invented so the Apollo mission was seen as something truly magical. Notwithstanding the conspiracy theories currently littering the internet, which continually question the truth on whether the moon-landing actually happened and that perhaps it was just a NASA hoax to maintain government funding for future space exploration, nothing will alter the fact that for me at least, this was a life changing moment.

It is easy to understand therefore, that the very notion of going to America was for many Britons at that time, as likely as travelling in a rocket-ship bound for the moon. As a family and as a nation, we were already dumbstruck at the ability to fly from London to Malaga on a Comet or DC9, to take an annual two-week vacation on the beaches of Spain, so anything farther than that was just a laughable thought, still not even a distant dream. It wasn't until Freddie Laker began his groundbreaking, cut-price transatlantic routes in 1977, that the ordinary British working man could realistically start to think about journeying to and exploring the USA. Although to be fair, even Freddie's 'bargain' prices were out of reach of most of the working-class population in Britain.

But until my late twenties, and despite my own pre-teenage worship of US television programmes, I'd previously had little interest in exploring the USA and it was only a business related trip that saw me purchasing a ticket for my first transatlantic flight. I'd long forgotten my first childhood memories of America, transmitted to me via my parents' monochrome television set. But when I finally landed for the first time in the USA, courtesy of the poisonous smoking cabins still maintained by the airlines of the late 1980s, a love affair began and my mind was forever changed when I first discovered this vast and intoxicating, brave new world.

Chapter 2

The Emigration Process

As soon as I began writing this chapter, I realised that I may have been making a grave error of judgement by putting the dullest section right at the start of the book and in doing so, I might be testing the boredom threshold of the reader. It is however, an important chapter and one that cannot be excluded so a little patience is required over the next few pages. I could write a whole book on this subject alone but in the absence of space, time and patience, I will keep this section brief and concentrate on the main points and on the obstacles that will be placed before the American Dream seeker. As a general rule, most of the problems outlined in this book are aimed at those people who decide to come to the USA on an independent basis without the soft landing afforded to new immigrants who move here on a company-sponsored relocation.

Since 9/11, the date-named event marked by the abominable terrorist destruction of the World Trade Centre in New York, the original Immigration & Naturalization Service (INS) has since been renamed and restructured to form The United States Citizen & Immigration Service (USCIS) which is now backed up by the oddly and ominously titled Department Of Homeland Security, both of which are extremely powerful government agencies. Relocating to the United States was always a reasonably difficult process, but it's now been transformed into something which is daunting at best and near impossible at worst.

If you thought emigration to the USA was problematic prior to the events of 9/11, it is fair to say that it is now almost impossible, particularly if you are English. I say English and not British because the likelihood of successful immigration if you are Irish, or even Scottish or Welsh is much more weighted in your favour than if you are English by birthright. Much of this is due to the fact that in the pre-9/11 era, the transfer from the UK to the USA was reasonably painless and more English people took up that opportunity than their counterparts in the rest of the British Isles. Therefore, a stricter quota limitation had already been applied to England before the 11th September in 2001 but soon after, the rules became far more rigid and complex.

The interesting thing for me is the reaction from most Americans when you inform them that England is so far down the pecking order for immigration approval to the USA. The stock response is "But surely we're allies and we have a long-standing friendship between our two countries..." As a rule, they are shocked to think that the English languish somewhere between India and South Korea in desirability as new immigrants to America. It is probably worth stating at this point, that although job associated visas to the USA are reasonably easy to get, provided that your company sponsors you, Green Cards for anyone who just wants to try the American way of life, are 'rare as hens teeth'. To better illustrate this, it should be noted that the number of Green Cards awarded for this pursuit is in the low hundreds and not in the thousands. The Green Card isn't green by the way, it's more a creamy tan colour and no mention of the word 'green' appears anywhere on it. Its actual name is Permanent Resident Card.

It is crucially important at this juncture, to make absolutely clear how vital it is to have a Green Card in order to permanently live full-time in the USA. You cannot live in the USA without one. While the USA Visa Waiver Program entitles you to vacation in the USA for up to three months with the simple completion of a form during your flight, it does not entitle you to set up home here. Additionally, the B-2 visa, which involves a visit to the US

Embassy in London, allows a pleasure-only stay of up to six months in America. However, when the time allowance has expired for either of these two visas, whether it's for three or six months, you are required to return to your home country. To live in the USA, you must be in possession of a Green Card and the process of attaining resident status is limited to a very small number of English citizens. In truth, your chance of success is probably so slim, it actually probably isn't worth trying unless you truly believe you have a uniquely valid case. But without wishing to dampen anyone's spirits, US immigration is possible if you have time, money, ambition and stamina as well as the necessary credentials for the application.

In reality, there are only four generally accepted methods of immigration to the USA although for the average English citizen, none of these avenues will likely prove viable. I have listed a fifth method here which may provide a better opportunity and this is more fully explained later in the current chapter. Let me begin by stating the most popular and legitimate avenues of relocation so that we may fully understand the huge problems facing any would-be British immigrant coming to the US:

1. Immigration via an internal transfer within a company that has a US base.

2. Immigration using the link of existing and immediate American relatives currently living in the USA.

3. Permanent/temporary residency based on business investment (requires a high degree of risk on capital).

4. Permanent residency via the Diversity Immigrant Visa Program. (also known as the Green Card Lottery)

5. Immigration as a 'Person of extraordinary ability in their field' (available to an applicant who is one of the small percentage of people who have risen to the very top of their field in the sciences, arts, or business).

So, what are the problems that you may encounter with any of these routes?

With a company relocation, the main benefit is that in most cases, the company itself will handle the entire process. This would include filing the relevant forms and petitions, assigning a law firm to handle all the tricky questions, finding suitable housing in the US, locating schools for children, arranging lines of credit and mortgages with banks and credit card companies, retrieving visas, permanent resident cards, social security numbers, driver's licences and so on. The downside in this scenario is that you are only an accepted resident in the USA whilst you are working for that company and as soon as you leave or are asked to leave the firm, you will quickly find yourself persona-non-grata as far as future residency is concerned unless you can find alternative US-based employment with similar sponsorship. From the three sad anecdotes I've heard so far, I would hazard that this is not a particularly comfortable or enviable position.

In the second example, residency through birthright will probably only apply to a relatively small group and it should be noted that the basis of this claim is extremely limited. Parental US nationality is pretty much the only thing that will be accepted much less the thin notion of hope that a paternal or maternal American-born grandparent might suffice. Of course it is sometimes accepted but don't put your house on it.

The third route, via business investment is feasible but risky. The visa is called the Treaty Investor Visa or E2 Visa. (There is an E1 version which requires an even greater financial investment) The E2 Visa allows the owner or developer of a new enterprise from a treaty country to take temporary US residency, provided 'he or she has at least 50% ownership in a substantial US business which is creating local employment and wealth'. This temporary residency may lead to Green Card status later. Generally speaking though, expect to make an investment of a sum in excess of $300,000. There is also a requirement that the business employs at least four local residents to fulfil the application and of course, there is no guarantee against the company failing. It's up to you to make it work in order to maintain resident status.

The Diversity Visa, or Green Card Lottery as it is more commonly referred, is just that, a lottery. Effectively, hundreds of thousands of applicants worldwide, are thrown into a lucky dip from which, around 50,000 Green Cards are available each year with a limit of some 3,800 annually awarded to any one nation. The successful applicants are drawn once a year from a random selection of people from countries with low rates of immigration to the USA. You would be forgiven for thinking that this might be a reasonable opportunity to gain residency. However, British applicants, along with the citizens of China, India, Russia and South Korea, aren't eligible to enter the Diversity Immigrant Visa Program.

Unfortunately, England has a historically high immigration rate to America, so now the UK (except Northern Ireland) is excluded from the qualifying list of eligible nations. I'm reasonably certain that many readers of this book will find this somewhat surprising and ultimately, depressing. I'm also given to understand that if you are from Northern Ireland, Iraq, Iran, Afghanistan or North Korea, then you are primarily eligible for the Green card Lottery and therefore theoretically deemed to be a suitable applicant.

I suppose I was initially a little shocked at the UK's exclusion in the Green Card Lottery but when I stopped to mull it over, I began to understand. Think about it. You have a large middle-class section of society in the USA, mostly college educated, many wanting to be doctors or lawyers (The USA has 43% of the world's lawyers) and a dwindling manual labour workforce, not helped by the fact that most kids want to spend their working lives sitting in front of a computer. Essentially, you have a nation that moves less, eats more, gets fatter and tries to remedy this life-threatening obesity with surgery. And all this time, the surgeons are scared to death of being sued by the lawyers who had probably been their room-mates at college. Meanwhile, try and get someone to put a new roof on your house after a hurricane in Florida or a tornado in the Mid-West or maybe find a contractor to rebuild your valley-descending home in California after the mudslides and earthquakes and the annual forest fire damage. Slim pickings if you want a home grown American company. In fact, try getting your lawns cut by someone who speaks English anywhere in the lower 48 states or even a restaurant meal in the whole of Texas that hasn't been cooked by someone from Mexico, Cuba, Guatemala or Costa Rica. It's difficult.

I'm not saying that any of the above is wrong, just that it's now a fact of American life that the core of the American manual labour market is now a different nationality to the one that originally built this country. The USA actually needs a healthy, strong, less educated, desperate-for-money workforce to shore up the whole labour market. It just doesn't need further additions of educated and literate immigrants from the UK so the general negativity towards our country as far as immigration goes, is suddenly understandable and ultimately I suppose, forgivable. It also comes as no surprise that many officials in the US government are currently so keen to hand over Green Cards to the 30 million or so illegal Mexican and South American immigrants who are already living and working in the USA.

In my own case, I was directed by my US attorney to the fifth method of gaining Green Card resident status. A small number of applications for residency are accepted on the basis of "outstanding achievements in the arts, sciences or business" and fortunately, I was able to fulfil the necessary criteria for this category. The method is also more usually described as 'a foreigner with extraordinary ability'.

The definition of a 'foreigner with extraordinary ability' for immigration purposes, means a level of expertise is required indicating that the individual is one who has risen to the very top in their field of endeavour. In order to demonstrate to the USCIS that you qualify for such a category and that your achievements have been recognized in your field of expertise, you must provide evidence of a one-time achievement (that is, a major and internationally recognized award), or at least three of the following:

"Proof of nationally or internationally recognized prizes or awards for excellence in your field."

"Proof of membership to associations in your field, which require outstanding achievements of their members, as judged by recognized national or international experts in that arena."

"Any article that has been written about you and/or your work that has been published in trade press or national media."

"Participation as a judge in your field having presided over and judged your peers' or others work in the same or associated area of expertise."

"Proof that your position and your decisions in your field of expertise have had a positive effect in that arena."

"Proof that you have written articles that concern your field of expertise and that these have been published in trade or national press."

"Proof that you have maintained a key role in your company and been critical to decisions made within that role."

"Proof that your remuneration and salary is at a high and senior level in recognition for the role that you fulfil within that business."

Of course, even after having met the necessary criteria of all of the above, there are still many more hoops to go through before a Green Card might finally be awarded. I've always found it ironic that the permanent residency my own pets now enjoy, was altogether more easily achieved. They had a check-up at the veterinary surgery in England, hopped on a plane and I collected them from the airport in the US. No interview, no hurdles, no official forms to speak of, and all achieved without a hugely significant impact on finances.

However, I digress. Once you have gathered up all the required evidence and associated paperwork and the Permanent Resident application has eventually been filed, expect to wait for at least 18 months to two years before being allocated an interview appointment at the US Embassy in London. From experience, I would say that this would be a hopeful time-frame as others who have been less fortunate, have waited many years for an interview. Prior to the interview, your application will be examined by a case handler in the USCIS. Without doubt, evidence of income, net worth and proof of self-sufficiency will be required prior to an interview being granted.

Before attending the US Embassy for the interview, it is also a stipulation that all applicants submit to a full medical screening at one of the UK Nuffield Hospitals. (As well as checking that your heart and lungs are fully functioning, you'll also be screened for obesity and for any contracted venereal diseases) For us, this meant leaving London for an overnight stay in the delightful city of Birmingham in order to be on time for our 9am appointments. This is a private hospital and due to the fact that the three-hour visit here was costing us approximately £1000 in fees, we were made to feel most welcome and although the medical itself is pretty invasive, particularly for my wife and daughters, it was a reasonably smooth and trouble-free experience. The results of all the tests and examinations along with a set of chest x-rays are then sent on to the US Embassy at Grosvenor Square in London.

Finally, you will be given a date for an interview at the Embassy and at the appointed time, you join a queue of similarly optimistic applicants in Grosvenor Square who have oddly identical appointment times and you wait patiently to pass through security into the assembly hall of the visa department. Hours will pass until you finally see your ticket number pop up on a giant TV screen urging you to go immediately to a counter window to validate your documents. In my case, I struggled in earnest to understand the Chinese lady who was yelling at me from behind the Plexiglass screen in a dialect of English I'd not heard before, informing me that I didn't have all of my documents in order! Having vilified me for several minutes, (yes, I was a British Citizen in my own country being yelled at by what seemed to me, a recently imported student of the Mao legacy) I was sent back, suitably humiliated, to the vast and noisy assembly hall to wait for an interview with what would be, the final arbiter of whether I was fit enough to live in the United States of America.

I must confess that after the initial sub-English interrogation, I was more than a little apprehensive that the impending interview would fare any better. As it was, a most charming member of the Embassy, a delightful American lady, guided us swiftly through the process and together with my wife and daughters, she promptly welcomed us as the latest newly approved residents of the USA.

Of course, at this juncture, you are not actually in receipt of a Green Card or a Social Security Number. The Embassy will then send a package of documents via a secure Embassy courier to your home in the UK. You are forbidden to open these envelopes and just instructed to hand them over to an immigration official at the US airport of destination. This must be done within the given timeframe (from memory, within six months) and then a couple of hours spent in an immigration room will precede the final rubber-stamping of documents and the addition of a one-year visa to your passport. In my case, the requisite paperwork was finalised by a quite delightful immigration officer by the name of José Manuel Fernandez-Gonzalez. Being processed by a man of Hispanic origin did feel a little odd, given the fact that the USA was for some time under British rule as a result of the

Treaty of Paris back in 1763. However, I digress. Mr. Fernandez-Gonzalez did a swift and excellent job and I gratefully received Green Cards and SSNs approximately two months later.

Emigration to the USA is not quick, easy or cheap. You can swiftly move from the position of having an awe-inspired love and passion for a country that is so vast and with almost unlimited boundaries to a complete and utter disdain for that same country but for completely different reasons. I vaguely remember my American lawyer joking with me that it would be far easier, cheaper and quicker to don a sombrero and walk across the Rio Grande in Mexico. He was jesting of course, but I slowly began to sympathise with this sentiment.

In my own experience, the whole procedure took around five years from initial enquiry to the point of actually moving to and living in the United States and I am told that on average, this was a pretty short period of time. It required an enormous effort and vast amounts of research and form-filling on my part and probably cost around £20,000 in fees of one kind or another once the legal costs were added in. It isn't a recommended journey for the impatient, the naïve or for anyone who is marginally strapped for cash and I would more likely confess now that if I had truly known what pitfalls awaited me, I would never have bothered in the first place. Of course, in my case I was doing all the work myself as I wasn't moving to America on a company relocation. Without doubt, it is a far simpler and less harrowing process for those who have a team of company specialists acting on their behalf. However, notwithstanding any of the hurdles mentioned so far, nothing should deter anyone in the UK who has the unbridled desire or just the mere idle notion lurking in the back of their mind of what it might be like to do this, to live The American Dream.

Chapter 3

Financial Pitfalls Facing New Immigrants

One of the more ego-bursting scenarios that face new British immigrants is the fact that they will most probably have arrived from the United Kingdom with a superior credit rating, capable of commanding tens of thousands of pounds of available credit and the easy procurement of a mortgage with just a couple of signatures. Sadly, whatever financial history you may have had in the UK, it is now irrelevant and consigned to history as your credit rating will be set firmly back at zero in the USA. In most cases, a credit history is sought by any potential lender using one or more credit agencies, the most common being the Experian credit checking bureau. Experian is a British company listed on the London Stock Exchange, having previously de-merged from another UK business GUS (Great Universal Stores), the company that spawned the likes of Argos and Homebase. To be brutally frank, your credit rating will begin at a lower level than that of a college student struggling with copious amounts of college fee debt and for many British people who have become accustomed to being treated as high net worth individuals, the effect of this new reality can be depressing at best and at worst make them want to give up on the American life altogether and go home.

From experience, it comes as no great surprise that the USA is strangling itself with credit card debt. It is also no real shock that

America's ratio of debt to population could be viewed as being little better than that of most Third World countries. The banks and credit associations happily give out endless credit lines to individuals who have absolutely no chance of ever paying back the debt and at the same time, the credit institutions continue to ignore anyone who has any genuine creditworthiness. It is not dissimilar to the British banks of the late 1980s who had lent vast sums to dozens of impoverished African nations, knowing that there was no real chance of repayment but continued to carry the loans on their books as assets with large interest sums attached. The sub-prime lending market in the USA is quite frankly, a disgrace and the government should have taken action years ago to prevent the potential financial chaos that is bound to ensue. It would appear that the basis of all credit decisions is made solely on an Experian computer report and with absolutely no respect or consideration to the human individual. In the main, this is completely understandable given the size of the US population as there simply isn't the opportunity, manpower or time available to properly check and evaluate every individual case on an individual basis. However, the real problem is that by relying on computers that aren't programmed with the power of human rationale, many mistakes are made and the applicants who are both smart and devious, are inevitably likely to abuse the system.

I realised that at some point I would need an American-based credit card once we were living in the States but I didn't place much importance on how difficult it would be to procure one, even though I was already in possession of a Green Card and a Social Security Number. Naïvely, I had assumed that because I'd been an American Express card holder for over twenty years in the UK, it would be a formality to obtain an 'American' AmEx card. Not true. The US American Express company isn't really related to any other American Express company in any other part of the world. Effectively, they would appear to run as individual companies and do not share information on their customers with any other territory. In fact, as far as I can tell, there is absolutely no cross referencing or communication at all. You may be part of the American Express family and they will promote theirs as the only 'world card' but in reality, they are outstandingly non-international and parochial in their rules and methods.

When we first bought a vacation home in the USA, the country was oblivious to terrorist threat, having never suffered a foreign attack on American soil, save for the bombing of Pearl Harbour in Hawaii in 1941. So at the time we purchased this holiday home, the mere fact of being a homeowner and part-time resident in the USA made it very simple for me to open an account at a local bank and send funds from the UK to pay monthly outgoings on the vacation property. It was actually quite refreshing in that the local banks were so customer-friendly and it reminded me of the way UK banks used to be, back in the 60s and 70s. I only ever stepped inside the bank a couple of times each year but I was often greeted by name whenever I visited my branch. However, since the post-9/11 Patriot Act was introduced, it has become somewhat difficult now to even open a US bank account. And without a bank account, it is pretty much impossible to ever achieve the absolute honour of being awarded a coveted VISA, American Express or Master Card.

As an example, when I finally came to live in the USA, I had to pay cash for everything I bought unless I used my UK-based credit cards. Unfortunately, UK credit cards are of little use when buying a house or a car. They are also worthless when trying to buy US-sourced air tickets, paying property tax bills, utilities, insurances or even for anything ordered online. For all of these, you need a credit card based in the USA and one that is issued to a US residence. As far as buying a house or car is concerned, you'll be ineligible for either a mortgage or a lease without an extensive history of reasonable credit scoring.

Of course for many new British immigrants, the equity in their UK homes may be sufficient to buy a home outright in the USA but this will be largely dependent on the area that they choose to live and the price of property in that area. But even if the house is bought outright, there are many other problems to consider that will require immediate liquid funds. What I'm really saying is that if the USA is the place for you, don't go there unless you have sufficient and available financial resources otherwise you will be hugely disappointed with the system and often, new immigrants feel an even greater degree of isolation than they could ever have imagined while still resident in the UK.

So how do you go about creating a credit score? Well, there is a sly method that some people use which takes a little time and although it's slightly devious, it is lawful, painless and in the main, successful. The method was described to me by an employee at my bank when I asked her the very same question. Effectively, once you have a bank account that has been used on a daily or weekly basis and it consistently remains in moderate credit, you can the ask the bank for a small short-term loan of around $2000 over a repayment period of approximately twelve months. Once several payments have been made, maybe five or six of the twelve required to repay the loan, you should then make a full and final repayment of the balance. Then, after a couple of months or so, request another similar short term loan and repeat the exercise. Once this loan has been repaid, the Experian computer will now recognise you as a moderately reliable borrower and a credit score will then be applied and the only real cost to you is the interest accrued on the loan while you have been making payments. (You can offset some of this loss by placing the capital in an interest bearing account or Certificate of Deposit). From this moment on, expect to be inundated by every credit card company in the country with countless offers of gold, platinum and VIP cards. Silly, but this is how it works.

Now, given the fact that most people who arrive as new residents in the USA from the UK will mostly have been checked and re-checked for their personal wealth and self-supporting ability and will therefore land in America with fairly substantial dollar wealth, there is a more direct and blunt way of forcing a degree of credit worthiness and that is by sending a message to the top of the banking tree in plain English. In my own experience, after selling my home in England, I was lucky enough to have a reasonably large sum of money sitting in my bank account waiting to be used for the imminent purchase of a new home, deliberately earning me zero return in interest. Therefore, with those funds sitting in the account, I applied for a VISA card with my bank. I realised prior to my application that the Experian computer would check my credit history and would subsequently return my application, marked 'rejected'. With this response in hand, I then wrote a letter of outrage to the President of the bank that had the use of my money in its account and asked that he transfer all of the aforementioned funds to a new account that I had set up at a rival bank. Needless to say, I received an immediate response from the bank president himself, apologizing for this error and informing me that my credit card would be fast-tracked and couriered to me within a week. The following extract is from a letter that was sent on my behalf by a Senior Vice President to some poor unwitting employee of the bank's credit card section advising him or her in no uncertain terms that I was indeed a very good risk:

"Mr. Robson has contacted us to discuss his application for a Visa Credit Card as referenced above. The application was declined by Experian Inc. due to "Insufficient Credit File" (copy of notification enclosed). While it is true that Mr. Robson does not have a borrowing relationship, he has been a valued customer of this bank for the past 4 years and has maintained substantially high balances with no overdrafts. Based on his excellent account relationship with the bank, we hereby recommend approval of the above application as requested. If you have any questions, or if further information is required, please feel free to contact me."

Having secured my first genuine American credit card, it should be stated that I then immediately used those dormant bank account funds to purchase our first American home, leaving the account somewhat leaner than it was at the outset. It will also come as no surprise that since receiving and using that first but vital credit card, I now receive no less than a dozen credit card invitations each week and usually at least two a month from American Express.

However, in order to be able to work in the USA, it is imperative to have a Social Security Number or SSN. Without this, life will become extremely limited. The SSN is really the equivalent to our own National Insurance Number and most Americans know their SSN off by heart. Conversely, I am certain I'm not alone in saying that I would have to look at my UK tax files to quote my own NI number. However, without the SSN you will have no chance of getting a job, bank account or even insurance. It is the most important document in your wallet and most everyday requirements revolve around this nine digit number, whether it's for auto insurance, credit card applications, telephone service, power supply or even schooling. It is pretty much the first thing that will be requested for any mundane exercise. It does not however, provide an automatic inclusion for any social security payment. That is only a possibility once federal tax payments have been made and the basis of any social security payment to you in the future will be judged solely on the amount you've paid into the system. This is very different to the UK where just about every immigrant to the country is immediately entitled to some fairly healthy financial, medical and social assistance. My own take on this is that the Americans have got it just about right.

Finally, for anything in the normal course of daily life that necessitates an ongoing utility account, a hefty deposit is required by the supplying company to protect them from potential losses. For example, if you require a power supply for electricity or gas, a pre-paid deposit of the equivalent to one month's usage will be required before they will authorise your continued supply. The same goes for a telephone service and for water utilities. This deposit may be held by the utility company for up to two years although they will pay interest on the sum while they hold the money. This is not a problem to most people, just something that may differ from practices in the UK. In summary, just because you have finally managed to secure residence in the USA, don't for one moment think that it is plain sailing from hereon in, as there are still many hurdles and obstructions waiting for you around the corner.

Chapter 4

Credit, Credit & More Credit

"Neither a borrower or lender be" was the advice given by Polonius to his son in Shakespeare's Hamlet. Like many everyday expressions that originated in the legendary Bard's plays and sonnets, this one has stood the test of time and has remained in the English language ever since but sadly, it is one that is seldom adhered to. In the 21st century, it is nigh on impossible to climb the steps of success without borrowing somewhere along the line and you can't help thinking that old Polonius was being just a little smug and self-satisfied when handing out this nugget of advice, having never personally suffered any real hardship himself but to paraphrase the old man's warblings, there was method in his madness.

The American psyche demands that nothing in life should be paid for, up front with good old-fashioned greenbacks. If you ever thought that the UK was a nation of credit junkies, then look no further than the masters of accrued debt in the USA to find out where that discipline first began. If you were ever under the misapprehension that it was just a small group of dreamy foreigners harbouring the idea of living the American Dream, then you would be somewhat mistaken in that thought. Believe me, the American Dream is alive and kicking in the hearts and minds of most American-born citizens, and it is particularly prevalent in the middle classes.

Let me recount a short story on how desperate many people become in the attempt to attain a lifestyle that in most cases is clearly beyond their earning capacity. Recently, some friends of ours had put their house up for sale and soon had a confirmed buyer who, once the deal was agreed, visited regularly to make decisions about the many changes and improvements that he wanted to make once his family had moved in. Bear in mind that this was a million-dollar-plus home and that a significant sum would be required as deposit in order to secure the sale, around 10% or $100,000. Our friends sensed a problem when the deposit was distinctly absent, just an offer of an old Mercedes valued at around $5000 as a form of collateral. Needless to say, the would-be buyer was unable to raise the other $995,000 required to complete the purchase. This wasn't funny, it was just extremely sad that this family was willing to risk so much to secure a dream that was clearly beyond their resources. It is though, absolutely indicative of how far people will go in America to secure a foothold on the ladder of perceived prosperity. Although in fairness, this is probably a similar scenario now played out in many parts of England.

Over-extension of finances does not end with the purchase of the home. On any road in any part of the USA, it is reasonable to assume that 90% of all cars around you aren't owned by the drivers. The very idea of going to a dealership, choosing a car and then writing a cheque is somewhat frowned upon. In fact, the salesmen will go to some lengths to convince you not to write that cheque but instead to take a lease or hire-purchase agreement. It is in their personal interest that you do not pay at the outset, quite simply because they would lose the finance bonuses normally received from selling a payment plan.

Most cars are leased and to that end, if you see a commercial for a car on TV or an advertisement in the newspaper, likely as not it will be the monthly payment that's promoted and not the selling price of the car. The actual price of the vehicle is largely irrelevant. The number of monthly payments is also irrelevant. These days, the cash-back sum that the dealer or manufacturer will offer, has become much more important, often amounting to many thousands of dollars. So really what the customer has in mind is the absolute maximum he or she can afford to pay each month, using the cash-back sum to pay off other debts, in order to determine which car will elevate them up the perceived ladder of success. Remember, in the USA, even more so than in any other credit-fuelled western economy, the perception of wealth and success is of far greater importance than the actuality itself.

It has always baffled me when driving through any working-class American neighbourhood to see the endless lines of new cars and SUVs sparkling proudly in the driveways of sometimes, terribly neglected homes. In many instances, these run-down shacks would appear to be worth somewhat less than the vehicles parked outside them. Pride in their vehicles is paramount to every American so let me say this loudly "CARS ARE VERY IMPORTANT HERE!" And Harley-Davidsons and boats and all-terrain-vehicles…. But to be fair, I'm not at all sure that these people really have got it so wrong. In the UK, we are brought up with the belief that the main focus in life is to buy a house and we're then content to be saddled with a mortgage for the rest of our working lives. It is just a basic education we receive on how we must bring purpose and reason to our lives by having finally paid for the roof above our heads by the time we've reached the age of 65, regardless of the fact that we'll probably only own it for another ten years or so thereafter. It should be noted however, that the rest of our European neighbours are not raised on this same principle. Due to the accepted notion that a defined rental sector should and must exist, and in fact thrives without social stigma, many Europeans have enjoyed a far greater lifestyle than their British counterparts for decades. The all important target for the British to own their own home is often counter-productive to the quality of life that they wish to lead. If you stop to think about it, you never really own the home you live in, you're only renting it while you are visiting this world. But the end result of this staggering mortgage burden is that more and more British people every year seek a new and improved life overseas. To quantify this, it is a fact that more than five million British citizens have emigrated in the last ten years, an absolutely substantial figure given the relative size of the UK population.

In the States, there is a basic ethic or principle that all the toys and trimmings in life are the things that make life worthwhile to the average American and if a buying solution is offered that makes it simple to procure these items, then most of them will grab it with both hands. Back in England, I often bemoaned the plague of television commercials, pumped out incessantly on the mainly blue-collar targeted channels offering debt solutions to the unsuspecting and presumably naïve viewer. The introduction of Sky Television to the UK brought with it the opportunity to advertise cheaply to specific demographics. Short-term relief with long-term pain to satisfy the torrents of commercials daring you to go out tomorrow and buy that new car or television.

Only recently, and with the use of the Tivo freeze function, I studied the legalese on the end frame of an American TV commercial, offering quick cash to an under-educated audience. Not only was this disclaimer miniscule in its legibility but the terms were quite unbelievable, an incredible 101% total interest charge on a four year loan, requiring that the borrower pay back more than double the capital sum after 48 months. Having been involved in advertising for many years prior to moving to the USA, I know that this isn't just innocent advertising, catering for the needy, but a very carefully and scientifically planned attack on the blue collar population as well as one that now frequently targets the white collar community.

So, "a word to the wise" (Charles Dickens, this time I believe), the USA doesn't operate under the same strict financial regulations we rely on in the UK, although most Americans believe it does, and it's better to avoid any organisation that offers you a debt-free existence for just the price of a free phone call. There's no such thing as a free lunch in the UK and you certainly won't find one here either.

Chapter 5

Buying The Dream Home & The Curse of Property Tax

Buying a home in the USA is a more straightforward process than the tenuous, lengthy and uncertain method that we have in the UK. There is though, a completely different approach to buying and selling property in the USA when compared to the process in the UK, or more precisely, England. (Scotland has its own rules which are a little more akin to the American way). If you are already aware of the procedure for buying and selling property in England, then you may want to skip the next two or three pages but for comparison purposes, I have included the English process as well.

Let's start with the basics. In England, you decide on the area in which you would like to live and then a visit to the various High Street estate agents will have you added to their mailing system with any appropriate properties subsequently mailed to you in the form of a hard copy listing although many agents now use the internet extensively. Details are initially emailed and then sent in hard copy later. If the required particulars, photos and floor plans are available on the agents' websites, buyers can download these themselves. Property portals are now popular, covering larger areas and representing greater numbers of agents, enabling the buyer to 'one-stop shop' without the initial need to contact an agent. It would also be rare in a mid-sized town for there to be more than a dozen agencies covering the chosen property area. Many of these agencies are owned and operated by the names over the door, although there are a number of national and international companies available, Savills, Hamptons and Sotheby's immediately spring to mind. Depending on the value of the property and also how much money, time and effort the agent is willing to invest in its marketing, the hard copy will range from a simple A4 printout to a professional, glossy, multi-photo heavyweight brochure with full floor plans drawn to scale.

(For anyone reading this who is not au fait with the estate agency system in England, it should be stated that a seller can choose between appointing a 'sole agent' or having 'multiple agents' although a buyer can use many different estate agents (realtors) to find a suitable home. A sole agent means that only that listing agent can sell the property and because this narrower band of marketing is likely to reach fewer buyers, then the selling commission will be lower than if it were with multiple agencies. Invariably, multiple means three or more agencies, although this can sometimes extend to seven or eight and 'joint sole' will mean that two agents are listing the property and both will share the costs and split the commission more or less equally. It is very important to remember that only the appointed agents are allowed to sell the property for the duration of the agreed contract period, which is absolutely not the case in the USA and it should be noted for American readers that the MLS (Multiple Listing Service) does not exist in the UK – more about that later).

So once you have been inundated by the local English agents with their own office listings, you would then make appointments with those agents to view properties that may be suitable. Once you have decided to put forward an offer on a property, the agent will submit this verbal offer directly to the seller. If it proves unacceptable, the agent will let you know and you can revise the offer until both parties have agreed the deal or you can simply walk away. At this point, even if a price has been agreed, a deposit will not yet be required and will probably not be needed for some time yet and at no time during this period, will a formal contract be signed by either party.

Your obligation now is to have a surveyor check the property, firstly for your own peace of mind and also, to establish a property value on which a bank might provide a mortgage, if required. At the same time, your solicitor will make contact with the seller's solicitor and establish the terms and conditions of the sale. The next target is to work towards an 'exchange of contracts' at which time a cash deposit will be required of usually between five and ten percent of the purchase price along with the signed sale/purchase documents. During this time, your solicitor will have performed local searches and obtained a copy of the property or land title along with any other documents that may pertain to it. Any alterations that may have been made to the land or building structure will require building regulation certification and local town council planning approvals.

Once contracts have been exchanged and a deposit made of between 5-10%, a date is set for 'completion' which is the day you will take over the property and the balance will be paid to the seller. Most buyers assume that once 'exchange' has taken place then they are guaranteed to complete the purchase. This is largely true but in some cases, the seller may decide not to sell and will cancel the deal. In this scenario, he can be taken to court to compel him to complete the sale, although this is rare. If it is the buyer who pulls out after 'exchange', then they cannot be forced to complete the sale but the deposit paid by the buyer would be retained by the seller, less agency fees. The main problem in England is that at best, it can take at least four weeks or at worst, several months to reach contract exchange and during that time, the buyer has effectively committed to nothing and in fact, neither has the seller. No deposit is required until almost the final part of the process and during this time, it is the seller who is on tenterhooks if he is desperate for a sale or the buyer if he feels that he might be gazumped by another buyer with a better offer. (Gazumping is when the seller accepts a higher offer from another buyer once a deal has already been made with the original bidder. It isn't illegal in England, but it should be.)

So how different could it be in the USA? Well, firstly the estate agent system as we know it in England, doesn't exist here. Yes, you do have private and national companies operating in just about every plaza in America but none of them has sole control over the sale of any home. The main gateway to researching properties is the MLS or Multiple Listing Service on the internet. Every property that is placed on this site is put there either by a realtor or private individual and every property is equally available for any other realtor to sell and take a cut of the commission, pretty much a free-for-all. Generally speaking, the selling fee on a home is around 6% and if an individual realtor sells a home that's listed by another realtor then the fee would be split 50/50 or at worst 70/30 in favour of the listing realtor. Having said that, sometimes the reverse is true and commission on lower priced properties may be as much as 10%.

There are also some fundamental differences in the buying and selling process on the east coast as opposed to the west coast. On the east coast, the contract has no real validity until the inspections are satisfied whereas on the west coast, the inspections are part of the contract period. Attorneys are used for closing in the east whereas a neutral escrow company will be used in the west. I cannot go into specifics on every area in the United States as there are far too many practical variations. In most cases, it is the realtor himself who will draw up the sale/purchase contract although there are many anomalies; in the state of New York, only attorneys are permitted to write the contract and I believe that in California, there must be third party representation in order to retain complete transparency. Really and truly though, the laws and regulations are very much state driven and it would prove impossible to look at all state variants.

In America, I've heard the phrase "everyone's a realtor" many times and it would be easy to assume that everyone in the US is a realtor because it really does seem that way. Statistics show that there are around 55,000 agents in England serving some 11,000 offices so if I were to make a comparison from what I've seen, then I would say that if there was one estate agent in the UK for every thousand buyers, then there is probably one realtor for every fifty buyers in the USA. Due to the fact that a realtor's licence can be attained with the purchase and completion of a 65 hour real estate course followed by a couple of exams and also in part because a realtor here does not need an office, just a PC, a cell phone and a car, the business is overcrowded and lacking in real experience in the main. You should be extremely cautious about using an agent who only dabbles in the business of real estate as they are unlikely to be able to give you the best service. Choose a full-time and experienced realtor and avoid part-time agents who only switch on their cell phones between rounds of golf. I would imagine that any American realtor reading this, will by now be feeling somewhat scorned and may be harbouring some fairly irate feelings towards me.

However, the good news is that there are still many experienced, talented and highly professional people out there who really do know their business and who will be quite invaluable in your quest so it pays to choose your realtor extremely carefully. The correct choice of realtor will not only find you the right home but will also save you time and money along the way. I should also balance the accreditation issue by saying that there is no formal training and certification required to be an estate agent in England. The skills and techniques are generally learned 'on the job', while working out of a recognised estate agency, although there is nothing to stop anyone practicing unlicensed.

The easiest faux pas that any British buyer can make when looking for a property in the USA, is to approach dozens of different realtors in the same area with the same property search. The rule is not written in stone but once you have chosen a realtor in an area, you should only view listings via that realtor unless you feel that they are just performing, in which case you have good reason to choose another. In reality, they are your personal agent and they don't want you to have any others lurking nearby. Even if you see a property in another realtor's office window or a For Sale board outside a house, the rule of thumb is that you should then contact your realtor and he or she will make the enquiry on your behalf. Or if a situation precludes this, ensure that you tell any other agents that you're already working with a realtor. Do not under any circumstances, try and circumvent the situation – you may think you are helping but all you may have achieved is the loss of a valuable commission to your realtor who may have already spent a vast amount of time and expense on your behalf, in the search for your home. From experience, I prefer to use a broker where there are perhaps a dozen realtors working out of the brokerage office. There is more communication and knowledge between these groups of realtors than can ever be found in a solo agent.

When you have decided on the home you wish to buy, the next step is the most refreshing one for English people. This is how it works. Your realtor writes up a legally binding contract with an offer to buy at the price you're willing to pay and this is then signed by you. Of course, you can insert any number of caveats or get-out clauses but this is the principle. A nominal sum of perhaps $1000 will be required at this point to prove that you're a serious buyer and not a time waster. This is called Earnest Money and it is refunded should the sale fail to progress further. The seller then has a period of time, let's say 48 hours, to accept, decline or counter. If he counters with a revised price, you can either choose to accept or counter his price. All offers and counter-offers are submitted in contract form and not verbally, as is the case in England.

Once the offer is accepted, the buyer must then arrange an early inspection of the home for anything that may affect the purchase. The cost of this inspection can range from $500 to several thousand dollars depending on the extent of the information required. Any adverse points that arise from the report may result in a reduction in price, an agreement to repair the problem or in some cases, the cancellation of the deal. This period of time is also utilised to allow the bank to appraise the property to determine a market value, if a mortgage is required. After the inspection period has elapsed, an agreed deposit is paid by cheque which is then held in an escrow account until closing (escrow is the usual method employed in the USA, whereby the deposit and the balance are held in a third party account until closing)

At the time of contract production, a closing date will be set, usually 30-60 days after the offer is made depending on whether the sale is East or West Coast where closing periods and general practices are somewhat different to each other. In California for example, the buyer has a period of 17 days for inspections and mortgage approval during which time, he or she can withdraw from the deal without incurring any costs or penalties and generally speaking, 30 days should see the sale concluded. After this 17 day period, deposits will likely be forfeited. The main bonus about the US system is that all doubt and uncertainty is removed from the buying and selling process and all of the anguish that UK buyers and sellers often experience is rarely felt in America. From my own experience, the first two properties that I purchased in the US, both took four weeks and six weeks respectively, from viewing to closing which is unlike any experience I've ever had in the UK.

One of the more shocking areas for UK owners when they decide to sell in the USA is the difference in selling fees between the two countries. In the UK, depending on whether the listing is sole or multiple, the fee will range from 1% to usually a maximum of 3%. As a rule of thumb, most agents will happily settle on 1.5% mainly because of the absurdly high price and clustering density of the available property in the UK. In the USA, as I have mentioned before, 6% is expected when selling but I know that 4% is sometimes negotiated. The one thing that British buyers and sellers should remember is that there is no Stamp Duty in America. For any purchase over £250,000 in the UK, Stamp Duty must be paid by the purchaser at 3% and if the purchase price exceeds £500,000 then the duty rises to 4% of the total price. (based on tax records at the time of writing)

There is something that should also be noted regarding profit on the sale of a property in the States. In the UK, there are no limitations regarding the profit made on your principal dwelling. That is to say that if you bought a house in January for £1m and sold it a month later in February for £2m, there is no Capital Gains Tax liability on the profit, provided that the house is your primary residence and that you can prove that you live there. There is also no minimum duration of ownership. It is therefore important to understand that if you sell your American home, even if it is your only home, before the second anniversary of ownership, you will be liable to a capital gains charge under US tax law. In a slow market, this may prove irrelevant but in a hot market it may result in a hefty tax bill and in some cases, state and federal income tax may also be applicable.

However, the biggest sting in the tale when buying a home in the USA, is property tax. Most overseas buyers will not be aware of the existence of these charges and will almost certainly be shocked by the size of the annual bill. To draw comparison to the UK, it is the equivalent of our Council Tax bill which we usually pay monthly. This charge in England also includes weekly collection of trash but it doesn't in the USA – this is paid directly to the waste haulage company.

Council Tax in England is a banded charge consisting of eight levels from A through to I, the latter being the highest band value so depending on the value of your home, the amount that you pay will be levied on whichever band you are in. However, Band I is for all properties valued in excess of £424,001 (approximately $800,000). Therefore, if your home is worth £30m, your charge will be the same as someone in the same area whose property is valued at £425,000. The annual charge for that highest band is around £3000 ($6000), at the time of writing. Really and truly, it is an unfair system where the very wealthy with large estates are paying the same charge as someone who owns a relatively modest home next door. (Currently in the UK, there are plans to revalue every home, as original valuations were carried out in the 1990's and are now somewhat out of line with inflation)

In contrast, the American system of property tax is based on the appraised value of your home and depending where you live, you will pay a percentage of that appraised value each year. This percentage is governed by the Millage rate for each particular county and town. For example, in Florida you will find that the Millage rate varies wildly, in some cases as low as 1.2% of the appraised value but in others, as high as 2.8% which is a somewhat hefty tax bill to pay each year, just for the privilege of living in your own home. But generally speaking you would expect an average rate of around 18.0 dollars tax per $1000 value of property value or more precisely, 1.8%. So for easy calculation, a $1m home would probably generate an $18,000 property tax bill which is payable annually, in advance and in one amount, not monthly and retrospectively as is the case in England. This is a simple illustration and the bill would be higher or lower depending on the exact location but use this as a general rule of thumb. (To keep it simple when comparing UK/US rates, I am only illustrating examples in the two most popular British immigrant destinations, Florida on the East Coast and California on the West).

It is also important to remember that the Council Tax Charge in England is paid by the occupier of the home so if a house is rented to a tenant by the owner, then it is the tenant who must pay the tax. The opposite is true in the USA. Whoever owns the home is liable to pay the property tax, regardless of whether they live there or not. I think actually, this is unfair. The main reason for having property tax in the first place, is to pay for all the immediate local benefits such as schools, parks and law enforcement. It ought to be the beneficiary of these services who pays the tax and not the landlord who is effectively paying for the state education of the tenant's children. The long and the short of it, is that it may pay dividends to rent a home in a good neighbourhood rather than to buy at high prices and then be saddled with the accompanying property taxes.

However, I digress. When looking at a potential home purchase in America, it is invariably the current property tax that will be shown on the listing itself but here is where the buyer should beware. The tax shown on the listing is likely the amount that the present owner is paying which may be an old homesteaded appraisal (a 'homestead allowance' on your main dwelling ensures that the property tax has a maximum increase of around 3% per annum and also allows a portion of the appraisal value to be exempt from taxation) and that appraisal may be from twenty years ago so as soon as you have bought the property, it will be re-valued within one year and an applicable tax levied which could be many, many times the amount that was being paid by the previous owner. This is often a huge belated shock to the unsuspecting foreign buyer.

For many residents in Florida, this high charge is acceptable mainly because there is no state tax on earnings. This is fine if you are a working household but for the retired population, which in Florida is enormous, the lack of state tax is not an incentive. In fact, because Florida has become such a popular destination in which to live during the past ten years, for Americans as well as foreigners, house prices have risen dramatically, sometimes by up to 500% in that period and the taxes, and ergo the city and county revenues, have risen in equal percentages. To that end, this is becoming a critical situation which could theoretically wreck the Florida housing market unless action is taken to modify the taxing system on property. My own view is that Florida should adopt the California rate of a straight 1% per $1000 for all homes and raise the state tax on all other purchases from 6% to 7% whilst also introducing a moderate state income tax. These changes would mean that it is not solely the residents who are paying for the benefits that the millions of snowbirds (those retirees who fly south each year to benefit from warmer climates) and tourists enjoy each year.

One of the most refreshing aspects of buying a home in America is the guarantee that on the day you move in, you won't be praying for light, comfort and privacy. This is to say that there's a caveat attached to the sale of any home in America requiring that all light fittings, fans, carpets, curtains and blinds should remain at the house for the new owner. It's part of the whole deal. I'm not certain that this happens in every home in every state but hopefully you'll never suffer the disgraceful post-sale looting of homes that we regularly see in the UK where the previous owner will sometimes remove all carpets, curtains and lights, in some cases even stealing the bulbs and switches, leaving the new owner with bare wiring for his trouble. Generally speaking in the USA, a walkthrough of the home on the eve of closing is suggested and advised to ensure that everything is in the home that was originally itemised on the listing. In some cases, it may be worth photographing all items such as washers, dryers, refrigerators and dishwashers to ensure that any high end items shown on the listing details, have not been replaced with inferior versions at the midnight hour. You don't want to find your Sub-Zero fridge/freezer replaced with a budget item on the day you move in.

On a lighter note, I've recently been made aware that snoring is no longer an acceptable facet of modern-day living. To that end, many homes are now being designed to cater for this problem. Architects are frequently being asked to design houses that have 'his' and 'hers' wings in order to eliminate the problem of disrupted sleeping caused by high decibel intrusion during the moonlight hours. Although I don't personally suffer from this malaise of palatal vibration, I know that for many wives and girlfriends, it is an insurmountable problem. Of course, the idea of separate male and female quarters may not be a bad thing in the long term, providing the female partner with a soundless environment whilst also providing the male partner his own sanctuary of neat and tidiness and a bathroom that no longer suffers the abuse of female chaos. However, the designers might also like to think about introducing a common area between the wings for other extracurricular, nocturnal activities.

The following words may help in understanding US real estate terminology:

Realtor = Estate agent
Offer on the table = Under offer
Pending, in escrow = Exchange of contracts
Closing date = Completion date
Lot or dirt = Plot or land
Owner financing = Seller may act as bank for the mortgage
Fixer-Upper = Needs work
Model = Show-house
Fee simple = Land & property bought outright together
Land lease = Building owned but land leased
Zero lot line = Built close to edge of property line
Carriage home = Semi-detached or attached
Town Home = Maisonette in development
Condo = Owned flat
Apartment = A rented flat
Duplex & Triplex = Single family homes split to suit occupants

Chapter 6

Education

Without doubt, the education of their children is high on the agenda of most middle-class American families. The post-code ethic, common in England, which enables access to the better state schools, is also alive and kicking in the USA. There are many stories recounted of families who move from one side of the road to the other, in order to secure a place in a better school just as we've repeatedly seen in England over the past two decades. In some areas, the state schools in the USA are not just good but actually achieve outstanding levels of academic and athletic success. Generally speaking, the more expensive the homes, the wealthier the county, and ergo, the better the schools. Nothing new there.

Schools in the USA have two terms or semesters, whereas in the UK, we have three, Autumn, Spring and Summer. (But oddly, no Winter Term) All schools in the USA are expected to provide a minimum 180 student days for each school year. There are no half-terms as such, although there is a week off in March/April, appropriately known as Spring Break and report cards are sent home at the end of each quarter and semester end. Unlike term times in the UK where all state schools share a similar calendar countrywide, the same is not true in the USA where each state may have dramatically different start and end dates for state-schools. For example, New York and California share similar calendars, whereby school starts in early September and finishes for the summer in late June, in fact not so different to the UK. However, having written to several California schools asking for exact information on the Californian school calendar, there did seem to be a huge variance on start and end dates, each school effectively able to set their own calendar. In New York, the picture was no clearer, the best response being the following words of wisdom:

"Once national/federal legal holidays (specifically mentioned in federal statutes) are taken into account, the calendar requirements here differ by state in terms of particular state regulations and laws (education being primarily a state level responsibility in the United States), and, in the case of New York City, local contractual negotiations with unions and educational factors that do not conflict with the aforementioned factors."

In Florida, school has traditionally started in early August and ended in late May, radically different to the UK and also to many other US states but this year, a new Florida state law now dictates that school may start no earlier than 14 days prior to Labor Day. The result was that school started on 20th August in 2007 and will end on 5th June 2008. Therefore, it is worth checking with the Department of Education in the state that you plan to settle before you set a moving date. As a side issue, it's also worth checking that your child has had the required inoculations because without them, a student will be barred from attending school at the start of term, no exceptions, period.

As a rule, students in the USA attend Elementary School from 1st Grade through to 5th Grade. Middle School is 6th to 8th Grade before moving up to High School which normally runs from 9th to 12th Grade. There are anomalies whereby Middle School is skipped, meaning that 6th Grade starts in High School and the student will stay there all the way through to 12th Grade, aged 18. A student's 'year' or 'grade' is also different in both countries. For example, a 12-year-old student would typically be in Year 8 in England but in America, the same student would be in 7th Grade. I remember my own daughter being slightly miffed that having left Year 6 in England, she was back in 6th Grade when she arrived at school in America for her next school year.

With the knowledge that the USA has a different perspective to the UK on the idea of when compulsory schooling should end and when the option of further education begins, it might be worthwhile at this juncture to clarify the framework of the American ladder of education and also some of the words used that describe the schools within it.

For the benefit of American readers, the following example typifies the course of events in a child's education in the UK:

Age 3-5	Pre-school or Kindergarten (optional but popular)
Age 5-11	Primary School
Age 11-16	Secondary School (in some schools, age 11 to 18)
Age 16-18	College
Age 18+	University

The following represents a typical framework for the USA:

Age 5-11	Elementary School (Grade School)
Age 11-14	Middle School (sometimes called Junior High)
Age 14-18	High School (sometimes from age 11 to 18)
Age 18+	College or University

In both countries, specialisation usually occurs after College or University.

One real difference in the two educational systems is that home-schooling is already very popular in the USA. This is the practice of teaching a curriculum at home where the onus falls on the parents to ensure that their children achieve or exceed standard grades. In two decades, the percentage of parents who choose this style of education, has doubled in America. Although nearly three million students are home-schooled in the USA and only approximately 45,000 in the UK, I am given to understand that the latter figure is twice the UK total of 1995, so in both

41

countries, there is clearly an increasing trend towards this new method of education.

In Britain, fee-paying schools are referred to as 'private schools' or sometimes as 'public schools', the latter often causing confusion for British people as much as for Americans. In Britain, non fee-paying schools are called 'state schools'. In the USA, there are simply two types of school, public or private which makes it somewhat easier all round.

The misnomer of the term 'public school' in Britain is still confusing to many, as public schools aren't generally viewed as institutions in the financial reach of most of the general public. As a brief side explanation, the term came about when English grammar schools began accepting brighter students from anywhere in the country instead of taking only the smart pupils who lived in the immediate vicinity of the school. In fact, one of the most famous schools in the world, Eton College, founded nearly 700 years ago, was the very first school to adopt this allcomers-accepted policy meaning that entry to this establishment was possible for any school-age member of the public, although in reality, hardly likely.

Therefore, if a person in England is described as being a 'public school type', it's more likely that he or she is being vilified as appearing snobbish or upper-class rather than as someone hailing from a state school. Eton schoolboys probably personify the very idea of perceived public school characteristics. They are nurtured and trained to believe that they are the best in the world at anything they care to put their minds to and they are taught to maintain a high level of expectation from everything in life, at all times. You will often see the boys, dressed in their waistcoats, cuffs and tails, walking on the riverside between the English Berkshire towns of Eton and Windsor. The look of confidence that they display is clearly evident when most of us would be too embarrassed to don the 18th century fashion that they proudly display as their uniform. In any case, these pupils can truly be described as 'public school' because Eton really was the world's first genuinely public school.

The big surprise for anyone moving to the USA is that in many cases, the public or state school might be more academically and athletically successful than their fee-paying counterparts. This is because America as a whole, places the importance of academic and sporting education right at the top of the agenda and public schools will often have manifold financial benefits awarded to them to achieve their goals, the type of funds that private schools are often unable to procure. Obviously, the higher the fees the private schools charge, then the greater the opportunity for the student but I was surprised to discover that most American private schools seem to charge less than half the annual fees of a comparable UK school. This is a generalisation, as many American private schools have outrageously expensive fee structures as can be seen at institutions like Concord Academy in Massachusetts and Hotchkiss School in Connecticut where fees are around $40,000 per annum. Compare this to Eton or Marlborough where average annual fees are in the region of £25,000 (around $50,000). Not so dissimilar.

Dwelling for a moment on the subject of private education, one practice that does disturb me in the USA, is the separate and quite differing fee structure applied to Catholic and non-Catholic students by some private Catholic schools. These schools make it absolutely clear that if you don't follow their particular faith, then you should expect the fees to be around 70% higher than those charged to the Catholic families. Maybe it's just me but this practice sounds just a tad sectarian.

Unlike England, where children often leave school at sixteen to start work, it is expected that American children should attend school to the age of 18, in order that they achieve at the very least, a high school certificate of graduation. This is pretty much deemed the minimum requirement although I should say that currently, there are plans afoot in the UK to raise the minimum school-leaving age to 18, which I truly believe to be a great move towards a better educated country. I am always surprised that the current school-leaving age of 16 is only a recent advance. At the beginning of the 20th century, most British children would be lucky to stay in school until the age of 11 and even by the end of the First World War, the leaving age was still only 14. A second world war had erupted before the age was raised once more, this time to 15. Unbelievably, another 25 years would pass before the minimum school-leaving age in the UK was raised to 16 in 1972. I can only hope that the current government acts quickly to implement a minimum leaving age of 18 and that it doesn't take another world war to match the Americans in their dedication to education.

Students in America work hard. When we first arrived here, I was shocked to see my own daughter getting ready for school at 6am and seated at her desk by 7.30am. Admittedly, school finished at 2pm and she was usually back home by 2.30pm but never a day went by when she didn't have an inordinate amount of homework. Awards are given for 'Straight-A Student' or 'Honour Roll Student' or 'Student of the Month' ensuring that the students work that bit harder to achieve the prize. The children are pushed hard to succeed and are given many goals and targets and the all important GPA is the number by which they will be judged at the end of the day. The GPA (Grade Point Average) is the figure that measures your success at school. It has a maximum value of 4.0 and anything above 3.0 is considered acceptable. (There are ways to gain extra GPA credits, meaning that a figure in excess of 4.0 is ultimately achievable) But if the GPA falls much below 2.5, the school will let you know quickly that action is required on your part. I like this method of putting the onus on the parents and making them take part in their children's education. The crucial factor is that unlike the schoolchildren in the UK, kids here generally seem to enjoy school.

I hope I'm not alone in the difficulty I've had in trying to fathom out what all the various terminologies mean in the American education system. Now, I can work out that 'trimester' means a single term of a three-term academic year and obviously 'semester' is one of the two terms of a twin-term period but Sophomore, Valedictorian and Salutatorian had me scurrying quickly to the dictionary. For ratification, the Sophomore year, which literally translates as 'second attempt' follows the first year at high school or college, that being the Freshman year. The Junior and Senior years are the third and fourth years respectively. (On a note of caution, it's probably best to avoid asking the meaning of JAFFY in the Australian education system as it may be a little shocking to find out what it means, safe to say though that it refers to a freshman, in less than glowing terms) Valedictorian and Salutatorian are the respective titles given to the highest and second highest achieving graduates of a high school or college, although the former is a little odd as the Latin origin of 'vale dice' really means that you are saying 'goodbye' and doesn't appear to be relevant to any scholastic achievement. The same also goes for Salutatorian, which would seem to derive from the French word 'salut', a friendly form of saying hello or goodbye in that land of fine wine and excellent cheese. But here's the new problem. There is now talk of new, Latin-originated expressions to be introduced to the American system which will have me even more confused. Valedictorian and Salutatorian will be replaced by Summa Cum Laude and Magna Cum Laude respectively and the plan is to throw in a Cum Laude for third place. Now I wish I hadn't given up Latin class when I was fourteen.

Like most parents, I take an avid interest in helping with homework. There's no doubt that children here seem to be pushed harder and they appear to learn more, earlier on in their schooling. However, and this may be partly to do with the size of the country, in world terms they appear to be under-educated. The educational targeting appears to be somewhat parochial when compared to anywhere else in Europe, not just to Great Britain. For example, even before she came to live in the USA, my daughter knew who was president of the United States and she could draw a pretty good approximation of the Stars and Stripes but even now, her peers at school would have no idea

45

who the British Prime Minister is or what the Union Flag looks like. However, this may be an isolated example and it may be the vastness of the USA and the enormity of everything that needs to be taught about it. But as far as knowledge concerning the rest of the world goes, there is a profound tunnel-vision approach, also borne out here in the newspapers, the international section often just a summary column hidden amongst the inner pages.

Most schools in the USA have a strict no-smoking policy for students. There is no quick fag (cigarette) behind the bike sheds; if you are caught, you are suspended and repeated violation of this rule will result in expulsion. No ifs and buts, no appeal, just immediate action. It's that simple. Most schools don't require uniforms but they do have very strict dress codes that must be obeyed. In general, students don't seem to abuse this privilege and from what I've seen so far, they are usually well turned out. If a student ignores the rule on school attire they receive a dress-code, effectively a yellow card in soccer terms. If they rack up too many of these warnings, suspension will be the next punishment followed by expulsion as the final resort. It goes without saying that the better educated the population, then the better the schools and ergo, the students.

The school transport system in America is just a breath of fresh air. The traditional yellow school bus that stops to collect the children in the morning and then delivers them back to their homes in the afternoon is one of the things that best exemplifies the American way of life. The sight of one of these custard-coloured leviathans is the sort of thing that conjures up visions of apple pie and white picket fences. It gives me a warm feeling every time I see one, all cars pausing behind and in front of the bus, to allow the children a safe route back to their homes. Rarely seen, the squabbles between bickering mothers scrabbling for the last available parking spot, a scene regularly enacted outside schools in England. The UK as a whole could learn a great lesson on school transport from our American neighbours.

The education process for most middle-class American children continues deep into their twenties and working life doesn't begin for many until the age of thirty or even when the ripe old age of forty is looming large. The cost of college and university education in the USA, is staggering. The average college student will attend at least four more years of further education, racking up a median annual bill of $30,000 which in the absence of any financial assistance from the parents, will need to be repaid over the course of the student's early working life. When comparing these costs with the £3,000 in annual top-up fees charged by universities in England, you can start to understand why college scholarships in America become such an important issue with parents and children alike. In England however, regardless of family or sponsored wealth, it is impossible to gain entry to a university unless the student has achieved the required A-Level pass results and in most cases these academic examinations are set at an extraordinarily high level. Merely being good at a sport, is not a relevant or salient skill and therefore, that particular prowess will not provide the cherished university (college) place. Academia rules at this level in Great Britain even if it doesn't appear so, earlier on in the school life of a British student.

In America, there are really only two methods used to achieve a partial or full scholarship to college; academic or athletic, smart or sporty and preferably both. However, there are many routes available to gain a scholarship and also more than one type of grant on offer. Specific awards are also available at most colleges, given to students with very high GPAs and for those who have received school honours or who might have unique strengths and qualities. These are known as Departmental Awards. Help can also come from local businesses, private organisations, religious foundations, national corporations, and even in some cases, from the different sections of the military. But without doubt, the most popular method of gaining college sponsorship is through the system of athletic scholarships. More than 125,000 of these scholarships are awarded each year at a cost of over $1billion, and nearly all of them funded primarily by the college or university itself. Details of these types of scholarship can be found at the National Collegiate Athletic Association (NCAA) although you should be aware that it's not the NCAA that awards the scholarship but actually the educational institution itself.

There are four levels of sponsorship that range from partial financial support all the way through to the complete underwriting of a student's college degree. The partial scholarship is given as limited financial assistance towards college fees whereas the 'full ride' means just that; payment of all fees and funding of any other extra costs associated with that particular scholarship. The latter type of funding is rare and therefore highly prized by all of those awarded the honour.

Finally, whilst my family and I have submerged ourselves in the American way of life, I have always been surprised that Americans, being the welcoming souls that they are, do not engender themselves so easily with new surroundings. My own town in England is home to one of the three American Community Schools in the UK, a group of private schools with ludicrously high fee structures. Bearing in mind that this particular town has probably the highest population of Americans outside of the USA, and that the local schools, state and private, are fine institutions, invariably the American kids will automatically be enrolled at ACS. It may be that the Americans feel they are temporary outsiders in the community or perhaps that the only valid education system is the American version but I strongly believe that in order to fit in to a community, it is important to fully embrace it rather than to shun it. Of course, it may just be that the wealthy corporations, responsible for bringing the parents to work in England, are also footing the stratospheric bill for the kids' education, which for any smart thinking individual would obviously be an opportunity to be seized immediately with both hands. "Carpe dollarè!"

Chapter 7

Health & Medical Insurance

If there is one aspect of life that could be identified as the fundamental difference between the USA and Europe, it is that a National Health Service does not exist in America. This is often the one hurdle that becomes insurmountable for Europeans who wish to settle in the USA. I still find it worrying that a leading First World country of this size has not yet adopted a system that cares for all and not just for the fortunate and successful. Even amongst Americans, there is an overriding fear of sickness. Not just the sickness itself or the treatment that they will go through to make a full recovery, but moreover the inherent worry and concern over whether this ill health and incapacitation will eventually bankrupt them. It is not enough just to have medical cover but in many cases, multiple policies and co-pays are essential in order to avoid financial ruin from hospital bills.

The current protagonists of the Democratic Party originally had National Health placed high on the agenda should they ever come to power (it was apparently one of Hilary Clinton's top priorities, were she to become the first female President) but it would still be a bitter pill to administer to the nation's taxpayers once the sheer scale of costs is revealed that would be required to adopt a care-for-all system. But before dismissing the idea that the costs would be too excessive, it is important to realise that even in England, the National Health Service is still only a fairly recent creation, having first opened its doors in 1948, less than sixty years ago. It may not yet be perfect, but it still works.

Of course, there are ways to launch an American NHS and the most obvious would be to fund it by some form of stealth tax. I've often wondered how the American public might react to a tax that added two or three dollars to the price of a gallon of gasoline in return for the guarantee of immediate and cost-free healthcare. Personally, although I'm not even sure that this amount of tax would be enough to subsidise the service, I truly believe that after the initial uproar from motorists, it would probably be gratefully accepted. It would put an end to the worries of many uninsured citizens who dread the thought of any type of illness and even at $6 or even $7 a gallon, the price of fuel would still be at least a couple of dollars a gallon less than in Europe. Strong medicine is often difficult to swallow but ultimately, the human race has a short memory. The petrol price-rise would soon be forgotten when the benefits of free healthcare were fully realised whilst also forcing people to use the car less and exercise more. Time to smell the coffee, methinks.

The problem becomes much deeper when you examine the knock-on effects of expensive medical insurance. Some of the major car manufacturers in this country are now complaining that the reason that they can no longer make profits is not because of the high cost of materials or the salaries that they pay their staff but instead, the unsustainable cost of providing health insurance for their workforce. If this is genuinely the case, then the future of the great American automobile industry has a much shorter life expectancy than I first imagined and that's without the mounting threat from Japanese, Taiwanese and Korean imports.

Many pension-age Americans are now working for the sole reason of receiving the medical cover that's provided with their job. A visit to the local supermarket will see that many of the employees are people who should be enjoying retirement but instead are forced to hold down these mundane positions just to continue living out their old age with the assurance of medical cover should they fall ill. My rose-tinted and slightly naïve childhood perception, that all those who lived in this great country were a healthy and happy population of men and women who lived the American Dream throughout their working life and beyond into retirement, was shattered when I began to fully understand the reality of the situation. Even for the prosperous and favoured middle classes, the sanctity and security of the American Dream is no longer a guarantee.

There's an old joke about hospitals in the USA that states that the first thing you'll be asked on admission to the building, is not one of concern about your condition but actually whether or not you have your credit card handy to pay for the treatment. In reality, this is not so far from the truth. On a visit to a local hospital a couple of years ago, the question of payment was slipped in during the course of measuring my blood pressure and temperature. Amazingly, once a credit card was produced, I was able to continue on for treatment. The interesting point here is that, should an American suffer a heart attack while stepping off a plane in England, he would be taken to hospital, made well again and sent on his merry way. And there would be no charge for the privilege, just a cheery farewell. Well, something like that anyway. The same is true for Americans who require a family doctor whilst living in England, whether on a temporary or permanent basis. Again, full service and no charge. Even prescriptions in England are charged at a flat rate of just £6.85 ($14), a fact that will doubtless shock many American readers.

An acquaintance of mine told me the story of his grandson who was not feeling very well, a pain in his stomach which had bothered him all weekend. A two-hour visit to the Emergency Room resulted in the simple diagnosis of gastro-enteritis and the subsequent issue of a drug prescription that would cure the problem over the next few days. The father had no medical insurance and therefore neither did his son and a week later, they received a bill for over $2000 for this unplanned visit to the hospital. I also read recently about a twelve-year-old girl who was unfortunate enough to be bitten by a venomous snake and was quickly rushed to the local hospital's ER and once there, she received a timely shot of antiserum to relieve the symptoms. The venom wasn't deadly but it would certainly have made the child extremely uncomfortable without an antidote. The invoice for that visit totalled over $12,000 but fortunately in this case, the parents carried sufficient health insurance to cover the cost.

As a final anecdote, a good friend of mine, supposedly covered by his firm's medical insurance policy, was unfortunate enough to take a tumble one day whilst riding his bike. The fracture suffered to his hand required immediate surgery along with a measure of post-operative therapy and although his firm's medical insurance paid a large part of the hospital bill, he was still saddled with a $7000 co-pay bill which was the difference between the total cost and the actual amount that the insurance company was prepared to pay for the treatment.

The good news is that Medical Insurance is available for all British citizens with varying degrees of cover and cost and it can be purchased within the USA or sometimes more affordably, directly from the UK. There are a number of recognised and reputable international insurance companies operating in the UK who will provide cover in the States but it is vitally important to read the policy conditions and exclusions very carefully to fully understand exactly what the cover will provide. The scope of cover can be adjusted according to budget with the most expensive and extensive policies offering everything from GP visits and dental cover all the way trough to emergency treatment and lengthy hospital stays which might involve multiple surgical procedures. At the very least, it's advisable to buy insurance that covers you and your family for any emergency treatment.

So why has health insurance become so expensive for Americans? A combination of different factors raises the annual cost. Firstly, more people need more treatment than ever before due to a poor diet and lack of real exercise. Secondly, the older American population is also not as fit and healthy as it once was but paradoxically, continues to live longer. The average life expectancy for Americans is now set at 78 years. Thirdly, the remuneration for surgeons has escalated into fantasy levels. It's somewhat sad that surgeons are now viewed in the same derisory fashion that has historically been reserved for lawyers in this country. (Although to be fair, if I'd spent fifteen years in medical school, surviving on a diet of beans, rice and ketchup and then found myself subsequently saddled with an enormous student loan for my efforts, I'd want to see a sizeable pot of gold at the end of the rainbow and hopefully not before I pegged out by the age of 45 due to the stress levels of being on call 24 hours a day). Hospitals are also producing bills that have no real relevance or cost justification to the treatment administered. None of which is helped by the fact that the poor family doctor who is trying vainly to provide an acceptable level of care, is forced to refer to the prescription-approval lists which dictate the brand of drugs to be prescribed that will be guaranteed to be paid for by the HMOs (Health Maintenance Organisations). Finally, and this is probably the biggest problem. As with any American company that provides risk cover, the health insurance companies themselves are making excessively high profits on the service provided and continue to do so at a staggering rate. I had always thought that our own private medical insurance companies in England, like BUPA or PPP, were expensive enough but in comparison to their American counterparts, they charge peanuts.

But the business of selling healthcare is not confined to the insurance companies. If you are a newcomer to the States, you'll doubtless notice an endless stream of television commercials, promoting pills to cure all manner of conditions. Whether you have heartburn, back-ache, amnesia, dyspepsia, rheumatism, arthritis, blood pressure, cholesterol, migraine, irritability or just a simple headache, there'll be a pill out there, just for you. There are pills for everything and then even more pills to combat the side-effects brought on by the original pills. I am particularly fond of the current crop of ads that deal primarily with E.D. (erectile dysfunction), or in plain English to you and I, impotence. The unabashed selling of Viagra, Levitra and Cialis to octogenarians, who really should have given up fooling around by now, continues apace during primetime television viewing. Gone is the embarrassment of genital failure, replaced by the promise of long-term and superhuman sexual prowess and presumably the added bonus of never falling out of bed again. Copywriters clearly don't see the pun when they write voiceover lines like "These days, you can't always find the right time with your partner (picture a 70 year-old necking with his wife as the door-bell rings to interrupt them) but with 36 hour strength and 4 hours of maintained erectile function, now you too can be flexible". Surely the main aim is to avoid being flexible and who in the world wants a four hour erection?

In fact, so concerned are the drug companies now with men's health, that there are new pills to combat the increasingly prevalent condition of BPH, (Benign Prostatic Hyperplasia) where the sufferers complain of 'going often', 'going urgently', 'weak stream' and 'frequently waking up at night to go'. I shouldn't snigger at this, because this condition is almost bound to affect me at some point in my life, although preferably not while I'm using Viagra with its 36 hour promise, but the advertisements which feature pensioner-age groups of men cycling through the wilderness, a hundred miles from the nearest restroom, just have me doubled over. Not from BPH of course, just from laughing so much. Anyway, if BPH is your problem, Avodart and Flomax will probably fix it for you.

Humour aside, all of these advertisements carry lengthy and ominous warnings to customers who might use these 'cures', for the sole purpose of protecting the manufacturers from any class action suits that may follow due to the possible side-effects suffered from using the medication. Although the FDA would harbour what would seem to be a false pride in billing itself as the highest adjudicator on the efficacy and safety of the billions of drugs taken every day, by comparison there would seem to be somewhat fewer lawsuits in any other part of the world concerning the subsequent side-effects from prescription drugs. Either America is addicted and is overdosing or someone's not doing their job. However, I would stress now that most of the ads shown on TV are for everyday conditions that are brought on by the lack of real exercise and from the failure to maintain a healthy and balanced diet. The cure is often available without the need to medicate.

Dental procedures here are rife but also not surprising, given the amount of sugar that the American public devours each day, so the purchase of dental insurance is crucial. A trip to your local orthodontist will be perilous. The cosmetically-enhanced smile that greets you in the surgery is just the beginning of an arduous series of expensive visits that will seriously harm your wealth. And don't be surprised to find that your friendly dentist will ping-pong you backwards and forwards between his dental accomplices and cohorts when a particular procedure needs another type of specialist. The other dentists in his gang will always want to take new x-rays each time so remember to take the originals with you to avoid duplication of records and costs. As an aside to this snippet on dental care and bearing in mind the extortionate prices the dentists charge and the houses they live in and the cars they drive, I was somewhat surprised to find that, of all the professions in the world, dentists are more likely to commit suicide than anyone else. Strange, but quite true.

Dental care in America is treated with the utmost importance. Rarely will you meet anyone here who hasn't at some point in their life, conceded to the obligatory brace or retainer. In fact, it's got to the stage now, where it is so fashionable for children to wear these ugly metal devices, that it's considered 'de rigueur' to wear one and almost low-rent not to have it. I know that Jay Leno usually makes a humorous comment every other night on his Los Angeles-based talk-show, denigrating the lamentable state of the British tooth, but in our defence, at least most of our teeth are the ones originally supplied by Mother Nature herself and not those manufactured by a wealthy, but suicidal dentist.

Dental care notwithstanding, the recent increase in the requirement of medical treatment is not a blip, but an ever increasing trend towards a nation of malady in a country that previously exemplified the defining picture of good health. Some would say that the root cause of the problem is down to the quantity, quality and availability of food in the USA which has led to previously unseen levels of obesity and incapacitation. Having witnessed the escalating desire amongst food producers to make meat and poultry fatter and more attractive, coupled with the enormous quantity of trans-fats now used in all fast-food production (which has gradually become the main diet of the poorer classes), I am now inclined to agree with that theory. Is it foolish to think that whatever we inject into the animals or put in their food to make them bigger and fatter, might not ultimately cause similar effects at the human end of the food chain?

The use of pills and potions to provide a cure for something that is often the result of unhealthy living combined with a general lack of respect for one's own body, dictates that it is also important to be wary of medications prescribed by your own family doctor. If the pills don't work that they recommend, likely as not they will prescribe something else instead, such is the obligation to provide an administered cure. Compare this to your local GP at home in the UK where you have to almost beg for a prescription. British doctors tend to adopt the 'physician, heal thyself' view in that if the body is able to combat a condition then it should be allowed to do so because by submitting to medication, the immune system is undoubtedly compromised. I can't help but agree with this viewpoint.

Finally, given the spiralling influx of poorer immigrants from Mexico and South America, a free National Healthcare System will be required in America sooner, rather than later. It will happen, regardless of its opponents. Not only to support this new and desperate migrant workforce but also to provide universal healthcare for its own subjects who continue to suffer outside the private domain of the privileged. It isn't just a nice idea, it's absolutely essential, as the time will surely come when all businesses will eventually stop giving the 'bonus' of medical insurance, because it will no longer be a commercial viability to do so. After that, only the fittest and strongest will survive.

Chapter 8

Fast Food &
The Rising Levels of Obesity

I vaguely remember an American hit record whose lyric passed mention of all the cops being in the doughnut shops. It was a witty poke at the fact that in America, if you need to find a policeman in a hurry, look no further than the nearest dining establishment where you may find half a dozen police cruisers parked outside. As is common in England, these fast food retailers occasionally offer complimentary or discounted food to the local constabulary but over the years, it's pretty clear to see that the options on offer have taken their toll on the waistline of the average US policeman. Cops ain't skinny in America.

If you are lucky enough to have visited a small selection of the fifty states in the USA, you will have noticed that there are many physical differences in the people who occupy those states. For example, it's not hard to see the difference in obesity levels between New York and Florida and likewise, between Texas and California. New Yorkers seem to make up a tribe that is fastidiously aware of its appearance and the most devoted members seem to function almost entirely on a diet of stress, coffee and adrenaline and I'm not just referring to the inhabitants of Manhattan. In contrast, Florida is the antithesis of New York with its relaxed and care-free attitude and expanding waistline but even The Sunshine State has woken up and has now started to address the obesity problem. Although in truth, it's more apparent in the wealthier middle-class areas of Florida.

Texas is actually like nowhere else I've been before. I've never seen so many overweight, oversized people anywhere else in the world. They're a happy, convivial and extremely hospitable race but they are big, they're very big. In contrast, they also have their fair share of the most elegant and beautiful women in the world. Conversely, California is more like Europe than any other state I've visited in the USA. Not only is it recognised now as one of the 'greener' states, but its natives are extremely conscious of how they look, what they eat and the amount of exercise they must take on a daily basis. It may be the vainest state in the USA and sales of mirrors must be on a par with sales of shoes, but I have always had the general opinion that they are the fittest and healthiest Americans.

I have a simple image that has stayed in my head from the moment I saw it here on television. There's an old TV series from the early 1960s, called 'Shell's Wonderful World of Golf' which was made to promote and teach golf to the American public. But apart from being just a wonderful set of programmes depicting an America in its absolute prime, this is what I really found intriguing. When watching any of the episodes, the players are all stick thin. So are all of the people in the crowd. In fact, you would be hard pushed to spot even a slightly overweight American in any of the sequences. They're not unhealthily thin, just perfectly slim men and women who also appear to be in the best of health. (They're all dressed immaculately too, though it's not relevant for this point). Compare that programme to a present-day transmission from The Augusta National or the US Open and you'd be shocked at the overall difference in shape, size and appearance. The players are still likely to be the fitter looking group today but even that will not be true in every case. America may be the greatest single producer of first-class athletes and sportsmen, but it has now also become the obesity capital of the world. And in a shockingly short period of time.

One of the reasons this has happened may be due to the relentless expansion of fast-food restaurants in the USA, that have quickly replaced the privately owned diners and eateries; the mom and pop shops that had previously formed the backbone of this country. But most of the hundreds of thousands of chain restaurants that dominate the sidewalks of any American thoroughfare, are not really offering a genuine melting pot of different foods from around the globe but are in fact, weak impersonators of world food. The great American Hamburger was laid to rest years ago and replaced with a version of it by 'restaurants' such as McDonald's, Burger King and Wendy's. In my opinion, the hamburgers produced are a poor substitute for the genuine American article, even though McDonald's has already fed the world 115 billion of them – that's around twenty burgers for every man, woman and child on the planet. Similarly, if you've ever eaten a pizza in Italy, which in reality is something of a delicacy, you'd be sorely disappointed at the offerings from Domino's or Pizza Hut. It doesn't stop there. Olive Garden claims to serve authentic Italian cuisine and if you're Italian, you'll have no stomach for their menu. I could go on and list endless other food outlets like Red Lobster, Dunkin Donuts, Taco Bell, KFC, Denny's and Subway but I think you probably get the picture. It is food based on an original idea but with little respect paid to the original ingredients and methods of preparation.

The sad part about all of this and the real reason that these companies will continue to thrive and expand is that their customer base is poorer, less intelligent and now more obese than those wealthier and better informed diners at the more expensive restaurants. The last time I visited a McDonald's was about eight months ago and as I waited in line, I realised that the majority of staff and customers were either African-American or Hispanic and mostly overweight (many of them absurdly obese) and along with the lack of courtesy shown from either side of the counter, it seemed to me that they were relatively under-educated in language, communication or hygiene. I wasn't standing there looking on in disdain; I was just quietly appalled at the fact that these people were feeding themselves a horrendous diet, at what seemed to be pretty high prices. Impoverished, obese and under-educated people feeding other poor, obese and equally under-educated compatriots. It was incredibly sad to see. I don't want this observation to sound smug but it did made me think hard about where the problem will end. As an aside, this scene is one that plays out every day in America and the minority language being spoken on that day in that restaurant, was English so if ever there was an example that illustrated the subtitle of this book, it was right there, right then.

Since the documentary film, *'Super Size Me'* found its way into the public's mind, there has been a pronounced reduction in sales of McDonald's standard menu items but not nearly enough to make a real difference. The company tried to take evasive action to stem the dip in sales caused by the film, by introducing more salad-based or seemingly healthy menu items, but in many cases it was said that these new offerings may have had a higher calorific or trans-fat value than the original hamburgers and fries. But it did seem that the company was at least making a concerted effort to correct the problem by reacting quickly to the torrent of criticism that followed the showing of the film. When looking at the McDonald's extraordinary early history on their own website, it's easy to see that Ray Kroc's brilliant and entrepreneurial original vision, emphasised all that was great about the American Dream and a quick look at the photos that catalogue those early years, brings a warm feeling to the most cynical of souls. The great pity is that the American Dream that the McDonald brothers began and which Kroc nurtured to fruition, has now been reduced to something quite different and ultimately, quite depressing. I would love to have compared the 1955 McDonald's experience to the 21st century version. I suspect that the hamburgers, fries and shakes of the 1950s were of the same standard that Kroc also demanded from his staff's personal presentation and restaurant hygiene. His original mantra to his employees, "time to lean is time to clean", appears lost on the restaurant staff of today, English seemingly the minority language. But Ray Kroc was an extraordinary man and his vision, passion and courage, (he mortgaged himself to the hilt to get the business off the ground) should still be saluted and remembered as part of the original essence that defines the American Dream.

In all fast-food restaurants, the variations on a theme are incessant. In fact, the many varying ways these fast-food outlets can serve a beef patty or a piece of chicken should in some way be admired. They are able to take two or three menu items that would be reasonably satisfying on their own, and put them all together to make one big mess that is either too large or too repulsive to eat. In fact, I'd never seen pancakes and syrup on the same plate as bacon and eggs before I came to America, let alone the sight of an omelette in a croissant. I personally like McDonald's, Wendy's and Coca-Cola, but I know that for me, they could become addictive so I rarely frequent fast-food restaurants except in those situations when absolutely nothing else is available.

So what has happened to make obesity a genuine national problem in the USA? Studies have shown that there has been a dramatic portion size increase since the mid 1970s which is actually when obesity levels first began to rise dramatically. Snacking has increased by 50% in the last thirty years while fast food consumption is up by 150% and sugar intake is up by a staggering 210%. The original 6oz bottle of Coca-Cola was once a genuine treat for kids. The logo itself conjures up a happy and idyllic America. But it is now being served up in 32oz buckets which when taken on a daily basis, becomes a deadly threat instead of being that original treat.

Although much of the obesity problem can be attributed to these alarming facts, there is also a popular theory that one particular national restaurant chain had the idea in the mid-1970s to change their plate size from 10 inches to 13 inches. With this additional space, the meals that they were able to offer were 65% larger when compared to rival restaurants and the immediate effect was that this company's sales went through the roof. The other restaurants naturally followed suit and changed their plate size and from that moment on, America was effectively consuming a radically higher amount of food on each visit to a restaurant. This plate size increase wasn't confined to restaurants; plate sizes in the American home increased too. As the plates expanded, so did the American girth. The rest is history.

Even Starbucks, who brought to America, a European style of café society, selling a range of cappuccino, espresso and latte that actually tasted like there might be a quality coffee bean present in the potion, first began by offering short and tall versions of its products. I always thought this was a responsible and sensible approach. But it wasn't long before the cup sizes were eventually replaced by Tall, Grande and Venti, the latter meaning twenty in Italian and translating to an enormous 20oz serving – a whole pint and a quarter of the brew. I still find myself just pleading to make a choice between small, medium and large instead of big, bigger and biggest but this just isn't the American way of doing things and so I'm forced to translate my selection from the menu into something that the order-taker will comprehend. In America, you must be seen to be buying something that is 'large' at the very least, otherwise the value-for-money perception will not be realised. Whatever the case, I am, and probably always will be, a devout and loyal Starbucks customer, forever hooked like a junkie for my daily fix of the caffeinated liquid.

Fast-food commercials sit comfortably next to the auto and credit ads on TV and the message rarely touts the quality of the food, just a big shout as to how much you can get for your dollar. $9.99 will buy you a three course menu of gargantuan portions with equally gargantuan amounts of fats and calories. When you sit down in any of these places, you are immediately primed with a loaf of bread and a churn-load of butter and the idea of ordering hors d'ouvres is out of the question for most Europeans as the entrée often arrives, accompanied by an enormous salad or bowl of soup. The easy availability of food is also a hugely critical factor. In the last three decades, the USA has seen food outlets double in numbers and most of those businesses are offering cheap and unhealthy menus which are served in excessively large quantities. If you make something too easy to get, then the consequences are obvious. It's not rocket science.

Finally, there is tradition in this country which I cannot recall when dining in any British restaurant and that is the request or offer of a box or bag to take home any of the food left on the table. Of course, it may be that the European portions are so small that plates are left licked and shiny but over here, it's the natural thing to do. Any unfinished morsel of food is gleefully packed away to take home for further feasting the following day. It even happens in more expensive restaurants but not as often.

The threat of heart disease, hypertension and diabetes is real. There is an essential problem with the American national food supply chain that needs immediate attention. The day will surely come when the USA wakes up and smells the proverbial coffee and suddenly recognises the need to adopt a more European (or Californian) approach to the quality, quantity and diversity of food intake. This, along with a return to daily exercise and the abandonment of the sedentariness brought about by a technology-driven lifestyle, will provide the two elements that can restore the health of this country to the one that I first pictured nearly fifty years ago. We should hope then, that it happens sooner rather than later.

Chapter **9**

Retail Therapy

For many years, the UK has slowly been adopting the open-all-hours policy, pioneered by the American retail industry. Even with the opposition of church groups claiming Sunday as the sacred day of the week, Great Britain has gradually changed its identity from the 9-5, Monday-Saturday hours of opening, to a nation desperate to utilise every available hour for selling anything from groceries to garden equipment. Even Christmas Day, traditionally considered the 'closed' day in Britain, is now an available 24 hours for any of us to purchase that last-minute turkey that we'd somehow forgotten to grab during the wild-eyed and desperate season of goodwill.

To see where we learned the value of trading during every hour of available retail time, we need look no further than America for confirmation. Wal-Mart is the greatest single, private and national employer of people in the USA, with as many as 1.8 million staff on the worldwide payroll, and over one million employees or associates in North America alone, representing an incredible 1% of the American working population. In fact, it is the single largest private employer in the world with over 138 million customers passing through its doors each week. If these statistics are wrong at the time of this book's publication, it's probably not an error; just that Wal-Mart continues to grow at a staggering rate throughout the world, every day. The benefits offered to employees are second to none and for many of the staff, the pension plan, the medical insurance, stock options, paid vacations and discount cards are part of the reason that they work there in the first place.

It is therefore no surprise to see that Wal-Mart's 24 hours a day, seven days a week, 365 days a year opening-hours policy is part of the reason that it claims the coveted title of No.1 Retailer in the USA. This, coupled with the fact that just about any item or service can be found there, is the reason why so many Americans congregate at the 'church' of Wal-Mart on a daily basis. It is one of the most staggering success stories that America has produced and it was the brainchild of one extraordinary man, Sam Walton, back in 1962 in the town of Rogers, Arkansas. If there was ever an example of something that typifies the absolute essence of The American Dream and one man's decision to seize it with both hands, then this is it. Mr. Walton died in 1992 but his legacy lives on in the lives of every American, every day.

Personally, I don't like Wal-Mart or indeed any of the other retail stores of this kind, whether it is Target, Kmart or whoever – they're just not my idea of fun but they are to many others so my opinion here is largely irrelevant. Without doubt, their price promise, guaranteeing that you won't find the same item cheaper anywhere else, is absolutely valid, but the actual process of shopping in these grotesque superstores is not one that makes the thrill of purchase something to look forward to. Like any other shopping trip, it is always best to avoid the weekend for stocking up. In the case of Wal-Mart, it is even more important given that their sprawling car parks are hideously busy on Saturday and Sunday and the journey from car to store should be marked in Hansel & Gretel fashion to ensure that the retrieval of your vehicle is guaranteed at the end of your spree.

As with any retail business, the clientele is often identifiable by the price and presentation of the product on offer and Wal-Mart doesn't buck that trend. The stack 'em high, sell 'em low business ethic isn't designed to cater for the discerning customer. You go there to buy cheaply and, without wishing to insult Wal-

Mart's customers, this low-rent attitude is often characterised and personified by the type of customer queuing in front of you at the check-out. Wal-Mart sells everything, and everything is sold cheaper but don't go there if you want to pick up an Armani suit or a Coach handbag or even a ripe piece of Camembert to partner your eagerly awaiting Chateau Margaux – they'll most likely think you're speaking in a foreign tongue and they certainly won't stock it. Wal-Mart just isn't the place for it. But if you want to buy your kids a fifty dollar bicycle, or you need an electric toaster for six bucks, or even a new TV on Christmas Day, then you came to the right place.

Of course, the introduction of 24/7 opening hours has spawned a new breed of customer, the nocturnal shopper. These are the creatures that slip in during the midnight hour to feast on Wal-Mart's wares with the comfort of peace, quiet and certain serenity, and the added advantage of a Wal-Mart associate readily available to answer product questions. I should confess that I have also shopped at Wal-Mart at this late hour, mainly due to the fact that one evening I wanted to buy a large and heavy television whilst allowing me to park my car within binocular view of the store, lest I be required to enlist the help of a willing Wal-Mart staff member for the safe loading of the thing into my car. Human nature dictates that we use every situation to our best advantage and of course, I'm no exception.

Wal-Mart, like Kmart, Target, Best Buy and Circuit City is a national success. We may not like these megastores but most of us frequent them at some time or another. However, if I have one thing that stays in my mind and which troubles me most, it is the sight of perilously poor people in these stores, armed with the opportunity to shop round the clock, spending money that they just don't have, for the sole reason of satisfying their idea of the American Dream.

But if you forget about the unpleasantness of superstore avarice, some forms of shopping in the USA aren't only easy, they're fun too. Supermarkets here are a breath of fresh air. In Britain, we have five or six large supermarket chains like Sainsbury's, Asda and Tesco that can be found in most towns, with the more up-market stores like Marks & Spencer and Waitrose mostly found in the wealthier areas. It's a retail sector controlled by a small group of high end players, a situation verging on a monopoly. In the USA, apart from the superstores mentioned earlier, there are many smaller supermarket chains that can sometimes cover one or two states or perhaps an entire region of the country. In addition to those groups, there are the family-owned businesses in some cities that might have only a couple of stores.

Some of the larger chains are possibly names that will be immediately familiar; Waldbaum's and Food Emporium in New York, Ralphs and Vons in California, Albertsons (at one point a nationwide chain in 37 states but now mainly on the east coast) and Randalls in Texas but there are some names that you might not recognise, like Kroger (2,477 stores in 31 states under nearly two dozen banners), Food Lion on the east coast and Star Market and Shaw's in Connecticut, Massachusetts, Maine and Vermont. The Winn-Dixie and Publix supermarket chains, both of which are found in the deep south and Florida will likely be familiar to many British holidaymakers. There are of course the 'club' stores which in Britain we call 'cash & carry' and some of these names will be instantly recognisable; Aldi, Costco and Sam's Club, not to mention the oddly and inappropriately named BJ's.

Food shopping in England is a nightmarish thought. It wasn't always that way, it's just that the enormous choice and availability of groceries under one roof, breeds an addictive type of shopper. Notwithstanding the struggle to get to the store, the car-unfriendly parking-spaces in the over-full car parks, the general rudeness from fellow customers in the store and the outlandishly high prices that we are charged in the UK, it could never be deemed a therapeutic experience. However, in the USA, wherever you go to buy your weekly groceries, it is usually a surprisingly pleasant exercise. Supermarkets here are wide-aisled, conspicuously clean and well mannered examples of how the food shopping experience should be. Car parks are ergonomically designed with wide and angled spaces that avoid door, bumper and fender tragedies and the shopping carts aren't chained to one another demanding the insertion of more of your hard earned lucre to prise one away. The packing and bagging of groceries by the check-out staff has been obligatory for many years and in most cases, the shopping cart will be wheeled to your car and the groceries loaded for you without the necessity of the perfunctory tip. In fact, the stores frown on the idea of any gratuity for this service. It's just part of the whole deal. It is worth remembering however, that although American supermarkets sell wine and beer, they do not sell spirits of any kind. You'll need to go to the Liquor Store for that – I don't know why, but I just love that name.

The one surprising feature that has not made its way over to this side of the Puddle, is the now established service of online grocery shopping and same day delivery that we now take for granted in England. There are delivery services available in some areas of the USA, although these are more often in the high end sector. It should therefore be noted for American readers, that the main supermarkets in England, including Tesco, Sainsbury's, Asda and Waitrose, all offer online ordering and delivery, the latter often available the same day and in some cases it is free. It's a wonderful idea and in general, it works pretty efficiently.

If grocery shopping could be deemed therapeutic, then shopping at the mall in America is an entirely different kettle of fish. These oversized lumps of metal and concrete are air-conditioned and sanitised monoliths that use muzak to nullify your mind while you drift endlessly from store to store to sift through the same chain names that sell to the majority rather than to the individual. The line-up of retailers in these malls is familiar all over the USA. There will typically be three or four department stores available; Macy's, Sears, JC Penney, Neiman Marcus, Dillards, Saks Fifth Avenue or Bloomingdales and the usual suspects of clothing retailers like Old Navy, American Eagle and Abercrombie & Fitch. Not forgetting the old faithfuls, GAP, Foot Locker, Pottery Barn, Body Shop, PacSun, Radio Shack and the ubiquitous Starbucks at every rest-point, as well as the litter of Sunglass Huts and cell phone cubicles that line the centre of the mall walkways.

At every intersection in the mall or at any of the department store entrances, there are always plenty of places to sit and rest. Some of these seats are courtesy benches and others are seating products placed there by vendors trying to promote their latest electric recliners or massage chairs. I often find myself grinning inanely at the huddled masses of aging men who sleep peacefully on these cleverly positioned benches or vibrato chairs, snoring gently and impervious to the clattering throng that imperiously passes by them. They've either given in to their wives' inexhaustibility to plunder the never-ending choice of stores or perhaps just surrendered to the impossibility of finding an exit through which they might relocate their cars and plot their escape. I've never yet seen one of these old chaps wake up so I assume they're either dragged off by their women once exhaustion has finally taken hold or that the mall staff merely wheel these poor souls into a storage facility for the night and push them back out again the following morning to repeat the exercise.

The similarity of each mall across the United States is also understandable, given that all of them are owned by large real estate investment groups who are building new and bigger versions at a rate of knots in every town in America. The largest of these property groups is Simon Malls, which at present owns 285 shopping malls of varying sizes in 38 states, covering over 200 million square feet of retail space. Simon Malls is a member of the S&P 500 companies and is also the largest publicly traded retail real estate company in the USA with a value approaching $50 billion. Don't be surprised to learn that Simon also owns 53 sites in Europe and five in Japan with plans to spread further still.

My first visit to a mall (I still have a huge problem saying the word as it's not pronounced mall as in Pall Mall but rather 'mall' that rhymes with 'tall'. With the word's origin dating back to

1737 and meaning 'a shaded and tree-lined promenade' it seems to have missed the point of the original interpretation) was to a relatively small version and even at that size, I found the place intimidating and devoid of any sense of naturalness. In fact, it reminded me of the Las Vegas casinos that deliberately avoid the use of clocks or natural daylight or anything that might alert the gambling inhabitants to the time of day or night, lest they decide to stop handing over their money to the casino for just one brief moment. In a similar way, these malls have had the layout scientifically designed so that there are rest-rooms, rest-points and restaurants at exactly the right spots to ensure that nothing should interrupt or shorten your shopping expedition.

In fact, expedition is not such an inappropriate word. To paraphrase from Simon Malls themselves, they run four types of outlet from the smallest, which are the regional malls, all the way up to the power-centres, mega-town centres, premium outlets and community & lifestyle centres, which are less a shopping trip and more an adventure. There is however, one mall in particular, actually not owned by Simon, which is in Minnesota and boasts the title of "the largest mall in the USA". It is appropriately named Mall Of America. This mall is the champion of all malls. Complete with a theme park featuring a roller coaster and thirty other rides, a shark infested aquarium, a dinosaur museum, hotel, casino and even a Lego Land, this is not so much a place to shop as a weekend vacation between school days. And apparently there are stores there too, where you can buy things. They actually suggest you plan your trip to avoid missing anything – God forbid.

Fortunately, malls aren't the only retail stores around. Small privately owned businesses litter the towns and cities the length and breadth of America and currently, there is still the opportunity for the discerning shopper to choose and purchase goods in a more leisurely and sophisticated fashion. The problem is that the destruction of these local businesses, caused by the emergence of the giant malls and outlets is gradually eroding the fading image of Main Street America and that loss adds to the depersonalisation and character-stripping of the great American trader and its loyal customer base. I'm sure that many of us would like to turn back time and rediscover the old style of shopping but it's just not possible now as the relentless construction of the mall phenomenon continues at an unending and unnerving rate.

Plazas or strip malls are the smaller shopping areas where all the stores are single units divided up from one long or sometimes U-shaped building. They are unenclosed, generally quite small, and usually surround a small car parking area. Amazingly, in the world of the mega-mall, these stores seem to survive and even thrive and the plaza still remains a popular target when you just want to pull up outside the door, buy what you need and depart without distraction or bankruptcy.

A brief note on DIY stores and pharmacies here. The two largest and most popular home improvement companies are Lowe's and Home Depot. You would be forgiven for inadvertently referring to Home Depot as either Homebase or B&Q. The name similarity is obvious for the former and the logo colour and branding is somewhat akin to the latter in the UK. Lowe's is altogether easier as it bears no likeness to any UK store. There are no real differences between the British and American versions except some of the words used to describe the everyday items you may want to buy. Filler becomes caulk, bath-plug becomes stopper, tap becomes faucet, rawlplug becomes anchor, spanner becomes wrench and my favourite – jubilee clip which translates as worm clamp. There are lots of variants on the American names and often you'll find yourself playing out a mutated version of Pictionary to a bemused staff member in your vain attempt at describing exactly what you're looking for.

With pharmacies here, the scope of what is available is far greater than in the UK. Boots The Chemist (which incidentally, is currently expanding to the USA and will be called Boots Retail USA) and Lloyds Pharmacy are our biggest chains at home but they are tiny when compared to the two equivalent pharmacies here, CVS and Walgreens. Both of these American giants sell very similar items to each other. They are more than just pharmacies, they also have departments for Food, Clothing, Toys, Electronics and my current personal favourite, Sexual Wellness. They also sell cigarettes, an idiosyncrasy that has always bothered me when their main goal as pharmacies, should be to provide a cure and not a way to die sooner.

As another little aside on health, for some odd reason the pharmacies here provide drive-through facilities similar to those found at fast-food outlets, rather than promoting the idea of exercise by making the customers actually leave their vehicle for a moment and take a few healthy steps. I know this may seem petty but the relentless pursuit of a sedentary lifestyle is as important as the harm done since the invention of the remote control by Robert Adler back in 1956 (Sadly, as I write this, I have just learned that Mr. Adler died yesterday of heart failure at a nursing home in Boise, Idaho. He was 93). When I was a boy, the remote control era hadn't yet dawned in England and we had just two channels on television so consequently, I was instructed by my parents to get up and walk over to the TV to change the channel, perhaps only five or six times an evening. Imagine the exercise that kids would get today without the aid of a remote control, now that there are a thousand channels to choose from? We'd be breeding six year olds with six packs.

I had never heard the expression 'Black Friday' until I came to live in the USA. I knew 'Black Wednesday' very well as that was the day on 16th September 1992, when the inept British government completely lost control of the economy and at one point during that day, interest rates raced up from 10% to 16% eventually culminating in Britain's withdrawal from the European Exchange Rate Mechanism. The ensuing chaos of that day found a nation watching on helplessly as Margaret Thatcher's Conservative Government flapped around like headless chickens while speculators like George Soros made billions of pounds of profit from the farce laid before them and desperate homeowners up and down the country were forced to surrender their homes to the banks because of their inability to meet future mortgage payments. I digress. Black Friday has an altogether happier meaning. This is the day in America that follows Thanksgiving (Thanksgiving always falls on the fourth Thursday of November) and it traditionally marks the start of the holiday shopping period that leads all the way up to Christmas. Black Friday is so called, because it is supposedly the first day of the year when retailers finally trade out of the red and back into the black. It is the biggest single shopping day in America and it is the day when you will see consumerism at its most frenzied.

I want to finish this chapter on what I think is a strange success story. There appears to be an American love affair with a lingerie store called Victoria's Secret and I just don't get it. I've looked at the store and its stock and can't think of a reason why anyone might get excited about any of its merchandise. Yes, the high quality packaging and bags are well designed and seem reasonably upmarket but the actual design and quality of goods on offer, leaves little to get excited about and Victoria's Secret feels more akin in originality to Marks & Spencer than a high-end knicker company. I will admit now, that being married to a woman who sold inspirational lingerie for twenty years, does make me a little biased towards the credentials of the more expensive and luxurious Belgian or Swiss offerings but come on, Vicky's real secret has to be her amazing ability to sell uninspiring tat to the masses, at extraordinarily wallet-damaging prices. I like the ads though.

Chapter 10

The Cost of Living The Dream

Unfortunately, it's not possible to make a true comparison between the cost of living in the USA and the UK as it's largely dependant on where you live in either country and given the wildly differing taxes and charges in each of the fifty American states, it's even more confusing to ratify costs in the USA. That said, it is worth looking at the overall picture to see if there is some way of evaluating comparative costs.

I have previously touched on property taxes in America and I've said that British immigrants will find them shockingly high when compared to council tax charges in the UK. However, every state has different weighting on real estate tax and this will be dependant on a number of issues. Again, I should reiterate that it would be impossible to compare every town, city and state so I will concentrate on the two most popular destinations targeted by the British; California & Florida. Again, an entire series of books could be written on the various differences in taxes from state to state, city to city and town to town, so I will use only broad brush strokes to illustrate the main points.

Proposition 13, was an initiative by the Californian voters that changed the constitution on property taxes in the Golden State. Its official title was "People's Initiative to Limit Property Taxation," It was effectively seen as a taxpayers revolt and finally, in 1992 after twenty years of petitioning, a tax cap of 1%

was set on the assessed value of property. It also maintained a 2% limit in annual increase over the previous year's bill, provided that the property had not changed ownership in that period. When resold, as in any other state, the property is then re-assessed at current values. The tax burden can also decrease if there is a drop in property value during for example, a downturn in real estate prices.

Therefore, in California, there is just one rate of annually paid property tax and that is 1% although there may be a number of other smaller local charges that will raise the bill as a whole, including additional items like the infamous Mello-Roos tax, so I am more comfortable in saying that the average Californian property tax charge will be around 1.1% of assessed value in total. As a simple example, if you buy a million dollar home anywhere in California, you would expect to pay approximately $11,000 a year in property taxes with a capped increase of 2% in subsequent years. Therefore, the second year's tax bill should be no more than around $11,220 and so on. Pretty straightforward.

In Florida, depending where you choose to live in the state, you would pay on average, around 1.8% giving an annual property tax bill of around $18,000 on a $1m property, a lot higher than California but the reason for this will be more fully explained later in this chapter. In Florida, there is also a cap on future increases which is set at a maximum of 3% and as stated previously, there is a 'homestead allowance' of $25,000 on the total assessed value which is completely exempt from tax ($7000 in California). This exemption isn't much and many Floridians want to raise it to a more realistic figure given the recent heady rise in Florida real estate value. It wouldn't surprise me to see a similar version of Proposition 13 pushed forward by the increasingly tax-burdened residents of Florida.

Part of the reason that Floridians continue to put up with high real estate taxes is simple; there is no state income tax. It is one of seven US states, along with Alaska, Nevada, South Dakota, Texas, Washington, and Wyoming where personal income is not subject to state tax. For many working residents, this is a very attractive incentive and makes high real estate taxes slightly more palatable. However, don't forget that Federal Tax is still payable, whichever state you choose to live in the USA.

At this juncture, I think it's important to clarify that Income Tax is a relatively new idea and it might be interesting to make a note about the origination of Income Tax in the UK. Prior to its introduction, taxes were levied at source; that it to say that anything you bought required that a purchase tax be paid to the government. The older and more amusing forms of taxation included the now famous but quite absurd Window Tax. King William III introduced this tax in 1696 to pay for the burgeoning military costs at home and in Europe and this charge lasted for over 150 years until it was replaced in 1851. Window Tax was a charge levied on the owner of a house who had more than the accepted number of windows in his dwelling. The limit was six windows and any additional openings would be subject to Window Tax. To this day, you can still see many examples all over Great Britain where the original owners had bricked up some of their surplus windows to avoid this extra charge. Eventually, Window Tax was replaced by House Duty, thus finally arresting the butchering of historic and architecturally beautiful homes.

However, it was only relatively recently, back in 1799 that the British Prime Minister, William Pitt The Younger, introduced a tax on earnings to help pay for the enormous anticipated cost of the Napoleonic Wars. As far as Pitt was concerned, Income Tax was always intended to be a temporary tax. By 1816, with Wellington's final victory over Napoleon at the Battle of Waterloo, Income Tax was formally repealed but recalled once again in 1842 by Sir Robert Peel, to pay for the growing burden of the public deficit at that time. This time however, the tax would remain in force for good and in 1945, Income Tax levels increased substantially to help pay for the cost of the Second World War.

The real point I am making is that Income Tax was always deemed to be a temporary measure to pay for extraordinary items, most of those as a result of the cost of going to war to defend the British Empire. Even to this date, the tax remains temporary, expiring on 6th April each year with the requirement that it be renewed yearly as a provision in the Annual Finance Bill. Unfortunately, Income Tax appears to have become a permanent fixture in Britain and because it is full of so many loopholes that can be exploited by the accountants of the wealthy, the poorer masses pay relatively so much more in tax than the very rich, who continue to pay a miniscule amount in relative terms and actually in many cases, no tax at all.

Of course, if you were to choose between California and Florida as an example of where to migrate to, you shouldn't rely solely on real estate taxes and income taxes as the governing issues regarding costs. There are many more points to look at including the differences in prices and rates for property, sales tax, fuel, cars, insurance, food and general living and entertainment costs.

If we look first at the enormous difference in the purchase price of a family home in these two states, it would be fair to say that California real estate is probably three times more expensive than Florida when comparing like for like. I won't go into detail and attempt to ratify this statement but from experience, I can confirm that this is probably correct. We also need to remember that this price differential will have an escalating effect on the real estate taxes you'll be asked to pay in the future. However, whatever the difference, the fact remains that American real estate is much cheaper per square foot when comparing like for like, than similar property in Britain so the British migrant will fare pretty well wherever he or she lands.

State sales tax in the USA is the equivalent of purchase tax in the UK, better known there as Value Added Tax (VAT). Whereas VAT is currently set countrywide at 17.5%, all state sales tax rates will vary in the US, depending on what you buy and where you buy it. Some states have different rates on cigarettes and alcohol and some will have varying levies on fuel and insurance. Some states have no sales tax at all and these little havens are Alaska, Delaware, Montana, New Hampshire and Oregon. (Although it might be tough for the newly immigrated Briton to get used to living in Alaska). It's true to say though that overall, California has the highest sales tax level at around 8% whilst Florida's is one of the lowest, at 6%.

It is important to remember that, unlike VAT in the UK which is usually embedded within the advertised selling price, whenever you purchase anything in America, the sales tax will not be displayed on the 'sticker price'. It is always added at the point of payment. I've always found this tradition of applying the sales tax at the till a little irritating, particularly when I'm buying something for 99 cents and the dollar in my hand needs fortifying with another 5 cents or so to make the sale. I rarely carry change – too bulky, so the 99c ice-cream ends up taking two of my dollar bills and fills my pocket with a jangling assortment of coins, all of which will be discarded when I get home. The whole sales tax system will irritate most British people, not because they have a problem paying it, just the method by which it is applied. I can confirm though, that it doesn't seem to bother Americans one iota – it's the way it has always been. However, if you go into a car dealership in the USA and buy a $50,000 car, the tax applied in Florida will add on another $3000 to the total cost and in California, because the sales tax rate is higher, you'll have to hand over a hefty $4000 to pay for the additional sales tax. I should also say that local state tax is payable even on the purchase of used vehicles. So if you privately buy a car from a friend or neighbour or via the Autotrader or eBay websites, then you must pay the sales tax on the purchase price when you register the vehicle in your name. Effectively, every time a car changes hands, the new owner must pay sales tax to the state. This is something that's uniquely different in the private buying and selling of pre-owned cars when compared to the practice in the UK, where sales tax is only applicable to brand new vehicles.

Fuel prices vary from state to state and typically, the price of a gallon of gasoline (petrol) in California will be around 30 to 40 cents more than in Florida. This is mostly due to the difference in sales tax levied on gasoline on the west coast. Although petrol prices in America are about one-third of those charged in the UK, California is currently well known as being the 'greenest' state and its residents appear to be far more concerned with the condition of the planet than its cousins seem to be, over on the east coast. Rarely sighted in the Deep South and Florida, are the smaller and more economical and European type cars and rarer still, the hybrid and all-electric 'green' vehicles. In Florida, you can buy a Toyota Prius hybrid any time day or night, but you'll find a long waiting list to acquire one in California. You'll also notice a marked difference in the amount of pick-up trucks used as the family conveyance in the south and south-east in comparison to the west. It always feels somewhat more wild-west in the east than it does in the Wild West itself.

Well now, here's the good news. Not only is gasoline cheaper here but just about everything is. As I've already said, if you're selling up in the UK and buying equivalently in the USA, you'll probably get a lot more bang for your buck. Everything costs less, including imports from the UK. All cars are staggeringly cheaper here, even with the sales tax added. The following story is an example that highlights the anomalies of international trade.

When I first moved here, I tried to fit in and do the right thing by buying American. After dozens of trips to Chevrolet, Chrysler and GM dealerships, I finally bought a Hummer and probably did so against my better judgement. (yes, I can hear the words 'stupid' and 'moron' being muttered as I write) Anyway, I could stand the thing for only six weeks before I had to get rid of it. To say that I disliked that useless, gutless and style-less piece of automotive junk would be a mild understatement. Now I think it's true to say that once the British have been away from their own country for some time, they start to cling to anything that is British or which has some British connection, whether it's Heinz Baked Beans or PG Tips, cricket, football or rugby. I slowly developed this same hankering and decided to order a Range Rover which I suppose is about as British, or English as it gets. However, the real point is that the car delivered to me, was built in England, shipped across the Atlantic and sold to me for the grand total of $63,000 including taxes. Had that same vehicle been delivered to my door in England, the total would have been some $110,000, a staggering price difference.

I'd like to say that the enormous price difference is solely due to the taxes imposed by the British government but I'm not so sure that the Revenue is completely to blame. I just think that we have always been and continue to be, the most ripped-off nation in Europe and sadly, we seem content for the situation to remain that way. What I don't understand, is why Americans (and me, actually) have the benefit of enjoying high quality British products at extremely competitive prices. The additional bonus when purchasing a new BMW or Land Rover in North America, is the invaluable offer of four years free servicing; 60,000 miles without a bill. This will doubtless infuriate European buyers as I'm not aware that a similar incentive is offered to them.

At the time of writing, the current dollar to pound rate is favourable to those transferring their sterling balance to US dollars. In fact, at two dollars to the pound, it is one of the best rates we've seen for many years. It may also distort the true price of anything we buy here. However, I tend to view prices as if the currencies were the same units. Therefore, if a new television here costs $500, then I would assume that the same or similar item in the UK would cost me £500 or if a joint of meat in the supermarket here was $20, then I would probably expect to pay £20 at Sainsbury's. What I am saying is that it feels as though you are getting everything at about half the price that it is at home in the UK. How long that lasts is debatable, as it wasn't so long ago back in 1985, that we saw the US dollar and Sterling hit parity, that is, one British Pound bought you one American Greenback. This was only twenty tears ago so the same could easily happen in the near future.

I've talked about food shopping in supermarkets in a previous chapter and sometimes it's difficult to gauge whether there is a difference in prices when comparing to the UK. Of course, currency fluctuation makes this even harder to calculate and the price of food differs from state to state, supermarket to supermarket. If I were to make a judgement, I would say that it is less expensive in the USA and quality would appear to be similar to the UK. The point being, don't treat it as a cost of living issue because it really isn't.

Utility costs over here will vary enormously, depending on where you live. It's not like the UK where the power providers supply the whole country at similar rates and the supply usage doesn't change dramatically, whether north, south, east or west. Each state in the US has significantly different pricing structures and unit costs. And even though there are nearly 1,000 public gas systems in the United States, it is worth pointing out that mains gas is not yet available to every home in the US. Many households that use gas ovens and hobs rely either on bottled gas or large underground storage tanks that are refilled when required. (The word 'gas' in the USA means petrol, a shortened version of gasoline rather than meaning 'natural gas' as we know it in the UK. Gas is generally referred to here, as propane). The majority of heating systems here are oil-fired or, as in the case of the southern states and Florida, the air conditioning is used to supply an electrically powered and heated forced-air circulation to provide occasionally needed warmth in the winter.

In the more sub-tropical areas of America, the use of air-conditioning is not a luxury, it's absolutely vital to make life a pleasant and bearable existence. The cost of running these systems in a home is extremely expensive and the average family in Florida will see annual power bills of $5000 or more plus the cost of frequent repair and service bills to maintain the systems. Again, there will often be only one electricity provider available so there is effectively a monopoly on price control so don't expect to be able to make a supplier change if you are unhappy with the prices being charged to you. The price per kW-hour charged, varies state to state but as a rough guide, electricity prices are around 6¢ per kWh in Florida and about 12¢ in California. However, prices on the west coast have hit staggering highs in recent years, sometimes as much as 20¢ per kWh. Bear in mind that electricity usage will be somewhat lower in California because the more temperate climate negates the constant use of air-conditioning, a crucial requirement in Florida.

Water rates are not necessarily higher in the USA but water usage in many parts, most definitely is. If you live in a reasonably nice home and you are working full-time, it's more than likely that you'll employ a lawn company to maintain your garden. It is also likely that your home will have an underground watering and sprinkler system that takes care of the lawn and plants. This is one of the many sensible things that our American friends do – whenever they construct a new house, they install a water pump and timer and lay rubber piping and sprinkler heads throughout the property. It is just such a smart idea and one which should be adopted in the UK. Except of course, that we would never be able to use the systems because of the summer-long hosepipe bans that we are annually forced to endure, despite the copious rainfall we experience in Britain all winter. However, the downside of the automated watering and sprinkler systems is that they use a lot of water and so unless you are lucky enough to tap from an underground well, you might find that water bills will be demonstrably higher here than in the UK.

Eating out is more common in the USA than in the UK. It is true that it's possible to take your family out to dinner and enjoy a relatively good meal at a restaurant without breaking the bank and it can sometimes prove cheaper to eat out than to cook a similar meal at home. In fact, Americans use their available time more effectively than we do and general entertainment is highly regarded on the monthly expenditure bill. They are also big sports fans and baseball, football and basketball games usually have capacity crowds although the same can't be said for the spectator rush towards soccer, not yet anyway. A day at the game is a great day out for the whole family and one that generally isn't subject to potential violence. To a man, they all seem to love boating, fishing, hunting and golf or even just a weekend up at a cabin in the hills. The pursuit of enjoyment and the best use of available time are paramount. It is also probably understandable, given that paid vacation in the USA averages maybe only a couple of weeks a year as opposed to the five or six weeks taken by employees in Britain. Weekends become mini-vacation periods and Americans get the maximum pleasure out of them. It's actually a pretty good blueprint for living.

The final part of this chapter deals with one of the heaviest costs of American life and that is, insurance. I have already touched on the extremely high cost of medical insurance but in America, insurance is not just big business, it's colossal and it's intimidating. Whether it's for life, auto, medical or homeowners insurance, the policy premiums are often so inflated that the very thought of them can stop you sleeping at night.

Auto insurance is commonly purchased as a six month policy as opposed to the annual premiums that we pay in the UK. This allows the American insurers to raise the rate twice a year instead of just once. A small scam, but a scam nonetheless. The first problem is that you cannot insure a vehicle in the USA without a current, valid US Driver's Licence. (Well actually, you might be able to buy insurance on a European licence but expect to pay many times more in premium costs). Of course, once you have gained your licence, the insurance company will view you as a new driver, even if you are middle-aged and have been driving for thirty years with an unblemished record. Because of this, you will be charged sky high premiums until you've had a ticket-less and claim-free driving record for a couple of years or so and then the rates will drop sharply.

There is however, a completely legal but slightly sneaky way to get around the fact that you've only recently gained your US driver's licence and it all depends on which company is quoting the policy. This is the sneaky bit. When completing the online policy form and the question comes up on driving history, phrased "How long have you had a US Driver's Licence?", you would naturally have to respond in honesty "less than one year". However, if the question is phrased "How long have you held a driver's licence?" then the honest response would be to refer to the date that you first gained a licence in your home country. The difference in policy premium will vary dramatically on the basis of this question. You'll still be required to furnish details of your US licence and the insurance company will ultimately have the ability to check it. Most auto-insurers in the USA work in a completely ignorant manner when assessing driver risk but there are some who are able to make the assumption that a middle-aged man or woman is probably not as big a risk as a 15-year old even if the former happens to hail from a different country.

In my own experience, the purchase of auto-insurance was yet another slice of humble pie to be eaten. When you're under the impression that you have finally arrived at an age in life where you're no longer treated as a potential credit risk, liability, felon or dare I say, as a teenager, there is nothing more humiliating than to find the rug sharply pulled from under your feet and that your new status in all aspects of American life, is now set firmly back at zero. My first auto insurance premium was astronomical and I could almost sense tears in the eyes of my broker as he repeated the cost back to my disbelieving ears for a third time. Not tears of sadness of course, just tears of joy at the percentage he would earn from selling me this exorbitant policy. I had no choice, I just had to pay it and swallow my pride. After a couple of years though, I was pretty much back to paying the same as I would have been paying in the UK. The one really positive point to note about auto insurance over here is that you can use your own US insurance policy when renting a car. This is a significant saving on the overall hire cost where many rental car companies will charge you up to $40 a day for Collision Damage Waiver protection, often much more than the actual rental of the vehicle itself. It is clear that these companies make enormous profits from selling insurance to tourists who have no choice but to purchase it at the time of rental.

The final part of this chapter deals with one of the largest annual outlays for any family, insuring the home. In England, we have two policies, one for the structure of the house, Buildings Insurance and one for everything in it, Contents Insurance. These two policies can be purchased as a combined policy or as separate policies. The American version is called Homeowners Insurance and covers both buildings and contents.

All areas in the USA seem to suffer from at least one natural disaster risk that is specific to the region. Whether it is earthquakes in California, tornadoes in the mid-west or hurricanes in the south-east and Florida, all of these potential risks allow American insurance companies to profit callously through fear of potential death and destruction. This is where cover can become a heavy financial burden. For this section, I will concentrate solely on my experience in Florida, the state which also has the largest insurance market in the United States.

Every year, Florida endures a sometimes dramatic weather period, officially referred to as The Hurricane Season. It starts on 1st June and ends six months later on 30th November. In the months prior to the start of the season, newspapers are filled with ads that urge you to protect your home with hurricane shutters or buy enormous generators for when your power is out or to stock up on gas masks, batteries, torches, tinned food, water supplies and other paraphernalia. With this frenzy, comes the dire warning annually rolled out by the insurance companies, that policy-holders will be facing huge increases in premiums.

One of the big problems in Florida is that historically, the quality and durability of housing construction has been poor. Many homes were 'frame' (made entirely from wood) and roofs were often shingled or just a simple layer of thin flexible linoleum-like tiles pinned to ply-board. This in turn means that older properties are much more susceptible to hurricane damage than many of the newer buildings which are constructed to a more stringent building code. It is only in recent years that the house-builders have started using CBS (cinder block structure or concrete block

& stucco) for the external walls and concrete tile or metal roof solutions. Even now, it is rare to find CBS used internally, relying mostly on the cheaper stud-wall method for partitioning.

Now, working on the assumption that our equivalently priced home in England was costing us around £400 per annum ($800pa) for buildings and contents cover, I had assumed that our new home in Florida, which had already survived three major hurricanes with minimal sustained damage, could only be a little more expensive to insure than our home in the UK. It was CBS on both levels and had a concrete tile roof – practically hurricane resistant. However, on my first visit to a broker, he informed me that he would be unable to find cover for my home and that I should try another company. I didn't bother asking why; I just made my apologies for interrupting his day and went off in search of another salesman.

The second broker said that he could find a company that was prepared to provide me with insurance, the only stumbling block being the premium, a staggering $15,000 per annum. (I'll be honest here; I actually thought that it was just a typo and that an extra zero had inadvertently been put on the price). This quote was obviously way out of my price range and a month or so later, I eventually and begrudgingly signed up with an insurance company that offered a homeowners premium, albeit loaded with deductibles, for the princely sum of $4,000 a year. Bearing in mind that I had truthfully answered in some degree of detail, all of the questions on the form, including whether or not my pool had a diving board and if I thought I might live in a flood-zone (I live on a rare hill in Florida) and having supplied the names and breeds of any pets that we owned, I was somewhat surprised to receive a letter six weeks later informing me that my policy had been terminated with immediate effect.

The sticking point was our daft and docile German Shepherd. Even though I had itemised him on the form, even though he had no previous convictions, even though he is mostly house-bound and completely fenced in when outdoors, the insurers had decided that they didn't want to insure me because of him. There was no refund for the amount paid for the insured period that had already elapsed and they wouldn't even deign to discuss their reasoning, they just cancelled me out as though I had never existed in the first place. This is something that just would not and could not happen in the UK. A contract is a contract, by law. A company that engages in this type of practice would be brought to justice by the Financial Ombudsman Service.

Fortunately, having used the equity from our UK home to purchase our Florida home outright, we were in the position to opt out of insuring our home altogether but imagine a family that has paid a high priced premium in January because their mortgage lender requires that the home be financially protected, only to find that they are in the path of a hurricane in June. The insurance company could merely decide that they didn't fancy the losses involved and send out a letter of policy cancellation just in time to avoid a potential payout. To describe the Florida insurance business as a scam, or that the people who operate it are crooks and thieves who profit from innocent home-owning victims, would be to make something of an understatement about the whole industry. There are exceptions, but not many.

For the benefit of American readers, if there is a mortgage on a home in the UK, then the lender will require an insurance policy to cover rebuilding costs to protect its own investment against flood, fire or other structural damage. The difference with the UK lenders is that they will also offer to provide reasonably priced insurance premiums as well as providing the loan – it's been the normal practice for many years in Britain. Therefore, the home owner is always reassured that he cannot have his policy cancelled as to do so, would see the lender effectively shooting himself in the foot.

It is alleged that most Florida-based insurance companies have such enormous revenue reserves that they could endure up to seven years of extreme hurricane damage payouts without really feeling any pain themselves. It is an incredible shame then, that the legislation isn't in place to firstly protect the hapless victims of inflated policies but also to build and enhance the reputation of Florida's insurance companies so that they might be elevated to a level of public respect that sits somewhere between lawyers and car salesmen. However, it should be worth noting that policy premiums differ throughout the USA and in the earthquake prone areas of California, I was surprised to learn that a similar priced home to my own would carry a premium of a mere $800 per annum which is much more akin to the charge I would expect in the UK.

To summarise, as I said at the start of this chapter, it is extremely difficult to draw any conclusions on the cost of living in the USA when making comparisons to the UK. A lot would depend on the dollar/sterling value at the time of relocation and also, the source of your income. It is true that many items like food, housing, fuel, clothes, cars and appliances are much cheaper than in Britain but equally, the extortionate costs for insurance, healthcare and property taxes are enough to deter even the keenest of dream-seekers.

Chapter 11

Driving In The USA

At the age of 17, having bravely taken my O & A'level exams and having previously submitted to the removal of my tonsils, adenoids and appendix, I was yet to encounter the stiffest test of my internal and external organs. The Great British Driving Test is for many, like no other examination, medical or otherwise, and it somehow manages to simultaneously challenge the strength of the mind and the sphincter alike.

In the days that led up to the test, I suffered from chronic diarrhoea and intense abdominal cramping at the very thought of spending ninety uncomfortable minutes in a vehicle with the universally despised British Driving Test Examiner. It was nearly thirty years ago when I took my test and I would doubt that much has changed in the interim. A sixty minute road test was followed by a fifteen minute examination on my intimate knowledge of the Highway Code. One bad move during the vehicle test or one wrong answer on the theory would result in the denial of the treasured British Driving Licence. The moments that follow the end of this torture are the most heart-thumping seconds of one's life and it culminates either in the triumphant signing of a pass certificate or the ignominious issue of that miserable scrap of paper that informs you that you've just failed in your quest. This is made even more depressing by the knowledge that a re-test will take months to schedule. It's one of those unique British experiences that really is, do or die.

It is therefore understandable that at the age of 45, in the run-up to taking my US driver's test, I suffered identical symptoms to those that I'd experienced almost thirty years previous in England. The good news is that I needn't have worried. Yes, you certainly do need a US licence if you wish to purchase, insure and drive a car over here but the truth is that it's nothing like as daunting as the harrowing experience you are put through in the UK. As an adult over the age of 18, you do not need to apply for a Provisional Licence, you do not need to take dozens of lessons to learn how to drive like a learner again and you need not worry about failing, as you can immediately schedule a re-test should it be required.

This is a typical example of the procedure involved. First you need to book a test appointment, which can be scheduled online in many states and the test can often be taken within a week of your initial enquiry. Then you turn up at the Test Centre, armed with your passport and any other documents that can prove your identity (you will need two, one primary and one secondary, the requirement will be listed on your local driver centre website). At this point, an eye test will be necessary (which doesn't entail reading a vehicle registration plate from a hundred yards) and you wait to take your road test.

In many cases, the practical driving exam is a mere trifle of a test. In my own experience, which was at a Florida test centre, the procedure began by my demonstrating that I could switch on the car headlights unaided, and that I also knew how to operate the windscreen wipers. After this, my very pleasant Puerto Rican examiner bade me in her best English, to follow her instructions. An adherence to the right side of the road for a few minutes, whilst obeying the 'stop' signs, culminated in a three-point-turn and the parking of my vehicle between a set of orange cones that could easily have accommodated a school bus. All this accomplished in a car park area without ever being required to challenge the perils of a public highway.

Ten minutes after I had first entered the car in search of the headlight switch, I was beaming in delight at having passed the first part of the examination. My stomach had made a miraculous recovery and I felt a certain sense of victory, knowing that I had prepared myself well for the final part of the endurance. In order to pass the theory section, it is important to bone up on every page of the Driver's Handbook to ensure that you are competent to answer any question regarding road signs, braking theory, speed limits or any other subject that may come up during the twenty-question computer test. I decided that for my own benefit, I would read the book, cover to cover, at least a dozen times in order that I wouldn't be surprised by any of the questions. This worked well for me although I was a little hesitant when I was asked to define the meaning of a big red sign with the word STOP written on it. I really thought that it might be a trick question – it wasn't, but you do sometimes get some extremely simple ones. As previously stated, there are twenty questions to answer whilst quietly seated in front of a computer monitor, all multiple choice and with no real time limit applied. In order to pass this final section, it is important that you answer at least 15 of the 20 questions correctly. You even have a second chance at the end of the test, if you haven't quite achieved the required 75% pass level.

Once you have earned the right to hold a US driving licence, by having fulfilled both practical and theoretical sections and having proved that you have reasonably decent eyesight, your final trip to the counter at the test centre will see you standing in front a camera to have your photo taken. This is followed by the real test, which is to see if you can keep your signature within the margins of a microscopically sized rectangle on a signing screen. My wife took several attempts to get this right and it was getting dark when she finally succeeded. At this point, a paper licence is issued with the promise of the plastic photo ID version to follow in the mail a few weeks later. And that's it. You can legally walk out and immediately drive any car that's insured for you to drive. In my own experience, it was not only stressless but in fact, quite enjoyable and the staff members at the test centre were incredibly pleasant and unbelievably patient, particularly with my wife.

I wouldn't say that the US driving test is simplistic or so easy that a child could pass, but in relative terms when making a comparison to the UK version, it is something of a cakewalk. I know that many of the Americans reading this may be fuming at some of the above but this is a generalisation and a description of the test that I took in Florida. Anyone who has taken a New York test will describe something much more challenging but anyone who has experience of driving on the Florida highway will doubtless sympathise and agree with everything I've said so far. Take a look at the myopic octogenarians queuing up with the 15-year-old tenth-graders in the test waiting-room and you'll see what I mean. In Florida, almost anyone can pass the driving test and in fact, most do.

Having now shown how different the driving test is in the USA when comparing it to the British version, there are also some interesting differences that are immediately noticeable when driving over here. Some are positive aspects but some are equally negative. For example, having driven in the USA now for some time, I am of the opinion that driving on the right-hand-side of the road does seem to feel more natural than driving on the left. Of course, I don't ever foresee the UK suddenly changing to the right hand side of the road as Sweden did (overnight in fact, at the start of rush-hour, one day in 1967) because the costs involved would be stratospheric. It would also result in the death of the 'right-hand-drive golden goose' which the car manufacturers call Great Britain.

Actually, I was surprised to learn that American cars were originally built with the controls on the right-hand-side up until 1908 when Ford decided that, in the better interests of their female passengers, the safer and more logical place to seat the driver was on the left. This is an extract from a 1908 brochure that explains its extraordinarily noble and caring thought process:

"The control is located on the left side, the logical place, for the following reasons: Travelling along the right side of the road, the steering wheel on the right side of the car made it necessary to get out on the street side and walk around the car. This is awkward and especially inconvenient if there is a lady to be considered. The control on the left allows you to step out of the car on to the curbing without having had to turn the car around. In the matter of steering with the control on the right, the driver is farthest away from the vehicle he is passing, going in opposite direction; with it on the left side he is able to see even the wheels of the other car and easily avoids danger."

One excellent feature of driving in the USA is that in general, you are legally allowed to turn right at a red light, provided that it is safe to do so. It does allow better traffic flow although I can't be absolutely sure that it doesn't cause more accidents than it's worth. Another positive point is that drivers mostly stick to the speed limits when driving in towns and villages. It is particularly refreshing to see drivers slow right down when travelling through school zones, the absolute opposite of what we frequently see in the UK. The extraordinary thing is that when these very same drivers find themselves on an Interstate, they change from Dr. Jekyll into Mr. Hyde and driving amongst them feels somewhat akin to playing Russian Roulette. The fact that any vehicle will pass you in any lane, at any time, is terrifying. It isn't legal to do so but it's the norm for most American drivers because most of them aren't aware that it's an illegal procedure. In England, where we drive on the left, the legal and courteous procedure is to overtake on the right when passing another vehicle and in general, it's the customary method employed, idiots notwithstanding. A safe and courteous distance is also usually maintained between you and the next vehicle on British roads. Not so in America. If a driver can find twelve feet of spare lane in front of your car, then it is likely he will grab it. The bizarre thing about this is that you don't often hear the obligatory blaring of horns or the see the hysterical flashing of headlights that you would commonly see in the UK. It is just accepted that any space on any highway is fair game to the quickest thinker.

In the UK, our motorway (Interstate) exits are labelled by consecutive numbering, Exit 1 being the first and if there are fifty exits on the entire motorway, then the last would be Exit 50. It's different and better in the USA. The exit number is defined by the distance away from the start of the Interstate. So Exit 1 will likely not be followed by Exit 2. Instead, if the next exit is 24 miles on from the start of the highway, it's labelled Exit 24. I like this, as it gives me a better idea of distance driven and distance yet to travel. There are also markers at the side of the road at one-mile intervals which are enormously helpful in determining the journey distance.

Toll roads aren't yet a common feature in Great Britain but they are utilised more and more in America. On the whole, they seem to be used by slower and safer drivers but though they're still fraught with danger I never see quite so many of the huge shredded truck tyres that seem to litter the Interstates. (This is a phenomenon that I've never seen in Europe but one that I assume is due to the enormous distances travelled by haulage trucks in the USA, the prolonged heat and wear from the road causing frequent tyre casualties) The most exciting thing about these pay-as-you-drive highways is that you are required to come to a complete stop at the toll booth to pay the fee, but once the barrier is raised, all drivers gun their engines and race away trying to beat every other car to the point where the lanes narrow from twelve into four. Sometimes I swear I can hear the immortal line that precedes the Indy 500 race at Indianapolis, "Gentleman, start your engines...."

If you see a STOP sign when driving in the USA, you must stop. I don't mean slow down to a crawl, check the coast is clear and then accelerate away, it means you must come to a complete stop. It's the done thing, mostly everyone obeys the rule and failure to do so will result in a ticket and a fine if caught breaking this important law. In the event that you find yourself at a four-way intersection (a crossroads), there will be a STOP sign on all four junctions. The rule of thumb here is simple. The first to arrive at the four-way should be the first to leave and so on. It is gentlemanly conduct to do so and the method is generally adhered to.

I noticed that roundabouts (circles) seem to be a recent introduction to American roads, their obvious advantages borne out in Europe duly noted by the US highway authorities. They are slowly replacing the four-way intersections, with the belief that traffic flow will be greatly improved. Many of the early roundabouts had a STOP sign at each entrance and so the traffic flow enhancement was initially negated. The STOP signs have gradually been replaced with YIELD signs so now a driver does not necessarily have to stop when approaching the roundabout, but should just yield to any traffic to his or her left. However, it is still easy to see that some Americans, particularly my octogenarian friends, haven't quite yet got the idea of how to proceed at a roundabout, with many of these drivers actually stopping at each junction as they navigate the circle, often taking several minutes to complete their orbital mission.

In England, we have become used to the prolific use of cameras that monitor our speed and provide photographic evidence of the motorists who stupidly pass through red traffic lights. It is now an accepted part of our daily lives to be aware of them and avoid the penalties that are issued by flouting the law. Not only are they used in the silent policing of our roads but also just about anywhere else too, including shopping areas, storage depots, car parks, housing estates and high streets. Great Britain is the largest user of public and private spy cameras in the world and to that end, the British public is the most surveillance controlled population on Earth, the epitome of George Orwell's prophesised Big Brother society. It is estimated that there are over four million cameras photographing the British public every day. To put this into some sort of perspective, that's one camera for every fourteen citizens. The positive spin on this, is that more crimes are solved and more criminals captured due to this clandestine method of filming and monitoring the UK population.

Compare this to the use of cameras in the USA. Although I haven't yet had the pleasure of driving in every state in America, I've yet to spot a spy camera on any road during my time here, though it may be that they are cleverly hidden and I just haven't seen them. The policing of US highways is largely left to the State Troopers and County Sheriff's Department. Unfortunately, with the amount of motorists using the roads, there can never be enough policemen to enforce the law or to maintain common driving sense, particularly in America. The economically sound implementation of speed cameras will also be eternally hampered by the nanny-state intervention of the American Civil Liberties Union (ACLU) who will probably denounce them as an infringement of personal privacy, but I still think that traffic cameras are necessary and will eventually be fully introduced in the USA. Not only have they been seen to curb bad driving and reduce the amount of speeding elsewhere in the world, they would generate far more revenue for each state than any number of State Troopers could ever do.

OK, so here's the soapbox. I enjoy driving in the States but I have to voice a couple more complaints apart from just airing my concern about multi-lane misfortunes. I originally thought that the British were the worst offenders in their knowledge of when and where to use their fog-lights or even for some, whether they knew what they were, where they were or how they were illuminated. In my own experience, I would hazard a guess that many Americans haven't even got a clue what fog-lights, let alone where they might find them on the car. The same goes for indicators (turn signals) – the manufacturers might as well save a heap of money and just not bother installing them because they rarely get used.

Secondly, the fatality rate on American roads is bewildering. Even with the American population being five times greater than the sum total in the UK, the fact remains that there are over 42,000 deaths annually on American roads compared to the 3,000 or so each year in Britain, which tells me that there are major flaws in the way that a driver's permit is so easily obtained in the USA. To put it in more easily understandable terms, it is a fact that you are three times more likely to die at the wheel in the USA than you are in the UK. The only positive aspect is that the state of California is 50% safer than Texas or Florida. And New York, which believe it or not is one of the safest places to drive in America, has even better statistics than the Golden State.

The real truth is, that having driven in many American states, I am staggered that there aren't more accidents and fatalities. There's good reason that the UK maintains its stance that the age of 17 should be the earliest age to be in charge of a motor vehicle. My personal opinion is that 17 is still too early and that 18 should be the appropriate age to allow a driver to take to the road. There is tangible proof too that the USA should revise its learner's permit age upwards to a similar position. I am shocked that the legal drinking age in the USA is 21 yet a 15 year-old, barely out of Junior High, is allowed to take control of a potential killing machine at such a young age.

Chapter 12

California Dreamin'

I will confess now, to a life-long fascination with California. There is a certain magical notion about the place that I've never quite been able to shake off and in fact, each visit to the Golden State does nothing to quell the secret envy I have for all things Californian. Songs like *California Girls, It Never Rains in Southern California,* and just about any song by the Beach Boys are not merely odes to a life cherished by the hippie- spawned love and peace generation, but in fact a celebration of a population literally blessed by being born into the coolest and hippest state in America. Of course, California has its fair share of problems concerning race issues and high crime statistics, particularly in the Los Angeles locale, but to mimic and transpose Mark Anthony's famous words in Shakespeare's *Julius Caesar*, I come here to praise California, not to bury it.

There is no doubting the history behind the naming of most American states. Many take their names from Native American Indian words but one or two of them have somewhat different origins. Florida for example, was given its name when Juan Ponce de Leon first discovered the region. The literal translation meaning 'flowery' was probably in line with the abundance of colourful and scented flowers that greeted the explorer when he first landed in 1513. But as far as I can tell, there is no obvious point of origination for the naming of California. There are some who suggest that the derivation of California may have come from the phrase 'caliente horno' meaning 'hot as an oven'. Others say that it's from 'caliente fornalia', Spanish for 'hot furnace', or even from the Latin, 'calida fornax', also meaning 'hot furnace'. Many of these suggestions use a mixture of Latin, Spanish and South American languages but whatever the root derivation, it's reasonably clear to see that California was likely dubbed for its inherently warm climate.

A recent magazine article stated that the climate in Southern California is the second best in the world, eclipsed only by an uninhabited island somewhere in the South Pacific. I would confirm this; it's a near-perfect place to live all year round with sunshine and blue skies engulfing a Pacific-cooled atmosphere, clear and pure with low humidity levels. (except for Los Angeles with its perennial and odorous yellow smog) Even the most vociferous of East Coasters who hold all of California and its people in utter contempt, will to a man, wax lyrical about the SoCal climate. I rarely hear any positive things said about the West Coast, apart from praise for its weather and in fact, from my minimal knowledge, California would appear to be the most despised US region by each of the other 49 states. Not the place itself, just the people who live there. Californians are regularly referred to as "those liberals" or the "nutjobs on the West Coast" but I've an inkling that this is more to do with an envy of Californians and their natural paradise than any real dislike for their politics and idiosyncrasies. Put it this way, I've never experienced anything but real warmth and good humour from the various west coast natives I've encountered over the years. They can't be complete fools in business and finance either. To try and put the wealth of the Golden State into some form of context, it is said that if California was an independent country, its Gross Domestic Product would be the seventh highest in the world, eclipsed only by the GDP of Italy, France, Great Britain, Germany, Japan and the USA itself, a quite staggering fact.

The Pacific Coast Highway, one of the more famous American roads and certainly the most breathtakingly scenic route in the

USA, creates a voyage that you can never tire of driving. My own favourite part of this drive is the stretch from La Jolla near San Diego which passes through Torrey Pines, Del Mar, Solana Beach and Encinitas before temporarily ending at Carlsbad and Oceanside. (Camp Pendleton is home to the military just north of here and it occupies a sensational piece of oceanfront real estate which necessitates a brief detour from the historic Highway 1) However, this is just a small section of the 600 mile route and it is equally breathtaking and beautiful at many other points, including the spectacular views at Big Sur and Pacific Palisades and at the towns of Santa Cruz and Monterey. Without doubt, the Pacific Coast Highway is thoroughly recommended to anyone who hankers after a scenic road-trip though it's advisable to begin the journey in the north of California, as this ensures you maintain the favourable view of the Pacific, best seen from the right hand side of the road. And although the entire coast of California is literally peppered with ludicrously high-priced oceanfront homes from the top of the state all the way down to the border of Mexico, there is still ample opportunity to pull over, park up and walk directly onto the cool white beaches and just marvel at that beautiful stretch of water that is the Pacific Ocean. Wherever I have travelled in the world, whether to Africa, India or even to anywhere in Europe, I have never previously experienced the strange allure that always draws me to the Pacific. It's almost magnetic and to be able to just sit and stare out to sea in the cool heat that is unique to this coast, is one of the most calming and Karma-inducing experiences known to man. And it's free.

It's understandable that the extraordinary and dramatic scenery in many parts of California has made the place such a desirable place to live. But the odd thing for me and probably for some of the other visitors, is the fact that many Californian natives, particularly the younger ones, seem to have no idea that they were born to a life of extreme privilege, even if only comparing the natural beauty of the Californian landscape coupled with its near-perfect climate to other areas of the USA or to other parts of the world. You only need to drive south along the PCH and look right to see the most magnificent ocean the world has to offer or glance left at the snow-capped mountains that glisten distantly in the sunlight. It's like having a year round vacation available right on your doorstep. It's probably my lack of intimate local knowledge but the under-30s in California don't seem to appreciate that they live in arguably the most perfect place on Earth in a climate which is just sublime. It does appear though, that the older generations are well aware of how fortunate they are to have lucked out on this particular piece of the American continent and they tend to exude a youthful, happy and positive attitude wherever they go. The hippie generation is still alive and kicking in California, a little older now, but just as vibrant.

So, as a perpetual tourist who can't resist the opportunity to people-watch, I've become acutely aware of these younger Californians, mostly athletic, tanned and more often than not, extremely good looking individuals, born into a near Nirvana-like society, but many of them completely oblivious to how fortunate they are to have inherited this particular life. There is a sense of boredom amongst them, an underlying feeling that they are waiting for something more from life and they sometimes display a slightly cold and impassive regard towards each other, as well as to anyone else around them. I realise that cafés like Starbucks now provide free 'office-space' with complimentary broadband internet connection to all their customers for just the price of a cup of coffee but when you stop to study the customers that habituate these 'hot-spots', almost each and every one of them is incognizant to everything and everyone around them, immersed in text, cell or email communication with their peers in other equally sterile environments along the coast. I know it is the same wherever you are in the world but to be bored with this region is to be bored with life itself.

On a recent visit to San Diego, and as a man born into a life of hostility and hopelessness in the melting pot of criminality of London's East End, I pondered this conundrum once more. For me as a boy, life held no promises, no worldly ambitions and no real chance for a rosy future, just a blank canvass as grey as the skies that perpetuate London's grim and bleak cityscape. Anything I wanted in life would be a struggle to achieve and the only way to avoid the depression of a pointless and unfulfilled East End existence was to escape it and find another route to realise my dreams. In fact, the exact polar opposite of the opportunities and cherished lives that are promised to, actually expected by the young Americans of California. These sun-kissed gods and goddesses possess an aura of aloofness that somehow tells the rest of the world who aren't members of their indigenous club, that they are better and superior to everyone else. In many ways, I suppose they are.

But unfortunately, my rose-tinted view of the Golden State has been further tainted by the smaller groups of spoiled children that populate the seriously wealthy parts of California. These areas, like Malibu, Beverly Hills and Orange County, are often popularised, satirised and characterised on television shows. But the over-produced dramas and fly-on-the-wall documentaries which portray these brattish, over-funded, rude and disrespectful teenagers do nothing to promote the true character of the Californian population. These children have already been given too much, too early and nothing and no-one in their lives will ever be enough to satisfy them. They are actually ruined individuals from an incredibly early age. It's a great shame that the highlighting of these nouveau middle-class families with high annual earnings and equally high expenditure but often low net worth, is sent to television screens throughout the world as an unfair example of what typifies the lives of Californian families. The other 90% of regular Californian kids must despise the spoiled obnoxiousness displayed by their witless counterparts.

But to that end, there is a serious, nationwide problem in the USA that's growing at an alarming rate. A generation of middle-class children across the whole country, are raised with the parental mantra that everything they want, they will most surely get. They are constantly told that they are special; that they are the golden children who can possess and achieve anything that the world has to offer. College or university will follow an easy run through high school and beyond that, a career guaranteeing opulence and a matching lifestyle that will eclipse even that of their parents. But in reality, the life that's realised post-college degree is more often than not, one of complete disappointment and not the idealistic fantasy that had been indoctrinated into them by their adoring parents. At the age of 22 or even sometimes much older, many young Americans find themselves educated to a high level but stuck in a dull and meaningless job paying maybe $30,000 a year. Not quite the million dollar salaries that Mom and Dad had promised. No real sign of the McMansions and Maserati sports cars either.

Now transpose this typical state-wide, middle-class scenario to the lives of the young über-wealthy Californians and it becomes much easier to understand why they often have such surly and listless expressions on their faces. For many of them, the task of independently emulating or exceeding their parents' success is made many times more difficult because of the paradisiacal life into which they were originally born. For me and for many of my peers, and I don't mean this disrespectfully, the task of exceeding what my parents had achieved was not nearly so difficult. My parents, like those of many of my friends, worked hard throughout their entire lives and struggled enormously just to maintain a roof over our heads and the idea of being wealthy enough to buy a new car was for them, not even an idle daydream. So by the time I was 21, I had a home that cost more to buy than either of my parents homes and I also had a brand new car parked in my drive. I hadn't done anything extraordinary, I'd just worked hard and along with a little luck, I found myself earning more than they ever had. This was not unusual as it was a similar situation for many of my friends. However, when this same task is set to the young Californians hailing from affluent families, they are starting at a somewhat headier rung on the ladder. Their parents already live in multi-million dollar homes and the exotic foreign automobiles that litter their multi-car garages are changed every six months along with the imported hired help so even the idea of these kids emulating their parents is almost impossible, let alone the notion that they might one day surpass this level of success.

Of course, if you only look at the stratospheric levels of riches that can be seen on the coasts of Malibu and Orange County and up high in Bel Air and Beverly Hills, then it is easy to see that this type of arrogant look-at-me wealth is clearly out of reach of most kids unless they inherit it or are given a senior position in the family business. But in the main, the California middle classes are just plain wealthy, even those that live in the outlying areas who don't share a fondness for the ostentatious lifestyles of the Los Angeles wannabes. These areas are secretly wealthy and the inhabitants strive to maintain a certain anonymity and privacy with a far greater reserve than is displayed in the more gregarious and celebrity infested locations. In fact, many of these quieter and more subdued towns share more than a passing resemblance to the wealthy stockbroker-belt regions back in England.

To get a better idea of what I'm talking about here, go and visit the town of Rancho Santa Fe in Southern California. (The golfer, Phil Mickelson, is one of the residents there) It has the beauty of a perfect English summer's day, white rail fencing running the perimeters of green fields, providing the playgrounds for the exquisite horses that frequent this region. Add to this the whitewashed and terracotta style of old Spain, stunningly illustrated by the magnificent homes that nestle in the hillsides and valleys, and you have the quietly confident conservatism of old money. Rolling hills and winding roads, surrounded by an abundance of ancient trees and deeply coloured flowers and shrubs, makes this area the number one, most desirable town to live, in the whole of the USA.

The history of this beautiful American oasis is as story-book as the vista of the place itself. The area was originally designated as a source of timber for the San Diego railroad companies but after the planting of thousands upon thousands of eucalyptus trees, it was decided that the wood they were growing was probably not suitable for the railway's requirement. The good news was that the trees were left unharmed and they flourished to provide densely wooded hillsides, an unusual feature of Southern California. By 1921, a decision was made to build a ranchito type of community in a Spanish Colonial Revivalist style. At the heart of this design was a central village; a collection of stores, restaurants and small residential units. A hotel was later added, The Inn at Rancho Santa Fe. (This hotel also serves the best cappuccino I've ever tasted) The architect responsible for setting the tone of this unique community was the renowned and incomparable, Lilian Rice. She was one of the first female architecture graduates from Berkeley and her vision for Rancho Santa Fe was founded on the simple idea of an idyllic and picturesque Spanish village. At the age of 33, she set about creating a community which still holds fast as a model in aesthetic design and planning. Unfortunately, she died too early in 1938, aged 49, but her great architectural vision remains unfettered and grows more beautiful with each passing year. On a recent visit there, my wife, referring innocently to the abundant flora and exquisitely perfumed air, asked me "What's that wonderful scent I keep noticing?" I jokingly replied, "Jayne, that's the wonderful smell of money!" Joking aside though, it is a veritable feast for the eyes and nose alike.

I truly love California, there is just something about the place which absolutely captivates me and the fact that the southern region has a near-perfect climate is such an enormous bonus. I know that I've been privileged to see some of the more beautiful and trouble-free parts of the state and that there are many poor areas where people live brutal existences on a daily basis but I can only write about what I've seen with my own eyes. I was born in the early 1960s and to be a true 60s child, you'd need to have been born in the late 40s so I was never a hippie as I was born too late to be a part of that peace and love, beatnik generation and I never fancied the idea of smoking weed. But in truth, I wish that I had lived in Southern California in the 1960s, probably on the beach in a VW Camper Van, quietly listening to the Mamas & the Papas, no cell-phones, no computers and in a world where people actually communicated with one another.

Chapter 13

Lost In Translation

It is no secret that language, like most things in life, is evolutionary. This is borne out each year by the addition and deletion of hundreds, sometimes thousands of words in what is universally regarded as the bible of the English language, the Oxford English Dictionary. However, along with our own destruction of the English language at home in the UK, the US version is developing a new and unique style of its own.

There is a style of speech here, commonly known as *'high-rising intonation'* best personified in the conversation of many young Americans. Each statement has now developed this new lilt at the end of the line that makes every sentence or phrase have the odd feeling of sounding like a question. I'm sure that most readers will immediately recognise what I'm trying to say here. It's not something that is easy to describe and it's certainly somewhat difficult for an adult to copy but it has recently become a youth manufactured language all of its own. Each time I valiantly try to impersonate an American teenager, I end up failing miserably and usually sound like some demented and aging half-wit trying to understand the language of hip and cool youth.

Many words coined in the USA are also exported to the UK. The word *'whatever'*, which has previously been seen as an innocent and innocuous word that implies a choice, has now become one of the most offensive expressions available. The arrogant and senseless way that teenagers use this word when they no longer care about a person, situation or conversation, fills most rational thinkers with a sense of frustration. If anything could describe the depth to which communication has sunk and the disrespectful manner that is endemic in some parts of British and American teenage society, it is the careless use of this single word.

The word *'awesome'* has also become a regular feature of teenage to twenty-something speech. The actual dictionary meaning is, *'impressive, outstanding or remarkable'* but in the context employed by the under-30s it is invariably used to describe most things that are far from awesome, in fact, quite ordinary daily activities. *"I just had breakfast". "Awesome!" "Hey, I just got dressed!!" "Awesome!!!"* But I don't at all mind the use of this word, as it wasn't that long ago when we were using a similar expression, *'far out'*, to describe something that really wasn't very far at all. It's better to show excitement about something than to show nothing at all.

But putting aside the idiosyncrasies of the under 18s, there are still plenty of oddities to explore in the day to day communication of any adult American. In my time here, I have often succumbed to the 'sliding' pronunciation of many words, using *'twenny'* when I mean *'twenty'* and inadvertently finding myself asking for *'warda'* or *'buddah'* instead of *'water'* or *'butter'*. It's one of those things that you haplessly slip into when living in a semi-foreign society. Sometimes it isn't a case of accidental mispronunciation but just the simple and innocent desire to make your fellow American understand what you are trying to say, therefore reverting to a form of English which I call, *Americanese*. I should say at this juncture that I haven't yet resorted to pronouncing *'Harry Potter'* as *'Hairy Poddah'* which seems to be the generally accepted pronunciation here, nor would I ever say *'Notre Dame'* as *'Knowdah Daym'*, the stolen French sobriquet for an Indiana-based American football team.

The one anomaly though, which I do struggle with is the word *'route'*. The song *'Route 66'* is well known throughout the world as is the highway itself and in this context, it is commonly pronounced *'root'* by English and Americans alike. But when route is used by Americans to describe a particular journey or used as it might be when giving driving directions, the word takes on a new pronunciation sounding like *'rowt'*, as in *'doubt'*.

Another word that I've only heard amongst a small number of New Yorkers is the word *'aks'* which is a colloquialism that has recently transferred itself to some of the rougher parts of England. It actually means *'ask'*, is meant to sound tough and is just a slang way of using the word. It doesn't sound pleasant and it hopefully won't last long in either country. I understand this word to be a remnant of the Dutch occupation of the New Jersey and New York areas, along with other oddities like *'dose'* and *'dem'* meaning *'those'* and *'them'*. The white origination of the word has now also slipped seamlessly into the African-American version of English.

But whether you decide to live here or whether you are just on vacation in the USA, it's worth taking the time to arm yourself with one or two of the linguistic anomalies you'll no doubt encounter. A woman's *'handbag'* becomes *'purse'* in America and *'purse'* becomes *'wallet'*. The word *'trousers'* in the USA, translates to *'pants'*, *'jacket'* becomes *'coat'* and heaven help any American who misunderstands the British meaning of the word *'fanny'*. Over here, it means your butt or rear-end, but of course in the UK, it has an altogether different translation, describing a delicate and private area at the front of a woman rather than any part behind her. (I think that's a reasonable way of describing the difference). *Pavement*, which is derived from the two words *'paved cement'*, is in fact the roadway itself in America and the pavement as we know it in England is called the *sidewalk* over here. Even the automobile has a whole new set of names, where *bonnet* becomes *hood*, *boot* is referred to as *trunk* and the *wing* is generally called the *fender*. Inside the vehicle, there is still more confusion. *Indicator* becomes *turn-signal* and *gear-change* becomes *stick-shift*. When driving, a *crossroads* is normally known as an *intersection* and *overtaking* is replaced by *passing*.

Words which are common in the English language in the UK, are often confused when used in the USA. The English word for *'crisps'* becomes *'chips'* in the States and conversely, *'chips'* becomes *'French fries'*, or on those occasions when the USA has a difference of political opinion with France, these somewhat innocent potato variants are then known as *'freedom fries'*. The good old English *'biscuit'* is known as a *'cookie'* and our traditional English *'scones'* are called *'biscuits'* although they aren't recommended here as an accompaniment to afternoon tea, more likely served at breakfast with home fries and smothered in *'gravy'*, a white and seemingly inedible concoction made from flour and pork dripping. In the USA, *'jam'* is referred to as *'jelly'*, while our own *'jelly'* becomes *'Jello'* but I've absolutely no idea how you would translate *'blancmange'*.

Modern day use of language breeds laziness and the spelling as well as the contextual use of words is often badly abused. Although I have become used to seeing the revised American spelling of words; *neighbor* (neighbour), *center* (centre), *labor* (labour), *favorite* (favourite), *catalog* (catalogue), *thru* (through) and *check* (cheque) are words that immediately spring to mind, I still have a problem with the varied pronunciation of words. I was always puzzled that the word *'aluminium'*, was pronounced *'al<u>oo</u>minam'* with the stress on the first *'um'* in the American version and the five syllables reduced to four. But when I looked more closely, I realised that it was actually spelt that way in the USA – *'aluminum'*, so I suddenly understood why. What I don't understand is why this well known element, appearing as Atomic No. 13 on the Periodic Table, had been re-spelt in the first place.

There's good reason that Microsoft gave us an English (UK) spell-check, as well as the English (US) version. Apart from the spelling variations listed in the previous paragraph, the letter *'s'* is often changed to *'z'* in America and many words will take on revised spellings. *Apologise, organise* and *sterilise* become *apologize, organize* and *sterilize* respectively, although *circumcise* miraculously survives the orthographic scalpel in America, retaining its original English form.

Sometimes, this revised spelling of words can be put down to laziness but more often than not, it can result from a simple mistake. I will never forget the story I was told of the car manufacturer Mitsubishi, when launching a new car back in the 1980s. Evidently, they wanted to emulate the thrusting magnificence of Ford's Mustang and so decided to call their new offering, the Colt Stallion, which sounded pretty damned good. However, given that the Japanese seem to have a minor problem with saying any English word containing the letter 'L', something was lost in translation between Japan and the rest of the world and the actual name given to the poor car was Colt Starrion, which didn't quite have the same desired effect.

'Oregano' is my current personal favourite in the Anglo/American language, always carrying the stress on the penultimate syllable in the UK but in the USA, that stress is moved to the second syllable. So in English, we pronounce it as 'orri*gaano*' and in the US version it is said as 'o*regano*'. Conversely, the word 'fillet' that we use in England to describe a prime piece of meat or fish is actually pronounced more correctly in the USA. In fact, Americans also use a more accurate spelling of the word which is 'filet', from the Latin word 'filum', pronouncing it with the stress on the second syllable and with the 't' remaining silent, the method typified by the French language.

However, bearing in mind the correct spelling and pronunciation of 'filet' in the USA, the one word I can't quite come to terms with in this country is the word 'herb'. In England, we correctly pronounce the 'h' because as a French word that has been adjusted for the English Language where our 'h' is not usually silent, the word is correctly said as 'hûrb'. In the States, where English should also be spoken with the use of a pronounced 'h', they instead make the 'h' silent as the French would do but continue to pronounce it as per the English version, 'ûrb'. My view is that if you are going to adhere to the French method of leaving the 'h' silent, then the French pronunciation of 'herbe' should also apply, therefore demanding that it be pronounced as 'èrb' as in 'air' with a 'b' on the end. It's not important, it just

113

sounds incredibly funny in Americanese when this 'Franglo' word is suddenly dropped into conversation.

Now we also know that the art of changing regular everyday problems into politically correct and acceptable euphemisms was invented by the Americans; *'vertically challenged'* for *short*, *'follicly challenged'* for *bald*, *'short-term thinking disorder'* for *stupid*, but to describe a thief as someone who has *'boundary issues'* is just silly. I can confirm, hand on heart, that I've even heard the term *'Auditory Processing Disorder'* applied to someone who is deaf. I recently heard a new expression, *'friends with benefits'*, which is a way of referring to an acquaintance who has the added bonus that he or she is a willing sexual companion, without the emotion or complication of love or jealousy ever being involved. A kind of no-strings-attached unpaid hooker service for both participants. But even this phrase, although reasonably new to my ears, has now been replaced with a shorter two word slang version, often spotted in your email spam bin, *'buddy'* being prefixed by another word that sounds not dissimilar to *'luck'*.

There are a number of words that are beginning to become redundant in America. For example, if a newspaper story states that *"There was a major freeway accident on Wednesday in San Francisco"*, it is likely that it will be written *"There was a major freeway accident Wednesday in San Francisco"*, the word *'on'* becoming surplus to requirement. Similarly, if you were taking a short weekend break for *"a couple of days"* then usually you'll find that in America, it would be said as *"a couple days"*, the word *'of'* becoming redundant in this case.

We live in a world where the communication process has accelerated to the point where we must now speak more quickly, use less words and take less time on the actual art of communication itself. The horrendous effects of MSN Messenger, text messaging and email have resulted in the debasing of the whole English language. Of course, we all understand and accept that language evolves but this often takes hundreds of years of the crafting and revising of words to be better suited to our lives, not by reducing the language to a set of letters that have more affinity to Morse Code than to a linguistic and communicative emotion. Teenagers use the three-letter-abbreviation *LOL* (which I foolishly took to mean *'lots of love'* not *'laugh out loud'*) and other similar shortened expressions to actually describe the mood of the text rather than have the text itself contain an inherent emotion that relays a feeling or point of view. I am one of those old-fashioned die-hards who will systematically write out in full, any text message that I might send. I may not be the most literate man on Earth, but capitalisation and reasonable grammar are in my view, deeply important but to any regular teenager, these issues are largely irrelevant. The post-literate society that has evolved since the birth of email and text-messaging, is symptomatic of the lack of thought and care that plagues our current day to day existence. If only the phone makers would render impossible, the sending of meaningless illiteracy and only allow properly constructed and correctly spelled sentences to transmit, then a better educated generation would emerge and the phone companies would make more money from the extra characters required to send the messages. Imagine the horror on a teenager's face when a text message is returned unsent with the warning: *"Error: misspelled word, grammar unacceptable, check syntax before continuing"*.

Television, as well as email and text messaging, is littered with expressions that are commonly referred to as *'three-letter-abbreviations'*. In fact, this particular phrase has itself become a three-letter-abbreviation, now just a *TLA*. The expression *COD* which I originally took to mean, *'cash on delivery'*, apparently now translates as *'cause of death'*. Similar gruesome phrases currently in use, are *TOD*, *'time of death'*, *GSW*, *'gun shot wound'*, and *GSR*, *'gun shot residue'*. The New York, Las Vegas and Miami based CSI shows are the best providers of the silliest TLAs on offer. I was horrified to learn that, in the interests of cramming into the programme as much abbreviated script as possible, even the poor victim in each episode is no longer afforded any respect in death, now just commonly referred to as the 'vic', saving a whole syllable of air-time. TLAs may well have originated on television in the various hospital dramas that frequent the American viewing diet. Only last night, I caught a fifteen second sound-byte from a popular hospital show, where three separate TLAs were used in one sentence, *ALS, MRI* and *DNR*, the first two meaning *'amyotrophic lateral sclerosis'* and *'magnetic resonance imaging'* respectively and the latter meaning *'do not resuscitate'* which was something I would've begged for if I'd had to endure much more of that particular bombardment of TLAs.

Of course, TLAs are nothing new and the practice really began at the highest level in the USA. Look at *JFK* for the late President John Fitzgerald Kennedy and likewise, *FDR* and *LBJ* for Presidents Roosevelt and Johnson respectively. It's been going on for some time, although *POTUS*, the common term used in law enforcement circles when referring to the President Of The United States, is elevated to a unique *FLA* (not FLA as in Florida, but FLA as in *Five-Letter-Abbreviation*). Even among the main American sports, TLAs have replaced the burden of actually having to speak in an understandable language. Baseball becomes *MLB* (Major League Baseball), US football is now the *NFL* (National Football League), ice-hockey has become the *NHL* (National Hockey League) and basketball is the *NBA* (National Basketball Association). Also, if you thought that *PAS* was an abbreviation for *'power assisted steering'*, think again as it's new and current meaning is *'physician assisted suicide'*. And *BFT* doesn't mean *'big friendly teddy'* but instead *'blunt force trauma'*. I know, I'm getting carried away with it now but I think you get the idea.

In much the same way that there are multiple meanings for any given TLA, depending on the subject at hand, one particular example comes to mind whose irony seems to be lost on the majority of Americans I've met. Only yesterday, I saw a newspaper headline which proclaimed *"Put IRA Funds Towards Your First Home"*. Now in England, we are acutely aware of what *IRA* means, the *Irish Republican Army*, a group that was originally named, The Provisional IRA, meaning that it was deemed to be a temporary military organisation. However, with the decades of terrorism associated with this group, the term *IRA* has always conjured a particularly violent image for British people whereas in the USA, *IRA* has nothing to do with terrorism, just an innocent TLA meaning *Individual Retirement Account*. In short, it's your Personal Pension Plan or PPP.

I have a deep and life-long fascination for the derivation of words and I can see how and why some words change in spelling and meaning so I'm not a complete puritan when it comes to the evolution of any language. Whether we believe that our American neighbours have hijacked the English language as we know it for their own personal version, is still a moot point. However, at the time of writing, the current US version of our language is still referred to as English and not American by most of the people who live here so we shouldn't yet regard the Queen's English as a completely lost cause, even if I can't quite get used to using the word *'Mom'* instead of *'Mum'*. It is also unfair to snigger at those Americans who struggle valiantly in pronouncing oddly spelled English names like *Leicestershire, Worcestershire, Caernarfon, Middlesbrough, Beaulieu* or *Edinburgh*. Even the innocuous name of *Surrey* can prove a difficult one to comfortably pronounce. I would also hope that no American is ever asked to correctly pronounce the name *Llanfairpwllgwyngyllgogerychwyrndrobwllllantysiliogogogoch,* the name given to a now famous Welsh town, loosely translated as, *"The church of St. Mary in the hollow of white hazel trees near the rapid whirlpool by St. Tysilio's of the red cave"*.

But there are just as many uniquely American words that will have British tongues tied in knots. I've practiced over and over again the correct pronunciation of exquisite and beautiful words like *Adirondack, Iroquois* and *Chappaquiddick* but I've witnessed many Britons tongue-tied over simple words like *Massachusetts* and *Okeechobee*. Most of these more elegant American words have their origins amongst the Native American Indian tribes, names like *Apalachee, Cherokee, Potawatomie* and

117

Shinnecock are good examples as are *Nantucket* and *Winnebago*, the former often used humorously in limerick form and the other finding its way to the rear nameplate of some of the enormous motor-homes that cruise the American highways.

Accents are wildly differing in the fifty US states, the New York variant being the least attractive for me, its machine-gun style of delivery that aggressively spits at you rather than endearing you to the speaker. It would appear to be a prerequisite that the minimum is said in order to achieve the maximum communication amongst New Yorkers. The whiplash speed of conversation matches the impatience that often typifies the New York psyche. Conversely, I've always found that the dreamier Deep South accents have the ability to entrance and intoxicate, often finding that their rhythmic, lilting and descriptive tones carry a grammatically enhanced mocking towards the recipient that is neither offensive nor hurtful. It's just beatific and warm, the intent of poking harmless fun beneath a friendly and affectionate overtone. Tennessee, Texas and Georgia have particularly good examples of these accents, best equipped for the elicitation of amusing one-liners and harmless put-downs.

I have one more thing to impart that never fails to trip me up in the American language. It's not to do with the written or spoken word, it's to do with the unique American way of quoting the date back to front. The rest of the world seems to accept that the date should be written down in a logical fashion that demands that the day precedes the month and the month precedes the year, effectively an ascending order of events, smallest to largest. *The 10th of March 2007* is therefore universally written down in numeric form as *10/03/07*. In the USA however, the month comes first and subsequently the American version takes the form of *03/10/07*. It's not a huge problem although I do have to think hard whenever I write a cheque *(check)* or whenever I am quoting my DOB *(date of birth)*. It's easy to see that 10th March can so easily become October 3rd when written by anyone who's not native of the USA.

Chapter 14

Litigation Rules OK!

America has the unfortunate reputation of being the greatest producer and user of lawyers in the world. It is not an enviable record; in fact it is one that breeds contempt for the law and instils a fear of everything in life. As I stated previously in this book, along with the statistic that the USA occupies 4% of the world's land mass and makes up around 5% of the world's population, it is also said that the USA employs 43% of the world's lawyers. I am assured that this is a staggering, but quite correct fact. There is far too much to discuss on this subject and it is not necessarily a topic that will interest the majority of readers so I will keep it very slim in content with just a couple of warnings about how different the laws are in this country and how easy it is to lose everything that you've worked for and also how easy it is for some people to get money for nothing.

Everything in American civil law is geared to taking money from unsuspecting individuals or companies via a lawsuit in order to line the pockets of would-be claimants and their lawyers. There is good reason that law-firm television advertisements litter the commercial breaks in this country, pushing devious methods at you in the hope that you might sue someone. Many of them will quote a 'no win, no fee' strapline – this is because they will take approximately half of any award or pay-out that you might receive. It's just lawyers playing the odds.

The terms 'ambulance chasers', 'class action suits' and 'mass torts' are just a sample of phrases that you may have seen when reading anything by the excellent authors, John Grisham and David Baldacci, but these expressions have an increasing presence in current American society. Ambulance chasers are exactly that – lawyers who will literally trail the unfortunate victim right into his hospital bed, proffering their business cards at the maximum point of vulnerability, in the hope of signing the patient up to file a compensation lawsuit. Mass torts and class action suits are filed by one law-firm on behalf of many people, sometimes thousands, against unsuspecting or negligent corporations. The main aim is to get the defending companies to settle compensation to all claimants in one hit, thereby making a large number of plaintiffs a little wealthier and the law firm, a great deal wealthier without the aggravation and expense of attending lengthy court sessions. Invariably, the mass tort will typically be as a result of the unforeseen side-effects of a drug made by one of the larger pharmaceutical companies, where the claim is duplicated amongst all of the plaintiffs and presented as one centralised and coordinated lawsuit managed on behalf of a large number of claimants.

When signing up to a class action or mass tort, one effectively gives up one's right to sue independently as an individual. In order to expedite the claim, many class actions are settled prior to attending court and for this reason, most larger organisations will have a fund set aside for this very purpose. Others, who hadn't foreseen the risk attached to the company's product, will often face bankruptcy, therefore avoiding a settlement and leaving the claimants unable to independently secure compensation. Drive through any American town and you'll see dozens of enormous billboards filled with the beaming and often repugnant faces of lawyers who want to sign you up as a potential client. Look through the Yellow Pages at the section for attorneys-at-law and you will be inundated by promises of successful claims for compensation against your employer, doctor, neighbour or associate.

You are also personally vulnerable to litigation in the safety of your own home. Home-owners insurance is not just for protection against hurricanes, tornadoes, earthquakes, fire and flood. It's also there to protect you from personal injury liability. It would be foolish to think in the UK that you should protect yourself against potential litigation in your home, the possibility of this a far-fetched idea. But in the USA, your home-owners insurance policy will carry umbrella coverage for accidents that may occur on your premises. There is good reason for this and the following story should be a stark warning of the pitfalls that may be encountered.

An acquaintance of mine, having just completed the construction of his beautiful new home, decided to hold a cocktail party for around a hundred or so of his friends, colleagues and relatives. At this point in time, he had forgotten to arrange his home-owners insurance policy, having only just moved into the house, a natural oversight. The evening was proving to be a great success with many of the guests congratulating him and his wife on the final result of his new-build. That was until around 11pm, when one of the partygoers tripped on the step of the patio as he went to look at the new pool. The result was that the guest had broken his ankle in the fall and ended up being taken by ambulance to the hospital. Of course, everyone was saddened to see this happen but it didn't interrupt the party for too long and after a short while, the evening recommenced and eventually petered out by 2am.

Unfortunately for the owner of the house, the injured friend filed a claim against him for the damage to his ankle and also for the subsequent hospitalisation and loss of business while he recovered. This claim was substantial, and was being filed by one friend against another, a quite extraordinary but not untypical American scenario. Without the protection of a home-owner's policy, the owner of the house was personally liable and he ended up paying out of his own pocket, forcing a second mortgage to be taken on his new home. Of course, there isn't a policy available for this type of predicament in the UK because the law simply doesn't allow for this ludicrous situation to exist in the first place, and rightly so.

Similarly, if you have workmen on your premises, whether they are repairing an electrical problem or just trimming the hedges, be very careful to ensure that they have their own liability coverage as you may be held responsible should they have an unforeseen accident whilst working for you. Because of these types of problems, the insurers take great care in avoiding risk. The inspection by the insurance company of your home and the potential risks attached to it, is normal in America when establishing the premium, although it's unheard of in the UK, where a phone call will secure a policy. If you are privileged to have a swimming pool on your property, make sure that you don't have a diving board as this could inflate the premium or void it completely. The same goes for the 'wrong breed of dog'; if you have a pet that falls into the undesirable category, then you may also be refused cover. If you are near water or in a tidal area, the premium will be drastically elevated unless your home is also similarly elevated.

When I heard the sad story of the proud new home-owner being sued by his friend, I was not only sickened and saddened by the whole affair but I was also made worryingly aware of the pitfalls that I might personally encounter if I were to suffer a similar predicament. From that moment on, I became increasingly careful about who was working at my home and I also became less inclined to have parties where I might end up with a bigger bill than I had originally budgeted. It's not a case of being overly concerned, just a case of making sure that your policy will cover you in the event.

Whilst playing golf one day, one of the other players in my group, described how in recent weeks, he had inadvertently driven his golf cart into a tree stump near the clubhouse. The result was that his cart was wrecked and he sprained a wrist. It should be pointed out that all of this was actually his own fault for not staying on the cart path and his cart, which was his own, was possibly not in the best of condition. However, after noticing one of the lawyer billboards on his way home, he made contact with the said attorney, filed a damages claim against the golf club and ended up with $8,000 in compensation.

Doctors, surgeons and hospitals are all in similar precarious situations of jeopardy. It is not necessarily the physician cost or the complexity of the surgical procedure that raises the bills from the hospitals. More likely it is the excessive insurance premiums that they pay in order to have you as a patient in the first place. The fear of being sued for negligence or malpractice is one that keeps many surgeons awake at night.

Therefore, in order to take part in The American Dream, it is vitally important to understand how real the threat of personal litigation might be so it isn't merely a case of "love thy neighbour", you just might need to sue him too.

Chapter 15

Cell Phones

Back in England, I rued the day that mobile phones (cell phones) were ever invented. The original versions, introduced back in the early 1980s, consisted of a large handset accompanied by a brick-like power cell weighing almost as much as a car battery. I had the use of one but it never left my car as it was just too heavy and cumbersome to take anywhere. In my own business, where film locations were often bereft of public telephones, these army-like gadgets proved invaluable, but in the course of normal day to day life, they were ultimately surplus to requirement.

However, and even though I own one myself, I truly despise these instruments that seem to relentlessly interrupt conversation, sending their owners into insular bubbles, oblivious and ignorant of the world around them. I remember an incident one day, whilst walking down Wardour Street in the heart of London's Soho district. My attention was drawn to a young girl ahead of me who, judging from her amplified voice and expressive use of both arms, seemed to me to be involved in a fairly animated conversation with herself. Realising my close proximity to someone who clearly wasn't at one with the world, I decided that the opposite side of the street might be a better choice for me to continue my stroll.

Of course, she wasn't lunatic at all – she merely had one of the first Bluetooth earpieces that had gone on sale in London, which whilst allowing her to gesticulate wildly with both hands, it also maintained that the phone itself remained hidden. When I realised that she was actually talking to someone else on another phone in another part of town, I was curious and as I followed behind her, she suddenly crossed the road, causing cars to slam on their brakes and swerve to avoid killing her. The 'bubble' that she was locked in was making her absolutely unaware of her own actions and of the actions and reactions of others around her. She was oblivious to me and to everyone else and in fact, she was a danger to herself and others too. This was the moment that I first regretted the invention of the mobile phone, or cell phone, as they say here in America.

You will be pleased to hear that cell phones are also ruining American society. They are proving to be instrumental in the abject destruction of manners and courtesy in all classes in the USA, as currently witnessed in England. Cell phones are proving to be potentially fatal as people continue to use them whilst driving and the worst culprits appear to be women who seem as a race to have their phones surgically attached to their ears. I'm sure that we've all witnessed the rush-hour traffic where endless lines of vehicles provide temporary mobile bathrooms for the drivers to shave, brush their hair, or apply cosmetics. (Actually, on many occasions driving to my office in London, I would watch in my rear-view mirror, the extraordinary metamorphosis from slug to butterfly by some of the female drivers queuing behind me). But whether the traffic speeds are slow or otherwise, the distraction caused by these belated ablutions is enough to cause injury or death to other drivers as well as to cyclists and pedestrians. My own opinion is that even the re-selection of a radio station is a distraction and can prove to be deadly.

However, as described in the previous paragraph and also in my ambulant study of the aforementioned mentally-challenged Bluetoother, the cell phone has now become the ultimate distraction in life. The use of these devices, again primarily by women, is pandemic. (This is not an anti-women chapter, just some examples of those instances I've witnessed since I've been here) No sooner has the soccer-mom, lady lawyer or female realtor started the car's engine than they are already in earnest conversation with someone in another part of town. I've seen it happen day after day and I'm still amazed that anyone can have a sensible conversation with another person at 7am. My own oral and aural capability is still in a pre-caffeine state of paralysis at that time of the morning, proving all conversational attempts completely devoid of articulation or comprehension.

Fortunately, as has already happened in the UK, the use of cell phones in cars is now beginning to be curtailed in the USA. In New York, it is already an offence to use a phone handset whilst driving, although a hands-free device is allowed. In California, they are also similarly outlawing the use of cell phones in vehicles, starting January 2008. In my opinion, the ban on the use of the handset is not enough because the distraction of conversation is still there, which is the real danger.

In fact, largely due to the recent ability of the cell phone to provide mobile internet connection, many people are using laptop computers in their 'vehicular offices', and more often than not they are surfing the net as they drive! In some ways, I suppose I am a little Draconian in my ideas when it comes to safety on the roads, particularly the American highways, but I'm also a great believer in the preservation of life. The selfish actions of ignorant drivers cause the deaths of thousands of innocent people every year and to that end, I believe that all of the following should be applied:

1. All cell phone use inside the vehicle should be made illegal, regardless of hands-free devices.

2. Any GPS or Satellite Navigation Systems that can be accessed or adjusted whilst driving, should be outlawed.

3. CD players and radios should be rendered 'locked' once the vehicle is in motion, making the changing of discs, radio stations or volume levels, impossible.

4. Dashboard television should be automatically switched off if the vehicle is in gear.

5. There should be no eating, drinking or smoking inside the car at any time. All of these actions are hazardous and distractive and an end for any or all of these activities would be beneficial to everyone. (This one will offend many people but if you want to eat, drink or smoke, then why not stop and enjoy it properly?)

6. There should be a maximum loudness level for all vehicle music systems in order to avoid driver 'insulation'. It is as important to hear as well as see, everything outside the vehicle.

7. All scanners, photocopiers and PCs should be carried in the trunk of the vehicle, so that temptation is avoided at all times.

Cell phones are not just a problem inside cars. They're often used in the USA by drivers when filling their tanks at the gas station. The use of phones on forecourts in the UK has been banned for some time, not out of fear that the phone itself is able to act as an ignition source for the petroleum but more to do with the inherent danger caused by its distraction. There are a number of recorded cases of accidents where a departing vehicle has knocked down another customer who had been engaged in cell phone conversation whilst walking from the car to the cashier. The isolation these things cause is incredibly clear to see.

My despair of the cell phone doesn't end with its vehicular use. I was recently standing in line (queuing) at a department store, waiting to pay for my items. The customer at the checkout was in deep conversation on her cell phone as she pushed her intended purchases towards a bemused cashier. At no time during the purchase, either when searching for and handing over her credit card, signing the receipt or taking the bagged purchases away, did she ever once acknowledge the existence of the poor cashier. I stared in shock at this shopper with her cellular addiction as she trudged away, down the escalator and out through the exit, never once pausing in her conversation and never once acknowledging that there was another living soul in her ignorant, arrogant and dreadful little world. I apologised on her behalf to the cashier but she told me that this was becoming a routine scenario in the store and she had now grown to expect it, although it made her furious every time it happened.

The very same day, I was waiting at the checkout in a supermarket and the same thing happened. A middle-aged man who evidently deemed his cell conversation more important than anything else in the world, literally checked out without courtesy to either the cashier or to the boy who was bagging his groceries. I was appalled. I'm not saying that this is endemic or unique to the USA as I realise that it happens in England and in the rest of Europe too. The difference that I have noticed though is that whereas it was often the teenage society that's guilty of this behaviour in England, I've found more and more, that it's the 30 to 50-year-old age group which provides the greater number of villains in the USA.

Even on the golf course, I regularly see the use of these damned phones. What could possibly be more important than a game of golf? I'm sorry, for a moment there, I was being just the slightest bit selfish. With most innovations, the human race benefits in some way although with any invention that makes life easier, there is usually a downside too. The invention of the motor vehicle has revolutionised transport, but at the same time, has caused excessive pollution. The microwave oven gives you a cooked meal in 45 seconds but the joy of cooking is being slowly eroded. The internet is an outstanding source of education and research but it is also home to paedophiles, addicts and conmen. Whatever my misgivings are with cell phones, there's also no doubt that they do have some benefits, whether it's their use in providing emergency communication or the added safety that they can provide for our children or even in the triangulation methods used by law enforcement agencies to track the bad guys.

My real frustration is not at the technology itself but more with the sadness that we are losing something which forms the very essence of the human race. We look around us, we see new things, we haphazardly and innocently interact with others near us, we make eye contact with passers-by, we smile at each other and we learn from our surroundings and actually, the real truth is that we are better for it. The use of cell phones as a function of everyday life is ensuring that we lose all of the above and that our humdrum existence is ruled solely by a device that was initially designed to aid communication, not kill it.

Chapter 16

Gun Culture

Nothing will ever erase from my memory, the ruthless and senseless slaying of those young and innocent children in the small town of Dunblane in Scotland on the 13th March 1996. On that day, a teacher and sixteen of her pupils went to Dunblane Primary School to enjoy a peaceful day of learning but before the end-of-school bell had sounded, they'd all died at the hands of a suicidal sociopath. It remains the single worst atrocity seen in peace-time Great Britain during the twentieth century.

The power wielded by a single individual when armed with a gun, is senseless. That said, the purchase of firearms in the USA is not only easy but it's happening as a common and everyday occurrence. The secretion of a weapon in a vehicle's glove compartment or even in a woman's purse in this country is not uncommon. For someone new to the USA, it is a frightening reality. It also seems that for every one citizen that opposes the personal carrying of firearms, there would appear to be at least two that would advocate it. In discussion on this subject I've found that I'm often directed to familiarising myself with the 2nd Amendment of the American Constitution and the American citizen's 'right to bear arms'. The actual text reads thus:

"A well regulated militia, being necessary for the preservation of a free state, the right of the people to keep and bear arms shall not be infringed."

I suppose the problem for me, is the current twenty-first century definition of the word 'militia'. I understand that the dictionary meaning is *"an army composed of ordinary citizens rather than professional soldiers."* But in current context, the word more likely conjures the vision of a group of extremists in a banana republic who have formed their own army and one that is neither well regulated nor lawful. The truth is that the USA, notwithstanding the Al-Qaeda terrorist attacks in 2001, has never really been under any real threat from external forces on American soil and therefore has never had any relevant reason to use this part of the Constitution for the defence of the state for which it was originally written and intended. There is a critical requirement that all acts, bills and laws be updated as the world itself undergoes change. Therefore, constitutional amendments in any country become an absolute necessity.

As an extraordinary example of English ignorance, it's worth looking back a few hundred years to see why there is a constant need for constitutional amendment. In 16th Century England, a woman suspected of being a witch, would be strapped in a chair affixed to a seesaw-like device and dunked in the nearest river. After several minutes had elapsed, she would be brought back up and if she was still alive, then according to the administrators of justice of that period, she would be found guilty of being a witch and she'd be executed. Of course, if she were to die during the dunking, then it would be admitted that a mistake had indeed been made and that she was probably innocent of all charges. She would however be dead either way. It didn't take too long for the witch-hunters of that era to realise that they might have to change the method of deciding witch, or not witch.

The fact remains, that 200,000 people die worldwide each year from gunshot wounds. These deaths are just the ones caused by private firearms, none of them as a result of any military activity. More alarmingly, is that 20% of those attributed deaths are by Americans, on Americans, in America. Half of the 400 million privately owned firearms in the world are owned by Americans.

You are 50 times more likely to die from gunshot wounds in America than in Great Britain and 100 times more likely than if you live in Japan. You don't have to be Einstein to work out that guns aren't good for you.

The human race has a fascination with weapons. Since the invention of firearms, there has always existed a natural desire for humans to shoot at a target, static or moving. To some, it is an act of violence and to others, it is simply a test of natural ability. Although I'm not a gun lover myself, I do understand the mental grip that firearms have on many and to that end, I fully support the preservation of shooting clubs. But that is where the guns should remain, in the clubhouse, locked and secured. My own passion is motor racing. Its high speed danger fascinates me but I race on a race track in racing conditions, I don't use a public highway to pursue the sport and I don't endanger anyone except myself and of course, some of the other idiots who follow the sport. Surely, the right to bear arms does not give us the right to take lives? Whether the terrifying scenes witnessed in Denver, Waco or Washington, too many people are hurt by the actions of a few.

The sad news is that many schools in the USA now have metal detectors at the entrances to try and eliminate weapons from the school campus. The relative ease in the ability to purchase a gun is one of the main reasons that there are so many firearms in American homes. The rules vary from state to state but in many cases, the mere production of a driving licence will secure the purchase of a weapon, provided that you are over 21. I find it disturbing that one particular leading American retail store will sell you a rifle or a shotgun, though I understand that they don't currently sell pistols or ammunition. I did read recently that this same company is ending sales of firearms in around one-third of their stores which seems to be a step in the right direction. But the sad fact is that you can still order high-velocity automatic guns direct from other traders on the internet, delivered right to your door.

If we believe that the removal of firearms from society is not relevant in reducing the numbers of gunshot crimes in the USA, it is worth noting that even at the highest rung of the ladder, it's not that safe in American society. Of the 42 men who have served as President of the United States since the great visionary George Washington in 1789, seventeen of them have been the target of assassination and four of those attempts were successful. Abraham Lincoln, James A. Garfield, William McKinley and John F. Kennedy all died from gunshot wounds, each murdered by American-born assassins. Effectively, if you are successful in your attempt at becoming President of the United States, there is a 40% chance that a gun-wielding madman will attempt to kill you at some point during your term of office and there's a 10% chance you'll end up dead. In Britain, there have been 52 Prime Ministers in the last 300 years and only one of them ever suffered an attempt on his life. Sadly for him, the attempt proved successful. The 17th British Prime Minister, Spencer Perceval, died from shotgun wounds on the steps of The House of Commons on the 11th of May, 1812. According to records, his last words being, "'Oh, I've been murdered".

Of course, my own thoughts are pretty much irrelevant on this issue. I am a guest of this country and if the current population decides that gun ownership and gun carrying is what it wants, then I have no position from which to argue. I wasn't born here and therefore have no say on the Constitution. It's always too easy as an outsider to judge others and just as the British public often becomes upset when accused or berated from afar, the Americans, quite correctly, have a right to be offended when they are also judged with criticism or cynicism by other nations. I would much rather leave the task of judging his own people, to the incomparable Bill Maher on HBO.

Therefore, this chapter is without doubt, the one subject that I least wanted to write about. It's not progressive, evocative or even particularly educational. I want to look more at the positive things that this country has to offer rather than to dwell on the negatives and for every reader that agrees with my own personal point of view on gun culture in the USA, there are just as many who wouldn't sympathise with my worries on the current legislation. However, for anyone who is thinking about making America their home, this subject should be mentioned and those potential migrants should be warned.

As an addendum to this chapter, I am learning right at this moment, of yet another horrific mass murder on a college campus, the consequences of which are still unknown as I write. A lover's quarrel on the campus at Virginia Tech in the town of Blacksburg VA, has resulted in the slaying of at least 29 people inside the college. This latest horror eclipses even Columbine and this is unlikely to be the final body count. For so many families and also for those thousands of people who are even distantly connected to these dreadful murders, today is a day that can never be forgotten or recovered. The sad truth is that the USA lives with a terrible new legacy that sees an average of two fatal college shootouts occur every year and it's been this way for the last decade. A Presidential speech of sympathy will no longer suffice for the majority of Americans, as the time for action against gun crime in this country must now be long overdue.

Notwithstanding the ridiculous and ignorant chants from the extreme lobbyists that claim gun control is not the answer to the problem, and whilst also acceding that a well connected criminal will always have access to firearms, I would imagine that had this particular student who decided to commit genocide at school today, not been able to buy his weapons from the local hardware store, then this latest atrocity may never have happened. Gun control is the answer, period. It won't stop all firearms-related deaths but it will make an immense difference. Surely it must now be time to stop citing the rights of a constitution that has for some time been out of date and to start living in a world that does not agree with the repetitive mantra that insists on the right to arm its people for an invasion that isn't likely to be coming anytime soon?

Chapter 17

Sport

OK, hands up! No, no, I haven't become a card-carrying gun lover since writing the last chapter. What I mean is, hands up, I confess to not knowing the first thing about American sports. I will admit right now, that most American sports leave me cold. This is no real surprise as we all tend to favour the sports that we grow up with in our home countries and in the same way that I have no particular love for any US sport, the game of soccer is a minor annoyance to most red-blooded Americans. The world's greatest and most popular sport called football (soccer) is relegated to the 'other sports' sections in the back pages of most American papers. In many ways, this is probably a good thing for me as an individual. For too many years in England, I looked forward with some delectation to spending three hours on a Sunday morning reading the sports pages and now that I display complete ignorance and a total lack of knowledge for any of the American sports that dominate the back pages over here, I find that I have more time on my hands to do other things. Like bemoaning the lack of decent sports pages in America, featuring football, cricket or motor racing....

However there really are only four main sports in the US and these are NBA, NFL, MLB, and NHL. These four associations represent basketball, US football, baseball and hockey, respectively.

So let's have a quick appraisal of the main ones:

US Football: It's commonly acknowledged as the jocks' game, requiring more brawn, less brains, the bulk and muscle competition between players and fans alike who seem tragically overdosed on testosterone, chauvinism and homophobia. It is completely confusing and over-long to Europeans but it is close to heaven for most male Americans. It's called football although the foot is rarely used and despite the fact that another sport called football had been using the name 'football' for over a hundred years prior to the invention of the American game, the US name never progressed to something more appropriate. The ball isn't ball-shaped either, more ovarian than round. The winners of the Super Bowl (nothing to do with bowling) are hailed as World Champions although to be truthful, I've never been aware of any non-American team taking part in the competition. An American, soccer-despising acquaintance of mine, recently described the Super Bowl as the equivalent of the World Cup. Well it's not, although it's probably a decent enough comparison to the European Champions League (the European club soccer competition). Around 100 million people follow US Football and of course, only about three billion worldwide follow the real football game, the one that's called football by everyone else in the world except Americans. Truthfully, US Football is a bastardised version of rugby except that the American players get the protection of full body armour which is absolutely not the case in rugby. I dislike rugby so I never really had a chance to like the American version of it. Cheerleaders seem to love this game though and I guess they're pretty nice to watch.

Baseball: This is rounders to anyone else. There's an awful lot of tobacco chewing and spitting and it would appear to be played by oddly shaped and overweight men in tight pants. This is a real guy game, Alpha Male's exclusive territory. The apparent aim is to win something called The World Series, although again, I'm not aware of any other countries taking part in the championship. Many people have tried valiantly to make comparisons to cricket but I don't really see it, other than the fact that the pitcher is like a bowler, the batter is the batsman, the catcher the wicket-keeper and the fielders, well, they're fielders too. The pitch is generally round-ish in both games and the batter's box is the equivalent of the crease in cricket, although a cricketer's box is something completely different that provides genital protection.... no, I'm sorry, there is no real comparison and baseball will just have to be seen as a version of rounders in my eyes.

Basketball: Again, netball to the rest of the world. Actually, of all US sports, I really quite like this one, having watched the Miami Heat take the championship in 2006. (I'm not sure what championship it was but it was the best of seven games and it seemed incredibly important to everyone else here so I just got caught up in the whole fervour of it all) I didn't realise until I started to vaguely understand the game, that it really isn't that physical at all. It's physical in the fact that it is non-stop end-to-end action played by extremely fit athletes but the players aren't really allowed to lay a hand on the opposition. They can block, but they can't touch the other team. If they do, it results in the penalty of a costly pair of free-throws awarded to the opposing team. It is an extremely clever game, it's the most tactical sport I've ever watched and it is absolutely time efficient with the team coaches keeping a close eye on the clock. The game can be won or lost, literally in the last fraction of a second. The players seem to be one of three things, very fast, very tall or just very big. Take as an example of size, Shaquille O'Neal who plays for The Heat, a colossus of a man who seems to cast a shadow over the entire court when he's playing. He is a giant in every sense of the word. These players are also paid on an equally giant scale, as are most American sportsmen. (The great Shaq apparently lives in a 65,000 sq.ft. home with a separate guest house covering another 15,000 sq.ft. Compare that to the average American home which is probably less than 2000 sq.ft.)

Ice Hockey: This is very fast, in fact it's so fast that I can't ever seem to locate where the puck is until it's in the net. The players in this game seem to thrive on a punch-up. In fact without the fights, I doubt that many spectators would show up to watch. If I understand correctly, it would appear to be more favoured in the northern states of the USA and Canada too. What more do I need to say about this sport?

All of the above is designed to be derogatory, inflammatory and calumnious but all descriptions herewith are made with my tongue held firmly in my cheek. I've just described US sports in the same throwaway manner in which any of my American buddies would pass comment on football, cricket or rugby. I am truly ignorant of the rules, protocol and techniques of all of the four main sports in the USA. I am trying to understand them but with the onset of age, there follows a diminishing ability in the mental acceptance of information. I suppose I'm lucky enough and proud also, that all of the world's major sports were spawned in various parts of Great Britain. These include football, rugby, cricket, golf, motor-racing, boxing, badminton, squash, lawn tennis, hockey and even snooker and bowls. OK, so the French and the Dutch may have had a hand in the invention of tennis and bowls respectively but the sports were shaped into the modern games in Britain. After all, tennis was originally called 'jeu de paume' and was racquet-less – the players instead using only the palms of their hands.

Apart from NBA, American sports seem generally to be based on that old-fashioned principle of testosterone and showmanship. While watching a College football game last night, it was interesting to see the TV director give us a multi-camera tour of the whole circus. It conjured visions of a Roman amphitheatre and there were defined ranks of the 'haves' and 'have-nots', the blessed and the luckless. I felt a sense of sympathy for the marching bands who were wearing what seemed to be extremely uncomfortable uniforms, mostly appearing to be a little overweight and not as good looking as either the jocks on the field or the cheerleaders who were dancing in between timeouts. But I suppose there's more than one way to get a free ticket to the game.

However, there are some sports where there remains a common bond and a universal understanding between Americans and Europeans. It would seem that golf is fast becoming the game that everyone can play and that everyone now wants to watch. It is more television-friendly than tennis, a sport which golf has somewhat overshadowed in recent years. It isn't just the men's side of golf which is attracting world audiences, women's golf has also undergone radical change in the last five or six years. No longer the domain of the aging middle-class blue-bloods and blue-rinses, the sport is now dominated by young, fresh and athletic female players who are not only excelling at the game but with their good looks and their desire to integrate style and fashion into the golf domain, they are fast becoming a sponsor's dream. The Americans have really taken the lead on this, sensing quickly the potential prize at the end of it. Natalie Gulbis, Michelle Wie and Paula Creamer are three shining examples of the ladies golf game in the USA, and the current World No.1, Lorena Ochoa, is now the most highly regarded woman in her home country of Mexico, such is her impact there.

If you want to see how this segment of the game is being nurtured in America, stop by at your local club when there is a girls' high school golf tournament in progress and enjoy a real treat. A quick look at the pre-match practice area will find rows of immaculately and identically dressed teams of slim, fit and athletic girls, all swinging clubs in a synchronised and clockwork fashion. It's like watching a display of immaculate and faultless human-elastic motion. The first time I saw this, I'd never felt so intimidated in my life at these extraordinary teenagers who gave the appearance of a group of exquisite and fearsome female soldiers, preparing for battle.

On one occasion, I happened to be playing in a group being quickly hunted down by the approaching teenage golf prodigy, Morgan Pressel, who was playing a practice round in her final county event before turning professional. I'd watched her practice for a few minutes earlier that morning and I was already terrified of this pint-sized sensation. As she approached the tee, my hands literally trembled as I was preparing to drive off. Fortunately, I made a good fist of it and didn't embarrass myself but I was taken aback as to how these brilliant young kids can reduce a grown man to jelly. My own daughter decided to take up the game at the age of 10 and in the two years she's been playing, she is already a formidable opponent. But whilst the likes of Gulbis, Wie, Creamer, Pressel and Ochoa have brought new life to the game by injecting the sport with style, panache and personality, women's golf is simultaneously in danger of losing the very momentum that these girls started. With the success of the Korean and Chinese players who are now making up almost 50% of the LPGA Tour, there's now a marketing dilemma for sponsors. Sadly, these brilliant young Asian girls do not naturally engender the same individuality and personality that is outwardly shown by the Americans and Europeans, and consequently their visual impact on television is not as powerful as that of their fashionista opponents. To put it in the bluntest terms, once the male viewers begin switching off, so will the sponsors and women's golf will suffer once more.

Motor-racing also shares a commonality between our countries. As I've said previously, I am a huge fan of open wheel motor racing, Formula One being the ultimate pinnacle of the sport. Unfortunately, the original concept of a group of like-minded and ambitious privateers developing a Formula One car to compete against other similarly focused teams, has really all but disappeared. Frank Williams and Ron Dennis at Williams and McLaren respectively, are the only remaining teams that still try to adhere to this principle but even their original hobbyist setups have become vast corporate empires.

The great names of the early years, BRM, Lotus, Cosworth, Ligier, Tyrrell, March, Hesketh and more recently, Jordan, Sauber, Benetton & Minardi no longer take their places on the Formula One grid. What's happening now is that the world's car manufacturers are using the sport as their own personal shop window. Honda, Toyota, Mercedes, BMW and Renault have managed to change the sport from something that was created by individuals, characters and enthusiasts, into a circus that is just another corporate event. Gone are the days when there was a genuine camaraderie on the race-track prior to the start where teams would often help out other teams if they had mechanical problems which might have prevented them from starting the race. It was a true gentleman's sport and I miss it.

The truly great drivers like Stewart, Fittipaldi, Lauda and Fangio and also more recently, Senna, Prost and Mansell are no longer the individuals that characterise the sport. Michael Schumacher has been the only real latter-day driver who has provided true excitement and controversy because he seemed to enjoy being the villain of the piece. I never liked him much as a person but I certainly admired the man. (I am often stunned to learn that this seven-time F1 World Champion is pretty much unheard of in the USA whereas in Europe, this iconic and idolised German racer is practically a household name). What I really mean is that it should be remembered that all sports need characters, heroes and villains. Without these, there is nothing to hold the interest of the viewing public and without an audience, the sport is finished.

But although Formula One doesn't command a lot of interest in the USA, there are similar open-wheel racing series that have enormous followings. The two obvious comparisons would be the IndyCar and the Champ Car series, both of which see speeds far exceeding those in Formula One. These American versions are not as refined and technical as F1 but the real bonus for Europeans is that in recent years, the drivers of these cars have changed from being predominantly American to a truly international and cosmopolitan array of characters. I use the word character deliberately as this is the one thing missing in F1 now and it is the ingredient that's providing the real pull that the American series' have on their international audiences. We even saw British champions at the end of the 2005 and 2007 IndyCar Championships. Dan Wheldon and Dario Franchitti dominated both seasons respectively, picking up the coveted Indianapolis 500 trophy on the way to their Championship victories. The introduction of women to these racing series, is also an added bonus. Not all of them are there just to provide a little extra gloss and glamour either – some of these girls are providing a real challenge to their male counterparts. Danica Patrick may be diminutive in stature but she has the heart of a lion.

The Indy 500 is the biggest race of all and it is the one event on the calendar when you will often see two or three overweight team owners desperately cramming themselves into an extra race car in the hope of finally getting their hands on that illustrious winning pint of milk, the traditional victory drink at The Brickyard. 2006 saw a final lap of intense rivalry between the 45-year-old Andretti-Green team owner Michael Andretti and his 19-year-old son Marco, both of them with a real chance of winning the race. Neither won, the chequered flag being taken by their American compatriot, Sam Hornish Jr. What it demonstrated though, was the inherent desire of all Indy drivers to win that single elusive event, a race that has been won by many F1 drivers as well, including Jim Clark, Graham Hill, Emerson Fittipaldi and Mario Andretti and more recently by Eddie Cheever, Jacques Villeneuve and Juan Pablo Montoya.

However, the really big auto sport over here would appear to be NASCAR. It actually stands for National Association for Stock Car Auto Racing or as I call it, GOBR, Good-Ole-Boy Racing. The drivers seem typically to go by the name of Jimmy, Bobby, Ricky, Kasey or Dale and they often have accents that evoke the sounds of banjos playing in my ears. There is a fair age range too although many of these racers carry the generic southern boy goatee beard. I should desist right now from further defamation of the sport as this is a true money-spinner. In fact, what began as a form of weekend hillbilly racing in the Deep South has developed into a nationwide sporting spectacle, with an enormous following and a business that generates billions of dollars. In recent seasons, I've also become a huge fan of the honey-tongued Michael Waltrip, his exceptional knowledge of the sport delivered in his inimitable Southern twang. The cars in NASCAR, mostly race around oval-shaped speedways, with the exception of a small number of venues which are road tracks and there are hundreds of monumental crashes each season, though rarely fatal, thanks to the hugely improved safety conditions inside the cockpit. These saloon cars travel at speeds approaching 225mph, heavily emblazoned with their sponsor logos. They look like high speed billboards, corporations racing against rival corporations. Prime examples of the companies who enjoy the benefits of NASCAR promotion are Target and Office Depot, Snickers and M&Ms, Budweiser and Miller Lite and Jack Daniel's and Jim Beam. Often you will see the UPS car trading punches with the FedEx car. In a recent race this year, it was outstanding to watch the Home Depot car pipped at the post by the Lowes car, these two companies being the largest DIY stores in the USA and bitter rivals at that. In a sense, it seemed like the CEOs of these companies were doing battle with each other on the raceway, stirring in me, memories of the Two Tribes video from the band, Frankie Goes To Hollywood, where a pair of oversized Gorbachev and Reagan look-alikes squared up to each other in a comic fist fight.

Commentary on sports programmes in the USA is so different to that found in the UK. British commentary is as reserved as American commentary is frenetic. It's wall-to-wall sound in the States whereas English commentary is more relaxed. Neither is better or worse, just fundamentally different in approach. It feels as though there's a strict rule on American television that any silent or quiet moment on any broadcast, is a television sin. Because of this, stock phrases are the way to go in the States and too many are used, *"we got us a race on now"*, *"gonna have us a showdown"*, *"the guy with the biggest cojones is gonna take it"*, and so on.

I think in many cases, it is more to do with which company is responsible for the broadcast. Sky Television in Great Britain is extremely corporate in its presentation which is the company's one huge disappointment. Contrariwise, the original national broadcasters in the UK, The BBC and ITV, are strangely far more relaxed in their presentational style. Blazers and ties are not a statutory requirement at these networks as they've always been at Sky. In many ways, Sky is more akin to the style prevailed by NBC, ABC and CBS. Compare the BBC's inimitable Peter Alliss to the corporate, suited n' booted identikit presenters of NBC Sports. It's chalk and cheese. Having said that, the combination of Britain's Nick Faldo and NBC's delightful and knowledgeable Kelly Tilghman, has been a revelation this year. The obvious mutual affection between the two has resulted in perfect golf presentation with a nice degree of humour too, although to be honest, Ms. Tilghman could make any sport worth watching,

I suppose for English ears, it's often the space between the words that means the most. Less is more. In American commentary, silence is non-existent and pauses are to be avoided at all costs. I'm guessing that US commentators are told that they are paid by the word or maybe the network bosses are simply telling them to keep the patter going or they'll be out of a job. The obvious is stated, just to fill a potential void in the sound. Often heard, are phrases like *"he pushed that putt"* – when we can see that the player missed it. And *"he's a good ball striker"* whereas I tend to assume that anyone who's playing professional golf on television is probably reasonably good at hitting the ball – that is after all, their job. However, all of that being said, there's no doubt in my mind that the American commentators seem to absolutely enjoy the whole spectacle far more than their British counterparts and you cannot help but get caught up in their unbridled enthusiasm so all in all, it works fine for me.

Golf as a sport, is now one of the totally international sports where players emerge from all walks of life from all over the world. The coverage in the USA, of all the world events is exceptional. No expense is spared in giving the American viewer the best view possible direct to his armchair. However, without wishing to suggest that the American networks might be just a little nationalistic, there is a distinct patriotism shown in the coverage of certain American golfers. If we look at the overall coverage of any of the PGA four-day events, I would estimate that possibly 50% is allocated to Tiger Woods and in his absence, Phil Mickelson.

Now I know that Tiger is already and will probably always remain, the greatest golfer ever, but I would suspect that even the most fervent admirers of the great man must get just a little tired of watching him for so much of the broadcast. It's got to the stage where all non-Tiger action moments are quickly cut away from, to slot in a brief shot of one of the rest of the other 150-odd players. Of course the vision-mixer is primed to return to Tiger immediately, lest we miss him re-tie his shoe or study his ball. Even as fillers, there are countless edited segments devoted to The Great One and even Tiger must feel a little embarrassed himself with this over-exposure. The fact remains though, without his presence, every televised golf tournament is downgraded to a minor event. The effect that his participation has on spectator and television audiences is unprecedented and will continue for many years to come. I am an enormous admirer and ardent fan of Tiger Woods and have often dreamed about taking him on in a match (obviously with Tiger only allowed to use his putter for every stroke on all 18 holes), but I do enjoy watching all of the other brilliant players too, so come on NBC, ABC and CBS - give us a break!

As a final comment on golf, I have closely watched the way in which Phil Mickelson conducts himself on the golf course. His manners are impeccable, he is courteous at all times and he's never short of a smile or an autograph for his many fans. His general deportment and boyish good looks, together with his ever-so-slightly meek manner, has historically made him even more endearing to female viewers, young and old. In short, he is a genuinely nice bloke. Since finally winning his first major and then backing it up with a couple more wins, the pressure and burden of achieving that elusive goal, seems to have now been removed from his still young shoulders. I don't think he will hang around too long to watch his game decline either. Along with his wife Amy and his three children, all of them charming and beautiful, they conjure up the very essence of the American Dream. The publicity that Phil and Amy Mickelson are currently receiving from the charitable works with which they are both involved, would seem to make him a perfect choice as a future candidate for the American Presidency. Surely Phil and Amy would make the ultimate President and First Lady, the type of leadership that America has been searching for and craving since the loss of John and Jackie Kennedy and wouldn't his candidacy probably be supported by Republicans and Democrats alike? Maybe I have an over-imaginative mind but I don't believe for one moment that I'm the only one who can see the foundations currently being laid.

Basketball, US football, baseball, and hockey are all synonymous with the USA but sadly, not with the rest of the world. The USA hasn't yet adopted soccer, deciding that it's a game designed for, and best left to girls but I hope it will become the biggest sport in America during the next 20 years. However, just try saying that to any male over the age of 30 and you'll be laughed out of the sports bar. The USA is still at the stage of importing over-the-hill ex-soccer stars from Europe, a hangover from the early 70s. The players then were the likes of George Best and Rodney Marsh and today they are best exemplified by David Beckham, having recently moved from Manchester United via a spell with Real Madrid to the LA Galaxy in the MLS (Major League Soccer). The big difference in America is that the boys begin playing the professional game of soccer, far too late in life. In the UK, many boys are playing at the highest level in the English Premiership at the age of 16 or 17, forgoing the opportunity for any further education and instead gambling on the chance of fame and wealth at a very early age. This route is unheard of in the USA and until some of the American kids take a chance on early glory then it will be impossible for the American game to ever emulate what's going on in the rest of the world.

But if the age that American kids start playing professionally is a problem, I believe that there is a much deeper problem that will prevent the immediate growth of football in the USA. Here is that problem. American sport is played with a distinct sense of gentlemanly conduct. There would appear to be a universal approach to the rules of each sport, and apart from the occasional accusation of performance-enhancing drug use, cheating does not seem to be the main focus in any of the national sports. Therefore, the original prediction that I made about the progress of soccer in the USA was a sweeping statement and the following point may prove to be a barrier.

The high theatrics of guiltless cheating employed by the Hispanic nations in Europe and South America have ruined the greatness of international football, whether at club level or on the world stage. There is no doubt that they possess the skills to impress but clearly they are also ardent students at their clubs' drama classes. Instead of using their inherent and God-given skills to play the game, they have reduced the sport to a sharp and unwatchable lesson on how to cheat. It is no longer possible to watch the histrionic antics of the Spanish, Portuguese and South American teams, their arrogant deception continuing to plague the reputation of all Hispanic players. It would be wholly unacceptable in the USA. I exclude Brazil from this list of cheats as they continue to provide exemplary discipline with artistry that shows everyone else where the future lies in the game of soccer. But it would be futile to expect Americans to accept and promote a multi-billion dollar sport, governed by one single aging official in the centre of the field. They would demand the electronic technology required to police the game and they'd be right to do so, we've been asking for it for years.

In the American game however, you will rarely see verbal abuse levelled at match officials and the hideous and heinous ignorance of rules because the US players seem to maintain a much higher and universal code of conduct, instilled in them at an early age by American coaches who'll not tolerate the tempestuous individual dishonour that might bring the entire team into disrepute. Even more refreshing, is the approach to the game by the women in American soccer. The manner in which they completely engender the sport along with their general deportment and elocution when interviewed, is a breath of fresh air. The game of soccer for American girls is still classed as a sport and not as a business and the players display none of the despicable aspects of the over-pampered and overpaid egotists of the English Premier League. When the United States Women's National Soccer Team won the Women's World Cup in 1991, it was an extraordinary victory for America. When they again emerged victorious in the 1999 tournament, they eclipsed the record of the English men's national team, who have been trying to repeat the success of the brilliant 1966 team ever since. Unfortunately for me, the likelihood of this happening in my lifetime is sadly, somewhat doubtful.

Although soccer is still a minor sport in America, it is viewed in almost religious terms in South American countries like Brazil, Ecuador, Peru, Costa Rica and Mexico. Brazil in particular, has a history of producing the biggest stars and legends of the game. It is universally agreed that they also play the most attractive style of football. It was interesting on a recent trip to San Diego during which I had a fascinating conversation about soccer with a hotel cleaner. He was ecstatic to be discussing his one true passion and amazed that he could have a chat like the one we were having, in America. He could have discussed soccer for the rest of the day and I guess that probably, I would have too. Wherever you live in the world, sport is important not only in emotional and sometimes religious terms, but it's equally important to the general state of the economy. After England won the World Cup in 1966, the United Kingdom experienced ten years of continued economic growth. It was unprecedented. Success in sport reflects well on the image of the nation and the economy will often flourish with that positive spin.

Finally, I am forever grateful to the Fox Soccer Channel and to the Speed Channel in this country, for the tremendous foresight they display in supplying me and others like me, our daily, weekly and monthly fix of Premiership football and Formula One motor-racing. Being the pathetic man that I am, and one with no other option than to suffer the degeneration of both sports like a brain-dead masochist, I would still find it more than a hardship to do without either of them so I thank those two companies from the bottom of my heart.

Chapter 18

Television

It goes without saying that when it comes to making high calibre television shows, the USA is the very best at doing it. As a recipient of the best available, the UK has long enjoyed a steady diet of quality sit-coms and drama from America. The list is endless and it continues to grow. Whether the beautifully honed one-hour dramas of *E.R.*, *The Sopranos*, *House*, *Six Feet Under*, *Sex and The City* and *24* or the half-hour golden nugget sit-coms like *Cheers*, *Friends*, *Will & Grace*, *Frasier*, *Seinfeld* and *Everybody Loves Raymond*, the United Kingdom has enjoyed the American crème de la crème for many years.

The redoubtable TV producer, Mr. David E. Kelley, has been responsible for a large part of this top quality output, beginning with his early writing for *LA Law* through to his creation of shows like *Chicago Hope* and *Ally McBeal* and then more recently, the brilliantly sharp, witty and politically challenging *Boston Legal*. He is also responsible for the script as well as the production which is one of the reasons the clever humour of the dialogue is of such high calibre. (I can't be the only one who's become an overnight fan of the superb dialogue and humour delivered by James Spader and the now reborn William Shatner) David Chase is yet another outstanding American producer. He is the creator of *The Sopranos*, the show which darkly portrays modern-day mafia life, and he is also credited with producing the quirky but brilliant *Northern Exposure*. Carsey-Werner is the production company of another successful pair of genius producers, Marcy Carsey and Tom Werner, responsible for *The Cosby Show, A Different World, Roseanne, 3rd Rock From The Sun, Grace Under Fire* and *Cybill*. All of the producers mentioned here are the bedrock of what makes American television so good; intuitive thinking by instinctive and highly intelligent people.

Quality in American television has been around forever. Pick any one from this list of shows from yesteryear and it will bring back more than one happy memory – *Here's Lucy, Bilko, Star Trek, The Munsters, Bonanza, The Virginian, Peyton Place, Gilligan's Island, Mr. Ed* and *MASH*. Even the hugely successful quality soaps like *Dallas, Dynasty* and *Knot's Landing* were memorable. They depicted a life which we in the UK had never seen before. These shows opened up new horizons as to what was achievable, notwithstanding the treacherous tactics of the ubiquitous J.R. that had the UK and the USA simultaneously gripped on the edge of the sofa, come Wednesday evening.

When Americans do it right, they do it absolutely right. As well as having the sharpest scriptwriters in television, the producers of these programmes ensure that the production value is writ large on the screen in 35mm celluloid. They use the best shooting stages, the best lighting directors and the best equipment. It really doesn't get much better than this. Even 30-minute sit-coms are not reduced to the horrendous inequities of shooting on videotape as is so often the case in the UK, instead insisting on the merits of 35mm cinematography to enhance the show's content and maintain the programme's shelf-life thereafter. I'm not saying that the UK is incapable of producing this kind of quality, in fact quite the opposite. In relative terms, there has been a superb offering of outstanding shows from the British Isles, including *Inspector Morse, Prime Suspect, A Touch of Frost, Poirot* and *Cracker*. The problem is that if these shows do manage to find air-time in the USA, you will invariably find them on BBC-America or some other minor channel buried in the 3am time-slots. Rarely will you see a primetime British programme on any of the main channels, NBC, CBS, ABC or FOX. If the show is aired, likely it won't be the British show but instead a reworked American version of it. This has been happening for years, more recently with the British drama *Cracker*, which is pointless without the brilliant Robbie Coltrane and once again with the sit-com *The Office* which has a completely different interpretation when missing Ricky Gervais and the surroundings of beautiful Slough. That said, Mr. Gervais has had a modicum of personal success with the superb show *Extras*, which is shown on the HBO channel, a company that continues to challenge the boundaries of television excellence.

It would appear from what I've said so far, that I am a big fan of American television and truth be told, I really am. However, there are obviously things that I don't like and elements that I would like to see change. I suppose my biggest problem is with the understanding of American dialogue. An animation artist friend of mine once told me that there are only five shapes used to animate a character's mouth, a,e,i,o and u. This provides for full oral animation for any script recorded. The problem in the American version of spoken English is that there is far less movement of the mouth when an actor is speaking in any kind of drama, be it on television or in the cinema. It's just a slightly more laid back or effortless way of speaking. For someone like me who is half deaf and who relies a great deal on partial lip-reading, it's a real problem. Fortunately, in this age of Tivo, I am able to rewind live TV and have another attempt at comprehending what's being said.

The other problem I've noticed, is that in the quest to cram as much script as possible into a 60 minute show (45 minutes if you take out the commercials), the actors are required to read their lines at a machine-gun pace. Couple this with the multi-angle filming techniques, the editors are able to ping-pong cuts between angles to maximise the effect of wall-to-wall sound. A great example of this is a show called *Studio 60 on The Sunset Strip* where each piece of dialogue from each actor is launched missile-like at each other without the characters taking a single pause for reflection and consideration in each scene. In reality, it is impossible to have this type of speed conversation without taking a moment for contemplation; people just don't converse this way. The real eye-opener is when these supposedly smart and sassy film and TV characters appear on the late-night talk shows. The actors who play them turn out to be nothing like their alter-egos, mostly just regular people who have to think hard about what they're saying, just like the rest of us. (I understand that *Studio 60 on The Sunset Strip* has now been cancelled, which is not a bad thing).

When there is a responsibility to fill the hundreds of cable channels available in the States, it is easy to understand why there is also an enormous amount of pitifully poor material populating American television. There is a low proportion of high-end programming and a high proportion of low-end material. The religious shows, shopping channels, brainless soaps and talk shows are the diet of daytime viewers who are fed a consistent stream of this drivel. It's almost Pareto's Principle at work here where 80% of the low-rent pays for the 20% high-rent.

The late night chat show was born in the USA. These shows are intrinsically different to the British versions. The type of show that was best personified in its heyday by Johnny Carson has lumbered on in the same format with hardly a change in style or delivery. David Letterman and Jay Leno are the kings of the late chat shows, transmitting from New York and Los Angeles respectively. Conan O'Brien and the Scottish comedian Craig Ferguson provide the follow-up for the late, late shows. All of these programmes provide the same fodder; actors and musicians promoting their latest offerings, people who do whacky things just to get on television or senators treading the star path in search of some vote catching. Rarely are we treated to any stimulating or compelling conversation, except occasionally by Craig Ferguson, the brilliantly funny and self-confessed, reformed alcoholic who succeeds in providing shelter for UK guests on his show in Los Angeles. Of all of the hosts, I probably like Mr. Ferguson the most, he's just on too late at night though.

I miss the likes of our own Michael Parkinson and Jonathan Ross. The former would delve deeply into the subject's mind in order to have intelligent conversation and make truly interesting and entertaining television. The latter would just ask the questions that the poor guest would never have dreamed of being asked to answer, usually buckling at the onslaught. They were often shocked into submission early on in the interview. My favourite interviews would have to be the unforgettable Michael Parkinson/Muhammad Ali meetings which will always remain part of British television legend. When Parky interviewed Muhammad Ali for the final time, I realised that this unique meeting of two people who had a complete and utter mutual affection and respect for each other, would remain in my mind forever and I was saddened to think that we would never see the two together again in the future.

With billions of dollars available for budgets, the USA has a film and television business that more than succeeds in filling the primetime schedules without the need to import anything from Britain. The unfortunate truth is that the UK shows which achieve any kind of success over here are the shows that you wish had been condemned to obscurity years ago. It would seem that the British are to be forever shackled to and identified by the inexplicable American fondness for shows like *Benny Hill* and *Keeping Up Appearances*. Even the timeless shows of *Fawlty Towers, Blackadder, Absolutely Fabulous* and *Monty Python* have failed to make a real impression and these are the shows that in my mind, better represent the true British character.

However, not satisfied with feeding the USA with the embarrassing diet of Mr. Hill and Mrs. Bouquet, the main American primetime schedule is now filled with another type of UK import. Check any of the current programme schedules and you'll see the mindless British shows that have invaded mainstream American television. *Millionaire, American Idol, Dancing With The Stars, America's Got Talent* and even the recent hit series, *Grease: You're The One That I Want* that ran a talent contest to find the lead parts for a new British-produced Broadway spectacular. All of these shows have been patterned on original UK formats with most of the US shows featuring at least one British judge, presenter or producer and in many cases, all three. Very few Americans are aware of this, happy to pour scorn on soothsayers like *American Idol's* Simon Cowell, blissfully unaware that the shows are pretty much owned by him and ex-Spice Girls guru, Simon Fuller. I can't imagine though, that Messrs. Cowell & Fuller are particularly bothered by these brickbats as they saunter gleefully towards billionaire status.

Whether you live in the UK or in the USA, it has become very difficult in recent years to take any news station or news agency seriously. All of these news services in both countries, have distinctly changed their format and content to re-emerge as 'shows' with the accent on lipstick and hairstyle, fashion and self-tan. The over-indulgence in the egos of celebrity anchors has long overshadowed news content and the gravity of delivery would seem to be practised in front of a mirror prior to transmission, rather than as a natural reaction to catastrophe. I can no longer watch any of the current American or British news programmes because so many of the overly made-up and overpaid anchors who present these shows on either side of the Atlantic, lack the integrity and sincerity of the original newsmen and women from the BBC, NBC and ABC. Nowadays, like many other people in both countries, I choose to gather my information from the internet news services where I can separate the wheat from the chaff.

At a young age back in the 1960s, I sat glued to every monochrome episode of *The Dick Van Dyke Show,* just desperately wanting to live in that family's life. I marvelled at the size of the refrigerator in their kitchen and even more at the goodies that were stockpiled inside. They lived in a house, the like of which I'd never before seen and they drove in enormous, expensive and seemingly brand new cars. Everyone was exceedingly happy and the sun always shined. It was a life I wanted so badly but it was also one that I didn't really believe existed and in truth, it was of course, a figment of television imagination. But many of these programmes that I grew up with were exported from the US to the UK; *The Dick Van Dyke Show, The Brady Bunch, Bewitched* and *I Dream Of Jeannie* all depicted a rosy, wealthy middle class life of fun, family and future fortune. The shows may not have been realistic but they still had an enormous effect on me. Even the more dramatic shows like *The Streets of San Francisco, Kojak, The FBI* or *Ironside* still gave off that air of American wealth and gloss but weren't nearly as violent as the equivalent shows made today.

I particularly liked those private-detective type of shows where there was always a gigantic and ostentatious 'Yank Tank' car, invariably synonymous with the show's lead character. It could be Frank Cannon with his snug fitting Lincoln Continental, Jim Rockford with his boy-racer Pontiac Firebird, Starsky & Hutch in the now legendary Ford Gran Torino or Thomas Magnum in the ubiquitous Ferrari 308. The only exception to this rule was Columbo in his Peugeot 403 Cabriolet which always seemed ready for the crusher. The shows still follow the same formula today, though much more violent now but without doubt, always as exceptionally well-made as they were then.

(On a completely separate note, it's interesting to see that in those TV shows listed above and in many others like them, all the cars shown in the background and foreground action would usually be American brands. Either Ford, Chevrolet, Buick, Pontiac, Cadillac, Lincoln, or Dodge but now those cars are more likely to be Mazda, Nissan, Honda, Lexus, Toyota, Infiniti or Acura. Not only did the Japanese bomb and subsequently buy most of Pearl Harbour but they have gradually destroyed and replaced the American auto industry. A sad fact when 2005 saw a dramatic round of price slashing from all of the major American car makers while the Japanese and German industries didn't even think to follow suit. It's also interesting to see that Japanese and European models now occupy the top ten spots of the most appealing cars for Americans and the best placed American brand comes in at a lowly 11th position.)

While there is little to criticise in American television production, it's worth making a final point regarding scheduling. In Britain, we've become accustomed to watching uninterrupted television series or serials for 13 straight weeks, the normal length of a season's run. Rarely do we have to wait for our weekly dose of *Prime Suspect* or *Taggart,* save for unexpected schedule disruptions due to World Cup or Olympic events. It is so different in America. In most drama or comedy series, scarcely will three or four episodes have been devoured by the salivating viewer than the programme will suddenly disappear from all future scheduling. Then a couple of months will pass and it's either back in a primetime spot or gone forever. There's no voiceover warning that the programme is being removed and never an explanation as to why it's gone or when it will return which is so incredibly infuriating to television junkies like me.

One odd aspect of American television that still baffles me is that whatever time of day or night, the showing of a breast is absolutely banned and will be covered up by electronically 'fogging' the offending area. I can understand that a watershed may be necessary before 9pm but surely it's OK after this hour? In Europe, there's no shame in showing a bottom or a breast, even in the commercials, something that wouldn't ever happen in the States. The irony of this is that whilst the channels won't show these inoffensive parts of the body, they are allowed to show ads, all day every day, promoting pills to allow penis enlargement. Violence on American television also appears to be bizarrely free of any restrictions or watersheds.

However, I have always been and will remain an avid fan of American television although I do despair of the relentless ad interruption over here, regardless of the fact that I worked for 25 years in the production of television commercials. I also wish the USA wasn't so puritan in its attitudes towards anything vaguely sexual. But, ignoring those two complaints, there's no doubt in my mind that the American production companies are the slickest ones around and their product is the best in the world.

Chapter 19

Religion

Although man's greed and desire to conquer have been the two main reasons that we've experienced so many wars, religion hasn't always been a completely innocent bystander. I am saddened that more wars have been fought and more lives lost over the disagreement about who has the biggest god. Conflicts over differing religious beliefs will in the end, be the deciding factor on whether or not this world and mankind continues or whether eventually, both are destroyed.

So, personal opinions aside, let's forget about the serious side of things for a moment and concentrate on what is unique about the religion business in the USA. America is without doubt, the single most religious country I've ever experienced. It cannot just be an unusually high requirement for forgiveness that sends so many people flocking to their pews each week or that so many are racked with guilt that they need a thorough cleansing every given Sunday. But many families habitually make the Sunday morning pilgrimage to their local place of worship which for golfers like me, provides significant opportunity to get a tee-time before midday on the Sabbath. However, with the knowledge of this huge weekly exodus by the American faithful, it might be interesting to find out if there is a higher level of burglary in American homes on Sunday mornings, just as the sermon begins. I'm jesting of course, but it does appear that most people here go to church at least once a month which for me, initially came as a bit of a shock.

America is the home of the free and the brave and also just about any religion you care to name. Don't forget that this is where you'll find the headquarters of the Mormons, the Seventh Day Adventists, the Lutherans, Scientologists, Kabbalists, Amish and Quakers, not to mention the inimitable Church of Christ with the Elijah Message. Basically, you can get all the colours in all the sizes. I'm not being disparaging, I think the whole idea of such a wide choice of denominations is in a way, quite refreshing. You follow the faith that most fits you rather than being forced to adjust your own ideals to fit into a preset religion. And it seems to work.

In my own country, the two main religions are Catholicism and the Church of England. Neither of these faiths would appear to be followed as fastidiously as any of the various religions pursued by Americans in the USA and I am often asked by Americans, which particular religion I follow. Although I'm not an avid church-goer, more scientist than theologian, I do tell them that as I was christened at birth in The Church of England then that would probably be my native faith, were I forced to choose one. This generally provokes an inquisitive response and for American readers, it is worth briefly outlining the history of this church, albeit subject to my own narrow-minded and ignorant interpretation.

The Church of England, which is the episcopal and liturgical national church of England, is a relative newcomer in terms of age, if viewed in religious context. It is probably the single wealthiest institution in the country, its riches lying primarily with the land in its burgeoning real estate portfolio, accumulated over the last thousand years, and also in the countless works of art that adorn those properties. Although the Church of England had been allied to the Vatican for many years, it was King Henry VIII who finally lit the fuse that would eventually result in the church's independence from Rome.

In 1531, the matrimonially-addicted monarch, King Henry VIII, was incensed by Pope Clement VII's long-running and continued refusal to annul Henry's marriage to Catherine of Aragon, who was by then, surplus to royal requirement. By 1533, and after many bitter arguments with Henry, the now exasperated Pope, finally agreed to hand over decisions regarding matrimony to the Archbishops of Canterbury and York. This effectively allowed Henry to divorce Catherine and marry his lover, Anne Boleyn. Unfortunately, poor Anne didn't last long though as Henry was already contemplating his next marriage to Jane Seymour and Ms. Boleyn was subsequently beheaded three years later in 1536. (It's a pity that Henry never discovered Mormonism) To cut a long story short, once all Papal control from Rome was ended in 1534 by the Act of Submission of The Clergy, Henry then awarded himself the title of Supreme Governor of The Church of England, made divorce lawful and also gained access to the Church's wealth. All of this because he had a personal problem with the idea of monogamy. The irony of the story is that even after creating a position in the Church of England where he could effectively divorce at will, Henry still managed to behead one more wife, Catherine Howard, nearly a decade later in 1542, apparently because of her adulterous behaviour.

The real truth is that the excommunication of Henry VIII by the Vatican in 1533, effectively made the Church of England an independent faith and save for the temporary reunion with Rome in the late 1500s, it was now free from the constraints of The Vatican. It became a more relaxed faith but one that found its congregation gradually decreasing in numbers over the centuries to the level that it's at today. From my own standpoint, I'm not a particularly religious person, relying more on the principle that I should live my life in a positive manner, a kind of Buddhist or Hindu Karma ideal, I suppose. The Church of England is not a 'pushy' faith and has never insisted on any input from any of my family, financially or emotionally, but I suppose it would always be there for me, should I ever feel the need for something more spiritual.

However, religion in the USA requires all of your spare dollars and to that end, it is fully tax deductible. There are hundreds, possibly thousands of denominations and from current statistics, close to half a million churches, pretty much one church for every 600 citizens. All of these institutions need financial support from their congregations and the donations that pour in every day, are not only excessive but in the main, free of tax charges. It wouldn't be unusual for an average middle-income family to make annual donations running to several thousand dollars which from my own experience, is a practically non-existent occurrence in the UK.

Religion here is also big business. You need look no further than your own television to find that the gospel is not only being spread on dozens of religion-specific cable channels, but the television stations, studios and arenas that are used as venues, are often owned by the churches running the shows. The pioneers of these religious circuses are the televangelists who became famous on a world level. We should all remember Jimmy Swaggert, Jim and Tammy Bakker and more recently, Pat Robertson.

Jimmy Swaggert is the head of the Jimmy Swaggert Ministries. He's been preaching in the USA since the late 1960s and from a European viewpoint, he would seem to characterise the image of a preacher in the Deep South, Swaggert being a native of Louisiana. As a Pentecostal preacher, his sermons are broadcast on 70 radio stations across America and he also appears weekly in the Jimmy Swaggert Telecast. In 2004, Swaggert, apparently a devout homophobe, allegedly preached that "I've never seen a man in my life I wanted to marry. And I'm going to be blunt and plain: if one ever looks at me like that, I'm gonna kill him and tell God he died". Seems a bit severe to me.

Jim and Tammy Bakker are even more well-known in Europe than the infamous Jimmy Swaggert. I vividly remember the photo-opportunities as they posed by their Rolls-Royces in the

British newspaper colour supplements of the 1980s. Their PTL (Praise The Lord) Television Network was an extraordinary success, partly due to the fact that they welcomed all-comers, even the gays that were banished by the aforementioned Mr. Swaggert. At one point during their career, they had national audiences exceeding 12 million and even commissioned a satellite to broadcast their gospel 24 hours a day. It's important to understand that the $50m that the Bakkers drummed up each year from their television viewers was a sizeable fortune in the early 1980s. But after various sex scandals, fraud, tax evasion and embezzlement charges, Jim Bakker was eventually sentenced to 45 years in prison. In 1993, having served just five years of a revised 18-year term and recently divorced by his wife Tammy, he was set free for good behaviour and went on to write several more successful books as well as launching a rejuvenated television career with the New Jim Bakker Show in 2003.

Pat Robertson began his televised preaching career with the purchase of a small and penniless UHF station in the early 1960s. After financial problems, Robertson launched a telethon with the task of finding 700 members who would donate $10 every month, which it is said, was the figure required to pay the monthly outgoings of the station. These 700 members coined the name for his long-running show, The 700 Club. He was extremely successful in his quest. His Christian Broadcasting Network spawned the CBN Cable Network and subsequently The Family Channel and finally, having undergone several metamorphoses, it is said that the channel is now owned by Disney, albeit with a new public face. However, a clause in the sale agreement stipulated that Robertson's 700 Club programme be broadcast twice daily forevermore, regardless of any future change of ownership of the channel, an extraordinary caveat. The show is broadcast in adapted formats all over the world, including a version in Great Britain. Like Mr. Swaggert before him, Pat Robertson also has an interesting opinion regarding homosexuality, allegedly once describing Scotland as "a dark land over-run by homosexuals", which seems a somewhat misinformed statement – well, at least that's what they'll tell you in Scotland. However, regardless of what Pat Robertson says publicly, it is also rumoured that his personal wealth is just a little shy of $1billion.

These are not foolish people. They are deeply clever individuals who implicitly understand the needs of their congregation and know exactly which buttons to push and what words to use. They know how to dress for the occasion and they know that the use of technology and high-end presentation will magnify the financial rewards that will spring from their followers' wallets. None of these businessmen ever got rich by being stupid and they understand more than most that there is truly a profit to be had in the repenting of sins.

On a final and lighter note, whenever there is a religious time of year in the USA, whether it is Easter, Christmas or whatever, there are enormous multi-page displays of newspaper ads in the local dailies. I love these ads – they literally bombard your eyeballs, offering all sorts of culinary temptations to muster appeal to the reader, the box ads occupying pages and pages of the newspaper. These are the times of the year when the churches take full advantage of the potential increase in their revenues. Easter Egg hunts, Continental Breakfasts and Evening Suppers are just some of the methods employed to lure the masses for a bit of wallet-massaging. I'll be honest here, at least the ads are executed with a sense of fun and colour and on one occasion, some of the breakfasts on offer looked so good that it almost had me tipping up on Easter Sunday. The problem for me was that the churches running these ads, declaring "He Is Risen", were serving bacon & eggs at 7.30am and there was little chance that I would be risen that early on a Sunday morning.

Chapter 20

Great Actors!

If the title of this chapter had you thinking that I was about to wax lyrical on the American legends of the silver screen, then I'm sorry to disappoint you. When I use the term 'great actors', what I really mean is that anyone in America who has any kind of day to day dealing with the general public, is usually a great actor. I don't mean this as a derogatory comment, more as a compliment in the way that they're trained. There is no doubt that the smiling greeting (made even better by the previous teenage employment of dental braces) and the initial conversation is always backed by a high degree of courtesy. However, this may often be just a shiny veneer (I promise you, this section isn't about dentistry) and I am forced to admit that customer service in the USA is sometimes shockingly poor and many Americans will, I suspect, agree with this declaration.

Prior to living in the USA, my only real experiences were those as a vacationer, tourist or delegate. All of these brief visits really only tested customer service in shops, restaurants, golf clubs, hotels and rental-car counters. Most of these facilities were excellent, except for the latter which I will comment on shortly, and my patience was never tested to any great degree. The initial impression, once you're actually resident in the US, is that every American salesperson is so thrilled that you're here and that they all want to be your new best friend. However, this notion is quickly extinguished when you finally realise that what they really want, is your money and a small piece of you.

America is a country chock full of salesmen. (and saleswomen). I'm not making a sweeping statement here and I'm not generalising. It is a fact that in every walk of American life there'll be a high degree of sales patter which is delivered in a honed and polished manner. It doesn't matter if it is the plastic surgeon who's recommending which size breast implant you should have, the pest control man warning you of life-threatening strains of airborne infestation or even the chummy car salesman who cheerfully tells you that this is your lucky day as he has a 'special' today, just for you. All of these people are what I have come to know as the Great Actors. They are the men and women who can certainly talk the talk but who rarely walk the walk. The sales pitch is brilliant but the follow-up is often appalling with any guarantees provided, really just pie in the proverbial sky.

For some odd reason, many Americans seem to have a particular penchant for the English accent. For me, I was always more impressed by the American accent, it just sounded more educated, more erudite and better informed. The speed of dialogue had always suggested a brain that was thinking faster than mine and I assumed that the predilection of using five words when one would do, indicated a higher level of education. In many cases this is true but in others, the speed of conversation often hides a high degree of ignorance, particularly when it involves customer service. Before I further antagonise American readers, it's worth reading on because I suspect that many of them will recognise some of the following scenarios and possibly sympathise with my viewpoint.

The longer I live in America, the more I find that dealing with any company, particularly those that use 1-800 numbers, is frustrating and repetitive. For many customers, including millions of annoyed Americans, the end result is often a requirement to take classes in anger management. The general defiance and pigheadedness that greets any complaint levelled at any large corporate company is maintained by employees with little or no education whatsoever. This is a deliberate ploy by these multi-nationals, the aim being to deflect complaint rather than to deal with it. By using clones who merely repeat the same scripted and mantra-like response to each question, the customer is soon worn out and eventually gives up on his mission. There would be little point in these corporations employing reasonable, sensible, civil, educated and sympathetic customer service representatives, as this would result in the need to correct or remedy faulty systems, services or goods, ultimately resulting in a negative effect on profits.

Over the last ten years, there has been a gradual change in the physical location of the customer service sections in the banking community, in Britain as well as in America. In England, several million pounds was spent on the pursuit of which British voice was the most acceptable and endearing to all British bank customers. Eventually, it was deemed that the northern English accent in Leeds was the most comforting, although Scottish accents also fared extremely well in the survey. But even if you are of the opinion that it was a complete waste of time and money to find that these Yorkshire voices were the best communicators to the rest of the country, at least some English companies seemed to be showing a degree of consideration towards their customers. However, when calling a customer service section at any company in the USA or in the UK, how often do you find yourself struggling to understand and communicate with a Pakistani or Indian accent? Although Leeds in England does in fact have an unusually high Indian population, it is not for this reason that your intimate knowledge of Urdu or Hindi is tested. It is because these companies have now taken the view that it is much cheaper to locate their customer service divisions in Bombay or Calcutta rather than continue to shell out some of their profits on something that provides real service to real customers.

Customers will invariably react to situations that don't match up to their expectations. A year ago, I had a PC that was faulty and I required some help from the manufacturer. Before I was able to talk to anyone, I was forced to hand over my credit card details to pay a one-off fee of approximately $80. When I finally managed to speak to someone about the problem and having paid my $80 to this American-sounding representative, I was transferred to the technical section. Unfortunately, the Indian technician who came on the line was impossible to understand. When I finally discovered that he was in fact, a resident of Bombay in India, I was angered by the fact that I had been deceived by the company. It wasn't that the technician was incapable or rude, in fact, quite the opposite was true. It was just that I found it absolutely impossible to understand what he was trying to tell me in his recently, semi-mastered version of English. After all attempts failed at getting a refund of my $80, including two letters of complaint to the female CEO which still remain unanswered to this day, I made my own protest in my own small way. When I bought new laptops for my wife and daughter, I made sure that the service department of the computer manufacturer was based in America. This loss of two sales to my original supplier went directly to one of their competitors. No big deal but read on.

On another occasion, I successively tried and failed to change my home telephone service. I had an enormous bill every month and the phone company had so many confusing and expensive calling plans that I found it hard to understand all of the various charges that made up my bill. In fact, the charge for placed calls formed a relatively tiny part of the bill. I also had ear-splitting static on my line which after further examination, I could see was due to poorly protected wiring in the junction box on the wall of my house. When I asked for a service engineer to come and find out why I had so much noise on my line, I was threatened with a call-out fee of $100 if the engineer determined that it was my fault. All of my phones were brand new and I had tested them elsewhere so I knew my equipment wasn't faulty and having inspected the external junction box which was actually owned by the phone company, it was fairly obvious where the problem lay. However, I had been threatened with new charges, I'd been treated like an imbecile and yelled at by an ignorant customer service representative so I decided to take action once more. As a user of broadband internet, I switched to Vonage who use this under-utilised connection for telephony. I haven't made a habit of pushing particular companies in this book, but this company is just superb. They organised the transfer of my number, sent me the new equipment and gave me a great call package too. For a monthly total of $25, I can make as many calls to any phone anywhere in the USA and make unlimited calls to land-lines in the UK, which for me is a real bonus. Effectively, all calls are free and you just pay one uncomplicated monthly fee. The only downside is that their call centres would appear to be in The Philippines but currently, I seem to get by.

Both of the actions described above, are minor events on their own and in effect, they are irrelevant but as part of a mass reaction, the effect on these offending corporations can be extraordinarily important. The computer company recently fired the CEO and the phone company has just been swallowed up by AT&T. Obviously, neither of these actions are as a result of anything I did as an individual but they are good examples of big corporations who couldn't back up their original sales patter.

Great acting doesn't end with the sales patter. The naming of his or her company position or grade is of huge importance to corporate Americans. Business cards that exactly describe how important they are in their corporations are equally craved and desired. How often has someone you've met, described themselves as vice-president of this or assistant vice-president of that? It must be the most overused and most irrelevant moniker in modern America. It isn't only used in large companies either; often you'll find a two-man operation with a president and a vice-president. Although there are many corporate employees who love the tiered systems of demarcation and crave badges of merit or superiority, the fact remains that the corporate shirking of responsibility is also inherent in their character traits. If you ever want to get any of these people to commit to something vaguely important then forget about it, it'll never happen as they just don't have the power or individuality to do so. Let's be honest here, how many Vice-Presidents of America have actually had any real power or have really done anything that merits the title in the first place? Rarely, have any of them been worth their salt in much the same way as the title of Deputy Prime Minister in England means absolutely nothing. No, I'm sorry but this term Vice is one of the most pompous and ridiculous words ever used to describe an employee's corporate level. For me, it is best translated using the fourteenth century, Old English description of the word 'vice', meaning jester or buffoon.

The greatest actors of all, live inside a world called Hollywood. Not so much the silver screen inhabitants but more importantly, the deal makers, the hustlers, the movers and the shakers. The lengths to which many eager employees will go to climb the Hollywood ladder of success, is disturbing. There are too many casting couch stories and just as many other tales that describe the level of self debasement to which some will sink in order to succeed in LaLa Land. So keen are some of the corporate underlings to please their masters that they will make sure that theirs are the first cars seen by their bosses in the car park in the morning. It's been known for some studio heads to play tricks on their most avid employees by arriving at work at 4am, thus ensuring that the keenest ladder-climbers are at their desks by 3.30 am. In Hollywood, because of this necessity to desperately maintain favour by getting to work in the early hours of the morning and thereby the urgent need to get to sleep by 7pm, the evening meal may sometimes commence at 4.30 in the afternoon.

In contrast, it is important to understand that the British film industry, when compared to the American version, is still in relative terms, a 'cottage industry'. The American film industry is a huge corporate giant which works and moves in a distinctly corporate and centralised way, whereas the British version is a scattered collection of small companies and the foundation of the whole business is still based on friendship, trust and craftsmanship and with absolutely no preset and corporate salesmanship anywhere in sight. The whole "I love your tie" and

"That suit is beautiful" conversation is unique to US executives, you just won't find that amount of mirror fascination in Britain.

And even with all the green-lighting, the audience testing, the sacrifice of originality in favour of standard-formula script and the general lack of risk-taking and real adventure by the main studios, no more than 3% of Hollywood's output is a standard of which to be proud whereas the British output of high calibre films must be closer to 20%. This may sound more than a little biased towards my home country, but from first-hand experience, I have seen successful British feature films made on the smallest of budgets, literally shoestrings, with huge assistance from favours and promises garnered from friends and colleagues in the business. Whether it's for stints of night-time editing, borrowed cameras, wangled dubbing time or even begging for free ends of unexposed film, nothing will deter the independent British film-makers. These films are more often than not, financed by the director and producer's personal credit cards, it's just not that unusual for this to happen in Britain.

To make a movie in the UK is not just to fulfil a dream but moreover to create and craft an art-form which has some meaning and a modicum of raison d'être. Of course, there is also the small hope that independent success will catapult them to a career in Hollywood and a multi-million dollar home in Beverly Hills. It really isn't the same in the US – the film companies have enormous studio overheads – the movies just have to get made, end of story, so you can't blame them. It's like a long conveyor belt that just keeps popping them out and every so often, along comes a good 'un. But having said all of this, and in America's defence, Hollywood is almost as big a tourist attraction as the Royal Family is in England so let's not knock it. It's Disneyland in a silk suit and it generates enormous income for the state of California and it's likely to do so for many years to come.

I said earlier in this chapter that I would return to the subject of car-rental companies. If you really want to see examples of outstanding customer service and simultaneously, the type of client-care that you wouldn't wish on your worst enemy, look no further than my two wildly differing experiences on the east and west coasts of the USA. As a rule, I tend to rent vehicles in Miami or San Diego. On occasions, I also need to rent vehicles out of Los Angeles. In San Diego and Los Angeles, I have never had anything but memorable experiences. On various occasions it might be a free upgrade from a Compact to an SUV or the waiving of late return fees or a free trial of satellite navigation. But the best example was the decision of a saleslady at Avis in San Diego. When I informed her that my wife and I were planning on driving from California to Florida, she offered to exchange our existing rental vehicle for a brand new car. She just wanted to make sure that we wouldn't be prone to breaking down on the 3000 mile trip and that the air-conditioning was sure to work, free of cigarette smells along with brand new window wipers in the event of rain during the journey. I'm not making this up, all of this is true.

Conversely, I have rented cars out of all the main rental companies in Miami, literally on dozens of occasions. The cars are rarely clean and usually stink of fags, (cigarettes) and you have to make particular note of all the pre-existing dents and scrapes on the vehicle. The treatment at the rental counter is largely hostile, rude and inflammatory. The queues are often ten customers deep with invariably just one representative occupying the entire sixty foot counter. If there happens to be more than one employee on duty, the behind-the-hand conversation is invariably in Spanish and you can tangibly feel the anger towards you because you have dared to interrupt their day with your pathetic request of a vehicle in which to go and do battle with the lunatics on Miami's I-95. No, these people are not the Great Actors that I've been describing, these are the real thing and they're scary.

Chapter 21

Viva Las Vegas!
The American Dream Vacation

There are so many incredible and beautiful vacation destinations in the USA that for me, it is completely understandable why the majority of Americans never leave their home country at any point during their lives. It also underlines the reason why only around 20% of Americans have passports compared to the UK figure of approximately 90%; there is just such an extraordinary choice right here on the American doorstep. What intrigues me more though, considering the amazing variety of different vacations available to Americans, is that there is such a morbid fascination with Las Vegas. It is unfathomable to me how anyone in their right minds can possibly think that this is an attractive destination for a holiday. The whole place fills me with horror and having spent five or six weeks there in total, albeit on obligatory conference duties, I can guarantee that nothing would ever tempt me to revisit this city, well almost nothing. I realise that I'm possibly in a minority in this thought and I also understand that not all Americans are of the belief that Las Vegas is their version of paradise but let's not forget that 40 million people visit the city every year, and hundreds of thousands of couples choose this hell-hole as a location to tie the conjugal knot. But the truth still remains that for many Americans, Las Vegas is almost a revered destination and for them, just being there is about as grand as life can possibly get.

A cab driver once told me while I was staying there, "I'm surprised that anyone would want to visit this place let alone make it their home, when God had never intended anyone to live here in the first place". I sympathised greatly with his comment and still retain visions of infinite rows of recently widowed octogenarian ladies, carelessly shovelling the remains of their husbands' insurance payout into the endless lines of slot machines that form the central feature of this gambling oasis, many of these women vicariously living out their late spouses' dreams.

I remember on one occasion, whilst waiting for the elevator to take me up to my hotel room, the sad sight of an enormously overweight man perched precariously on a stool in front of a set of one-armed bandits, all of which he'd commandeered as his own private mini casino. He was feeding six machines in tandem. It was 10.30pm and as I stepped into the elevator, I wondered how long he might stay at his post, armed with his 32oz plastic beakers brim full of quarters. When I came down to breakfast the following morning, I was astonished to find him still astride the same wilting stool, relentlessly feeding the machines ten hours later. He was either getting very lucky or he was losing his shirt, the latter more likely.

In all the times I've visited Las Vegas, I've never gambled one cent in any of the casinos or on any of the slots. I'm not some paragon of virtue, it's just that the only winners in Vegas, as everyone knows, are the hotel and casino owners. A documentary once detailed the construction of the Venetian Hotel which was built as a tribute to the owner's love of Venice. It may well have been a project that began as a true passion for all things Italian, but there is no doubt that the real driving force behind it was the potential income from the casinos and slot machines. With its motorized gondolas and Grand Canal Shoppes and the Venetian Living Statues that perform daily in the hotel's own version of St. Mark's Square, it should be remembered that the cost of building this billion-dollar plus hotel was recouped within nine months of opening. Gambling is the main event in Las Vegas which pays for everything that doth glitter and shine. I suppose that what I'm trying to say is that if you truly want to discover Venice then go and visit the real thing in Italy. Of course, if you don't fancy putting up with the canal stench and the daily excremental bombardment from the pigeons in St. Mark's Square, then stick with the Vegas version.

But whatever I feel about Las Vegas, I suppose there's no doubt that many British people will want to make the pilgrimage to this gambling shrine in the desert so whilst I myself have no love for the place, here is my outstretched olive branch to Las Vegas and its disciples in an attempt to describe the parts that I have enjoyed there and those which I would subsequently recommend to others.

Hotels: I've stayed at around half a dozen of them which is only a small sample of what's on offer, but the newer ones are The Venetian (with its motorised gondolas), Paris (featuring a scaled down Eiffel Tower) and Bellagio, which is probably the most up-market and most expensive. The Monte Carlo, which bears no resemblance to its namesake, is pleasantly calm for Las Vegas and somewhat more relaxing than the lively but atmospheric Caesar's Palace. Luxor is the giant, black glass pyramid of a hotel which was built in tribute to the famous edifice in Cairo that bears the same name. You can't fail to see this extraordinary monolith when you're approaching McCarran Airport; it has a massively powerful beam of light that points straight out of the top of it and can be seen for miles. There's also the MGM Grand, supposedly the biggest hotel in the world with 6,300 guest rooms and of course, New York, New York which is a miniature theme of New York City, complete with the Statue of Liberty and a condensed version of Central Park. It also has a terrifying roller-coaster that does a circuit around the entire exterior of the hotel. The Hard Rock Hotel which is just off the Strip is worth a visit too. This casino-hotel is very popular with music lovers so if you have a Hard Rock VIP Pass handy, you'll be thankful for it, as immediate restaurant seating will be guaranteed.

There's no shortage of hotels in Las Vegas with around 150,000 rooms available in and around the Strip. Hotels don't tend to grow old in Sin City, the bulldozers moving in and replacing them with shiny new themed hotels as soon as the originals have reached their sell-by date. It's unsurprising really as the town has a 91% occupancy rate which effectively means that nine in ten rooms are used every night of every year. Having experienced six or seven of these hotels, I can tell you that there's a certain Vegas stench that pervades even the non-smoking rooms. It's just impossible to keep these places clean enough with the human traffic that trundles through them so it's easier to build a new attraction rather than waste money renovating a dying one.

Restaurants: The Restaurant at the Top of the World which is situated in the Stratosphere Tower Hotel is not dissimilar to the Post Office Tower restaurant in London. It's a revolving dining room located at the top of the hotel's tower with the best views available over Las Vegas. There are helicopters frequently passing by which because of their close proximity, feel more like computer-generated images, so you would be forgiven if you feel as though you're in a *Terminator* or *Blade Runner* movie. It also has reasonably good food but you do need to book ahead and allow yourself time to get up to the restaurant (via rocket lift). This is not necessarily a place to go for a fine dining experience but the wraparound vista afforded by this sky high location is unequalled anywhere in Las Vegas.

There are a number of excellent restaurants in Bellagio but if you like steak, then you should go to Gallagher's in the New York New York hotel, where once seated, is akin to being in one of the best New York steak restaurants. All of the meat here is hung for three weeks in the glass cases surrounding this venue, an air-ageing process that makes you fully appreciate the taste of the beef. (It's not a place for vegans or vegetarians) Excellent food and very slick service combine here for a superb meal. Fantastic mashed potato too. Again, you should pre-book and slide the hostess $10-20 to guarantee an immediate table. I always enjoyed this restaurant each time I visited Las Vegas and the mini Central Park outside is an interesting place to wander afterwards in an effort to burn off the recently acquired calories.

There are two particularly good Chinese restaurants that I remember which both featured food cooked without the perilous monosodium glutamate. (It's important to look for restaurants that display signs proclaiming 'No MSG' as many people experience horrendous after effects from this food additive). One of these restaurants is the Cantonese Rik Shaw in the Riviera, which although one of the oldest hotels in Vegas (the movie 'Casino' was actually shot there because the interior has remained unchanged since the 60s and was therefore deemed accurate for the period) the food in this particular restaurant is excellent. The other recommended oriental restaurant is Jasmine in Bellagio. It's very quiet, very calm and very upmarket, has superb service and fantastic food. They practically spoon-feed you in this place.

Shows: The best show I've ever seen is *Siegfried & Roy* at the Mirage which was an illusion act on the grandest of scales. It involved lions, panthers and white tigers as well as a huge cast of performers. I once saw an elephant disappear in front of my eyes and I still don't know how they did it. Unfortunately, when one half of this famous duo was attacked on stage by a young tiger in 2003, the age-defying, surgically-enhanced Roy Horn suffered near-fatal wounds and the show has since been cancelled indefinitely. But these two German magicians are genuine showmen and if there is ever a chance of them returning to the stage, they will make it happen and it would be well worth queuing up to buy tickets for the experience.

There seems to be no end to the *Cirque de Soleil* type shows on offer, all falling under different names like *Mystère* and *Zumanity* but they are still well worth seeing. *The Blue Man Group,* currently showing at The Venetian is also a must-see show and although I haven't seen it in Vegas, I am assured it is an excellent choice. For entertainment, Caesar's Palace is unique for me, in that it is dually, a 'must avoid' and a 'must see' venue.

The former because Canada's Celine Dion set up camp there and I've no great desire to spend even two minutes listening to her, let alone being asked to pay an exorbitant fee for the pleasure. The latter because Elton John occasionally substitutes for Miss Dion when she's on a break and this brilliant British living legend is well worth your hard earned cash, any day of the week.

The other show that I would thoroughly recommend, totally different to *Siegfried & Roy*, is *Lance Burton: Master Magician* at the Monte Carlo. He runs a very slick comic/illusion act which is elegantly paced and extremely charming. It should be noted however, that ticket prices for some of these shows I've mentioned, can often be in excess of $100 per person so it could end up being a fairly expensive night out for the average family.

Shopping: The Forum Shops at Caesars Palace practically take the form of a full size shopping mall inside a hotel. There's a huge variety of retailers, from Versace to Burberry and Jimmy Choo to Valentino. An addition to this building, which can be accessed via the Forum Shops, is the two-storey car showroom, Exotic Cars. This is definitely worth a visit to see the incredible array of beautiful motor cars on sale there. The range on offer is mouth-watering and this company claims to be the busiest dealership in the world and I believe it. When you realise that over 7,000 people pass through their premises each day, it is an unsurprising claim. The oddly named Fashion Show Mall is the largest shopping area in Las Vegas. It houses over 250 retailers in more than two million square feet of commercial Nevada real estate. It's not my idea of fun but my wife and daughters would likely deem this an out-of-body experience. To find some real bargains though, which I am personally forced to seek out while my female family members batter their credit cards into a frenzied submission, it's worth taking a taxi out to Las Vegas Boulevard where you'll find the Las Vegas Outlet Centre. It's another of the Simon properties and houses around 130 retailers, all offering slightly more affordable clothes and shoes than are otherwise on display in the Forum Shops at Caesar's Palace or at The Fashion Show Mall.

When you first arrive at McCarran Airport, don't bother with cabs or hotel shuttles, just walk up to the driver of the biggest limousine you can see outside the terminal and ask him the price he'd charge to take you to the Strip. It will likely only cost around $30 and during the ride, you can try the limo sunroof experience made famous by Tom Hanks in the movie *'Big'*. En route, the driver can call the hotels I've listed above and check room prices and availability. Remember, if there isn't a convention going on in Vegas at the time, you can get $300-a-night rooms for about $70 and less. Ask the driver for advice if necessary as they're really helpful guys and inexplicably, they seem to like the English. It's impossible to explain how big Las Vegas is, so you should take a cab everywhere you need to go. You might think a hotel is just a brisk stroll along the Strip but in reality, it's probably about two miles away. (I made this mistake once and almost ended up needing oxygen to avoid premature heart failure) At the hotels, go to the taxi line and when the bellboy pulls in a cab for you, give him a dollar or two. Always have plenty of single dollar bills in your pocket, you'll need them. Tipping is a very serious business in Las Vegas and they expect it in cabs, bars, hotels and restaurants. I was once told in no uncertain terms that it's 20% to 30% for just about anything.

There are a thousand things to do in Vegas, all of which you'll discover when you arrive, but all of the above is a must-do, must-see list. Make sure you plan and book these and I guarantee you'll not be disappointed. I've been there six or seven times now, and I know the place reasonably well, but I always ensure that I make reservations at Gallagher's and at the Stratosphere Top of The World restaurants, because there is nothing better in Vegas at a price that's vaguely affordable. There are also numerous excursions available in Las Vegas. I've personally experienced a couple of short helicopter rides during the day which show in some detail, how far into the desert this town has spread in recent years. (Apparently, Las Vegas has one of the fastest growing populations in the USA) I've also flown around the Strip at night, courtesy of a small airplane, which was a singularly breathtaking experience. If time allows, take a trip out to the Grand Canyon and witness firsthand, preferably whilst flying through this gorge, how unbelievably dramatic nature can be. The Hoover Dam, one of the greatest feats of engineering the world has ever witnessed and also the scene of so many lost lives during its construction, is an absolute must as well. If you still have time to kill, a drive out across the desert to Red Rock should complete the tourist mission.

I knew I was missing something as I wrote this chapter and I've just remembered that there's something that makes Las Vegas absolutely worth the trek - the excellent choice of golf courses in and around the Las Vegas Strip. Two outstanding examples are Cascata with its breathtaking scenery and immaculate course and clubhouse and then Rio Secco, which is about ten minutes drive north of the Strip, nestled in the foothills of the Black Mountains. Even if you don't like golf, you couldn't fail to be captivated by the surroundings at both of these courses.

Licensed betting shops are a familiar sight in UK high streets. I don't know if it is the lack of these legitimate bookies in America that forces people to gamble in the licensed areas of the country or whether it is just a national and inherent desire to wager because it isn't only Las Vegas that has this almost magnetic and hypnotic draw. There are a number of other towns which are similarly attractive vacation destinations for Americans, including Vegas' neighbour Reno in Nevada and Atlantic City on the east coast. From a personal standpoint, these gambling meccas hold no real interest. Betting for me, has never been an attractive proposition, primarily because the odds are stacked so highly against the punter but also because for so many people, the dream of winning usually ends in abject misery.

In summary, if you really must go, try some of the attractions and restaurants that I've mentioned above but don't lose all your loot in the casinos and if a taxi driver offers you the 'menu' for the Chicken Ranch, don't go, it's definitely not a restaurant although the menu does make pretty interesting reading.

Chapter 22

National Identity

In a recent UK Census, there was a requirement on the government form to state one's nationality for the record. There was notable anger amongst some English citizens as the form didn't permit English natives to use the term 'English' to confirm their nationality. They were instead required to use either of the terms, 'British' or 'UK' in their selection. If the whole UK population had been instructed to use the same choice of terms when describing their nationality, there might not have been such a big problem. The bone of contention here was the fact that whilst the English were banned from using the word English, five million Scots were allowed to describe themselves as Scottish and this anomaly understandably made fifty million Englishmen somewhat irate. The English did not dispute the Scots' rights in their desire to be noted and recorded as Scottish, they just wanted equal affirmation and recognition of their own unique nationality.

In the USA, the definition of nationality can sometimes be confusing to the outsider. It is well documented that the current American population is made up of a number of different migrant nations from all over the world. In reality, I suppose it might be fair to say that the only real Americans are the Native American Indians as they've been here for more than a thousand years, although even this statement might be roundly disputed. In the 18th and 19th centuries, as a decision on how they would plan their journey to target a new home, the extraordinary method that many immigrants adopted was the mere memorising of one word, be it Chicago, New York or Detroit. In many cases, this innocuous name or word may have just been glimpsed on the side of a ship or in the title of a book or even imprinted on the lid of a packing crate but it conjured up visions of a bright new world. It might also have been the only piece of English these immigrants knew and many of them would live the rest of their lives in America, completely ignorant of the English language. I know some families even now, where the grandparents are only able to converse in their original mother tongue. They have managed to work their entire lives in the USA and raise families here without ever being required to speak one single word of English.

On the other side of the coin, I often hear people in this country, who look as American as apple pie, describing themselves as Italian, Irish, Scottish or anything other than just plain American. There seems to be a requirement by many in the USA to have an individualistic nationality that isn't solely American, even though they were born in America. My own favourite comedienne over here, Chelsea Handler, makes frequent claims of a German heritage. Whatever her birthright bloodline, she's about as American as the Star Spangled Banner and she even looks like Tabitha from the 1960s 'Bewitched' television series.

The point I'm making is that all of us are guilty at some point of playing the nationality card to self-enhance any given situation. If I had a dollar for every time I've heard an American proclaim he's Irish, I'd be moderately wealthy but I don't really understand the need for anyone to make the proclamation in the first place. The indefatigable Conan O'Brien certainly carries the obligatory thatch of red hair and is doubtless in possession of the appropriate surname but can I really believe his persistent claim of Irish nationality? Surely, with that Massachusetts accent, he is the all-American boy? I can't denigrate Conan as I am a big fan. He was a brilliant writer on Saturday Night Live and his enthusiastic energy often leaves me breathless when watching his late-night show. Go Conan. Conversely, the great Shaquille O'Neal has an Irish surname though I'm not aware that he's ever claimed Irish nationality. But of course, for many African-Americans who were brought to America during the slave trade era, their names were 'given' to them by the plantation owners, many of whom were English or Irish so it's easy to see why many African-Americans have British names. However, of all the many Americans that claim to be Italian or Spanish, and there are many, it is a rare occurrence to meet anyone who can actually speak the language of the country to which they claim their nationality. There are some, but not many. My opinion probably holds little relevance to the people of this country but my belief is that you are a product of the country in which you were born. I was born in England, therefore I am English. It matters not that my ancestors were probably an international cocktail of assorted nationalities, be they Nordic, Roman, Saxon, Celt or Swazi, I am for all intents and purposes, English, and I'm proud to be so.

In the UK, the stripping of the English nationality continues at a brisk pace. Watching from another shore, it's easy to see why so many ex-pats who have moved to the USA, choose never to return to the UK. It is also hard to believe that so many more English citizens, who do have the opportunity to leave for a better life, instead decide to stay in a country that is gradually being eroded of all national pride and individualism. I have no desire currently, to return to a country that bans me from being English, that will not permit me to fly my national flag but which continues to award 10,000 homes each year to immigrants, free of charge. All of this, as a sulking and petulant, pompous and puritan Scotsman is allowed to govern England while Scotland maintains its own 'no-English-allowed' parliament. Gordon Brown has become the first Prime Minister of England to have literally sulked and grizzled his way into No.10 Downing Street. The Scots must be laughing at this anomaly where one of their own can rule over the Auld Enemy, as it's no great secret that the Scots hate the English even more than the French despise us!

While Gordon Brown, as Chancellor of The Exchequer, continued to apply stealth taxes to the English, more money is still spent per capita, on his own countrymen in Scotland than is allocated to the people of the country he serves. It is well known that England massively subsidises Scotland, but to be truthful, it's of little importance. The North Sea of Scotland has long been plundered by English and American oil companies and it should also never be forgotten that Scotland made a significant military contribution in both World Wars. The loss of Scottish lives was in relative terms, far worse than the death toll amongst English soldiers. For the unerring bravery that the Scottish soldiers have always given for the protection of our island, they rightly deserve to be referred to as the Bravehearts. However, I'm still mystified that a redder than red and staunchly socialist Labour Party member like Gordon Brown consistently allowed the very rich to remain so wealthy while he was Chancellor. It is said, that in 2006, the 54 UK-based billionaires paid a grand total of a mere £14.7m in tax between them on combined assets totalling £126 billion. To put that in more relevant context, they were paying around £100 in tax on each £1m they had. It is also alleged that almost all of these businessmen avoided paying any Capital Gains Tax whatsoever.

I digress again. To many, the United States might appear to be born from a mongrel melting pot of diverse nationalities but when viewed from a neutral standpoint, it could also be interpreted as the greatest example of cosmopolitanism ever witnessed. The combination of European migrants that came from Great Britain, Ireland, Germany, France and Scandinavia along with the South Americans from Guatemala, Mexico, El Salvador and Puerto Rico, when mixed in with the Russians, Africans Japanese, Chinese, Koreans and Native American Indians, makes this nation of immigrants, truly the most multi-national country the world has ever seen. There is however, a growing phenomenon that will eventually change the cultural, social and national make-up of the USA and it is worth reading the following note to realise what is happening in other parts of the world where historically, there have been far greater and more rigid restrictions placed on immigration.

I once read an interesting piece in a magazine that discussed the problems facing Italy in relation to its indigenous population. I have no idea if it was absolutely accurate but the thought behind it was still incredible. It truthfully and naturally stated that Italy had always had the reputation of being a family orientated country with the typical Italian woman depicting the image as the perfect example of motherhood. However, using the formula required to maintain the current levels of any population, it would therefore be necessary for each Italian couple to produce an average of 2.2 children, the additional figure of 0.2 required to allow for child morbidity and also for the difference in the amounts of male and females born in any given society. However, as the modern Italian woman now invariably chooses a career over motherhood and moves further away from marriage, it is estimated that the average family now produces only 1.7 children per couple and at this rate, the Italian population would perish completely within 130 years. Moreover, while the indigenous Italian population declines, the overall population is increasing because of high immigration to Italy in recent decades. What can also be confirmed is that the Asian, African and Latin nations are simultaneously adding over 80 million to the global population each year while conversely, the European numbers decrease annually by one million people because the average birth-rate in Europe has now fallen below 2.0 per couple.

Taking the Italian example and applying it to the USA might not yet be appropriate, but at the start of this book I remarked that there is an element of educated thought that believes the USA may in time adopt Spanish as its national language and I suppose there is some good reason to believe this. While the American population increases by nearly 2 million each year, the number is only really swelled by Hispanic and African-American births while the number of Caucasian Americans continues to decline. The Hispanic immigrant population is growing at a rate that far exceeds the 2.1 children born to the average American household, (in fact Mexicans typically produce an average 3.1 children per couple) It is therefore not difficult to see that in a fairly short time, the American population might possibly become predominantly Hispanic and that Spanish could also become the primary American language thereafter.

It is also a fact that the city of Miami is now 70% Hispanic. This is an unbelievable statistic given the timeframe in which this has happened. Miami has only had a human population for little more than a hundred years as before then, it was mainly inhabited by alligators. I was in conversation with some American friends recently and the subject of the problem regarding illegal Mexican immigrants was raised. One of the group, mindful of the need for the USA to maintain a labour-intensive workforce, suggested that Mexico should become the 51st State. I was never sure if he was joking when he said this but I suspect it is something that many Mexicans would embrace immediately, and who knows, maybe a few Americans too.

While the British government continues to apply restrictions governing when and where we are allowed to fly the Union Flag or The Cross of St. George in England, our friends across the Puddle are staunch supporters and displayers of the Stars and Stripes. The national flag is everywhere, in gardens, on cars, in stores and in restaurants. In no other country will you see a symbol of a nation, so closely protected and so prominently displayed and although this may be seen by other countries as a slightly partisan affectation, there is no denying that Americans are proud to be American, regardless of the cultural and racial diversity of its national identity.

Chapter 23

The Race Issue

It is no secret that all non-white races in America have historically had a more difficult and encumbered route through life than their Caucasian counterparts and from the evidence I've seen, the black or African-American population of the USA has had the harshest road of all of them. It's been less than 140 years since the United States abolished slavery in this country but the memories and emotions of that despicable era still exist in the minds of many. This guilt continues to haunt America as a nation in much the same way young Germans today are still haunted by the nightmarish reminders of the cruel atrocities committed by their forefathers during World War II.

Most of us will have read about or seen some of the disturbing pictures of the many forms of racial separation and racist killings that have plagued the USA during the last two centuries and none of these events was helped by the introduction of the Jim Crow Laws. Although these barbarian rules, enforced between 1876 and 1965, insisted that the 'white/coloured' amenities be segregated and equal, the so-called 'coloured' facilities provided, were invariably inferior to the 'white' versions. These laws also maintained that even the renting of a room to a 'coloured person' in a white household was illegal and a heavy fine would follow. There was a penalty of six months in jail for even writing about the possibility of social equality between the races. Only last century, it was still illegal for a black and white couple to be married in Florida. Even sleeping together under the same roof would result in a heavy fine or 12 months jail time. Theatres and cinemas were instructed to keep a multi-race audience separated at all times and buses and trains could only carry one colour or the other, but never both at the same time.

Therefore, it should be remembered that only in recent years have black and white schoolchildren been allowed to ride in the same buses as each other, let alone share the same schools or classrooms. It is only in recent years that all races are able to use the same public convenience, at their convenience. And it is only in recent years that all Americans were allowed to eat in the same restaurants and vote at the same time, in the same polling booth, no matter what the colour of their skin. There are still many towns in the Deep South that have 'whites only' and 'coloured only' drinking-water fountains on display in their main streets. The signs are not there for current enforcement, but more to remind us of the arrogance and crassness of the Jim Crow Laws.

I don't believe it necessary to conduct a historical tour of the litany of racial misdeeds that have been inflicted on the black population of America, as this would likely fill a whole library, let alone one chapter of one book. However, the longer I live in this multi-cultural society, the more I have become disturbed and concerned at a growing phenomenon that is the very thing that black Americans have been campaigning against for so many years, and is the very thing that many of them are now guilty themselves of promoting. Segregation.

There are some subtle changes occurring in American society, which although I would find it difficult to describe any of these as reverse racism, they can only provoke a more separated and segregated society, but this time, one that is being fuelled and promoted by some black sections of the American population. When I first came upon the television channel BET, I was appalled and saddened to realise that this network's name actually stood for Black Entertainment Television. It wasn't that

I was opposed to the idea of a channel that catered specifically for one demographic as this has been going on ever since the introduction of multi-channel cable. It was just the name itself which shocked me. To try and put this into some sort of context, it would be difficult to imagine a channel called JET, where only Jewish comedians were allowed to perform or heaven forbid, a network called White Entertainment Television. It could not and must not happen because its very existence would cause an outcry from the non-white and hopefully, most of the white population. But more to the point, it shouldn't ever happen because it's just plain wrong.

Maybe it's because I'm an outsider here who just doesn't know enough about the racial history of this country and the anger that still prevails. Yes, I know that most African-Americans didn't have a choice in their country of birth, their ancestors forced to leave Africa two centuries ago to come to America against their wishes and sold as slaves. But then neither did I. I had no control over where I was born, even though my ancestry is likely not English, but I was born in England and therefore I am proud to be English because that is the country that adopted me and which first fed and nurtured me.

I may not be educated enough on the issues of race in America but I know enough about the effects of racism in my own country to know that the problem is not unique to the United States. I know that racial bias has often hindered the future prospects of many hard working African-Americans but I also know that an impoverished young southern girl called Oprah became the highest paid entertainer in television history. I know that Mr. Bill Cosby is one of the funniest and forward-thinking men I've ever listened to and I know that a mixed-race marriage produced the most brilliant player of golf this world has ever seen, in Tiger Woods. I know that Magic, Shaq and Mr. Jordan are the superstars of basketball, Willie Mays is the American baseball legend and Sir Colin Powell became the highest ranking officer in the history of the US military (although I still don't understand why his name is pronounced that way). I know that Condoleezza

Rice could become the first simultaneously black and female President although I think she's too smart to offer herself up for the job. I also know that there is a Martin Luther King Day every year which celebrates the cause of a brave, talented and enlightened man who changed the course of history in the USA. I know that on the track and field, black Americans have long reigned supreme in being fastest, highest and strongest and that they emphatically fulfil the Olympic Motto, "Citius, Altius, Fortius", but I also know they can't swim that well. I know that all races are equal, but not in all ways. It's just the way it is.

Whilst I never understood why there could be toilets, restaurants and buses that barred entry to a black American, I still don't understand why a form of segregation continues today but this time sponsored by black Americans. It seems not enough to describe one's nationality as American, it must be African-American. Why is that? It may simply be that a more accurate origin is now required. As I have mentioned previously, Jewish Americans will often describe themselves as Jewish rather than as American in the same way that Americans who have a hint of ancestral history originating in Ireland or Italy, will undoubtedly describe themselves as Irish or Italian but I just don't think it's relevant. Put it this way, I am English. I don't define myself as a White-Roman-Norse-Anglo-Saxon-European-Mixed-Breed. I'm just English.

The entertainment industry, while on one hand claiming to promote race equality, is possibly the guiltiest when it comes to promoting this new segregation. It isn't only BET that caters for a uniquely black audience. More recently, we've seen the introduction in America of The Black Movie Awards. I'll be honest at this point, when I saw this programme advertised, I couldn't believe what I was seeing. In fact, I thought it was the Saturday Night Live team doing one of their practical jokes. It just didn't seem feasible that this could be going on in twenty-first century America. This new segregated awards system is not limited to the black population. There is now also an Asian-only gong show peculiarly titled, the Asian Excellence Awards, promoted in another particularly uncomfortable and separatist way by AZN Television, the Network for Asian-Americans. Many of the participants draw on extremely tenuous ancestral links in order to gain access to the event, in the hope of winning an award. Some of the participants look about as Asian as I do.

To try and balance the topic and to indicate that this narrow line of thought is not limited to the USA, I should say now that I've seen a similar scenario in England too. We have a music awards show called the MOBOs. MOBO stands for Music of Black Origin. The show is primarily aimed at a black audience and these music awards are mostly given to black artists. There have been some anomalies to the rule but this has mostly been when white artists have surrounded themselves with black musicians or are working with a black production team. It is no secret that most black musicians are truly exceptional and natural masters of music production, but it would've been interesting to see how the Rolling Stones might have faired had their success been in 2007, an all white band using an all white production team but certainly performing music of black origin.

It seems an incredibly backward step and also somewhat archaic to promote this kind of segregation by staging single colour events in this age of apparent enlightenment. I am fully aware that the film and television industries are primarily populated and controlled by white executives and that the parts for black actors and actresses have always been severely limited, the actors often placed in typecast roles but it is also true to say that the music industry is a hotbed of diverse race and colour that works together and more importantly, thrives together.

I hope I never live to witness a White Oscars ceremony or a Caucasian Grammy Awards because I've always believed that everyone has a chance of glory no matter what their colour, creed or race. And this is not an entirely naïve thought. If it were true that black artists had only recently found success at the Oscars and at the Grammys with the likes of Halle, Denzil and Jamie in film and Kanye, Beyoncé and Alicia in music, it might be understandable to have a black-only series of awards shows. But if we look back to 1959 at the very first Grammy Awards we would see that the incomparable Count Basie and the divine Miss Ella Fitzgerald were deservedly amongst the first winners that night. Look even further back to 1939 and you'll see that Hattie McDaniel won the Oscar for Best Supporting Actress in her role as Mammy in the epic film of that year, *Gone With The Wind*. I know it took ten long years for the organisers to finally recognise black actors and they were often typecast in their given roles but the achievements stood there side by side with their white counterparts, and so finally put to rest the notion of a single colour ceremony. Sometimes it is just a question of perception, to avoid the adoption of a blinkered vision, seeing only what you want to see.

The United States of America has produced more than its fair share of great artists, writers, musicians, sportsmen, engineers, entrepreneurs, statesmen, pioneers and visionary leaders than possibly any other twenty-first century nation. For that reason, it is hard to imagine that white supremacy groups like the Ku Klux Klan still continue to form an irremovable stain on some parts of American society whilst perpetuating an ideal that is truly outdated. It took extraordinary courage for the late Rosa Parks in her abject refusal to give up her seat to a white man on a bus in 1950s Alabama. The subsequent bravery shown by Martin Luther King Jr. in his quest to defend the rights of all citizens, black or white, was immense, the great man eventually paying with his life for that vision of equality. Even now, since the physical destruction of the Berlin Wall, that once again united East and West Germany as a single nation in 1989, it may not yet be appropriate for young Germans today to utter John F. Kennedy's immortal phrase, "Ich bin ein Berliner". But it should by now, be an honour for all races and all colours that live in this extraordinarily physically and naturally blessed country, to stand up as one nation and simply say, "I am an American".

Chapter 24

Politics

This book wasn't written to make a stand or to take sides on anything religious, social or political but I think it is still worth commenting solely on the things that can be observed by an outsider looking in. As a resident of this country but also as one who still retains British citizenship, my voice or opinion regarding American politics is largely irrelevant because I vote in England and not in the USA. That said, the egos, greed and hunger for power that exist in excessive quantities throughout any country's political system, are there to be sniggered at, gasped at and mocked by all who are forced to live with it and under it. This is the citizen's privilege.

In the same way that British Members of Parliament have acutely embarrassed my country over the last fifty years with their continuing scandals of financial impropriety and sexual indiscretions, I am certain that the USA has also had its fair share of political offenders. The photographs that we've grown used to seeing in British Sunday rags, of perhaps a lingerie-clad middle-aged politician begging for his fix of dominatrix or the brown envelope payments passed to prostitutes at London train stations have now become almost routine. The faked and risible suicide of a British Postmaster-General on a Miami beach and the murder conspiracies that continue to beleaguer our own Parliament, do nothing to engender faith in the people who are supposed to be in charge of the country. We are no longer shocked by it but instead, we now almost expect it.

The same happens on this side of the Atlantic. Only recently in America, a congressman was scandalized by the discovery of his 'improper conduct' with teenage boys, forcing him to run for cover to the nearest rehabilitation clinic, the preferred celebrity bunker employed when the scandal bullets start flying. What is really despicable is the way that these so-called pillars of society always manage to blame someone else for their own shortcomings rather than shouldering the blame themselves and putting their hands up to admit, "Guilty as charged". They never seem to take the punishment, just crawling back, squealing like stuck pigs, "It wasn't my fault". And the odd thing is that more often than not, you will see those very same miscreants quickly reinstalled to another high-powered position of government, eager to ply their perversions on fresh and unwitting victims.

Putting the aforementioned villains to one side, there are many elected officials who work hard to achieve new levels, for and on behalf of their country. However, there are occasions when the choice of the leader may not be the best choice from a national and domestic point of view, yet the candidate may still prove to be a pertinent selection when viewed from a world standpoint. When Tony Blair became Prime Minister in 1997, there were many that doubted the wisdom of his youth, probably in the same manner that the USA was sceptical about electing John F. Kennedy in 1961, his date of birth not falling in the prerequisite 1800s. However, regardless of your political persuasion, (I have no allegiance towards any party) Tony Blair has done a pretty fair job overseas and is held in some esteem by our international neighbours, notwithstanding national scandals at home. And in recent years, there have been a number of American Presidents who despite their perceived inadequacies in the eyes of their own people, have performed supremely on the world stage.

When Ronald Reagan took office in 1981, it was too easy to denigrate him for his past career as a B-movie actor. We've all seen the endless excerpts of "Bedtime for Bonzo" featuring his acting scenes with a chimpanzee and many of us watched sympathetically as he was belittled on political and satirical television shows, his level of sophistication unfairly mocked. But outside of the USA, as he cultivated and promoted his new allegiance and friendship with Britain's Margaret Thatcher, he was a truly refreshing man. His seemingly genuine and sincere smile of warmth had such a positive effect on how the rest of the world perceived the USA at that time, in stark contrast to the very different image that currently prevails. Even after an attempted assassination, Reagan rebounded with a grin and a previously unseen presidential empathy won him even more supporters and followers. I can't be certain how the general American public now views his presidency or the mark that he made but from a European standpoint, he will always be seen as a genuine example of uncomplicated American honesty and devotion. I suspect that Clint Eastwood recognised early in his mayoral quest that politics, actors and chimps might actually prove to be a winning combination.

When Bill Clinton came to power, a man who also went on to enjoy the maximum allowance of two presidential terms totalling eight years at the helm, we were already aware of his sexual hankerings and previously documented dalliances with pretty and not-so-pretty political groupies. But even this adolescent behaviour didn't dissuade the American voters from electing him as their chosen one. He was a good-looking Ivy League type of man, physically similar in some ways to the Kennedy brothers. He had a smile that could disrobe a woman from twenty paces and wasn't half bad at playing the saxophone either. He also had the benefit like Mr. Reagan before him, of having a clever and powerful wife sitting permanently at his side. Of course, Nancy Reagan never had to put up with an impeachment hearing, fuelling a national parlour discussion on what might or might not be considered sexual activity, and what was just fooling around. She also never had to deal with a debate that discussed the President's perception on the primary employment of a cigar and she never suffered the humiliation of seeing an oddly unattractive intern proudly displaying the spousal spermatozoa on a particularly tacky dress.

But the fact remains that Mr. Reagan and Mr. Clinton stood astride the world stage as absolute and genuine statesmen. Not since JFK in the 1960s, had America had an international and presidential figure of whom they could be truly proud. The problem for any elected president, when viewed through the eyes of the rest of the world, is of the image portrayed and the inherent charisma that emanates from that person. If it isn't there, the task of being President is undeniably more difficult. Ask any average American to name three British Prime Ministers and the likely response will be: Tony Blair, Margaret Thatcher and Winston Churchill, regardless of the fact that in the sixty-odd years between Churchill and Blair there were eight other Prime Ministers of Great Britain. Americans just don't remember them as world leaders, in much the same way that the British don't really remember too much about Johnson, Ford or Carter.

All countries seem to have inherently bewildering political systems and for anyone who is a newcomer to American politics, it is confusing when drawing party comparisons to the British equivalents. In Britain, there are really only two main parties, Labour and Conservative although the Liberal Democrats in the UK are making steady inroads. The two parties in the USA are the Republicans and the Democrats. Red is the colour used for Republicans and blue for the Democrats. My first assumption was that the colours employed in the USA were the same as those used in the UK. Red, which has traditionally been the colour of the communist and socialist flags in Europe is also the shade favoured by The Labour Party (left-wing Socialists) and blue has always been synonymous with The Conservative Party (right-wing Tories). Therefore, I equated Republican for Labour and Democrat for Conservative. In fact, quite the opposite is true. The 'red' Republicans are the old money, blue-blood conservatives and the 'blue' Democrats are a cross between the Labour Party and the Liberal Democrats. It's a bit confusing for outsiders but eventually you get the gist of it.

The two states with the largest populations in the USA are California and Texas respectively. California has always been seen as a perennial example of the Democrats and Texas is regarded as one of the long-standing Republican states. And without doubt, Texas prefers Texan presidents. The problem is that Texas, being the largest and loudest American state and with its gun-loving reputation, tends to produce presidential candidates who are characteristic of that part of the country. George Bush Jr. may be an extremely affable man in private but in the eyes of the rest of the world, he's portrayed more as a gunslinger than as a modern statesman, a kind of latter-day cowboy on a mission and therefore it has proved difficult to identify with his persona on an international level. It was also his absolute misfortune to take the reins of the US Presidency just a year before 9/11, the act of terror which sparked a conflict that still continues in Iraq. Without doubt, his Presidential legacy will suffer horrendously. Initially, because of the US/NATO disagreement over the perceived existence of 'weapons of mass destruction' which resulted in a US/UK invasion of Iraq, but more importantly because the war has dragged on for far too long, with the terrible waste of so many young lives, British as well as American. While this war also continues to burn taxpayer's money on both sides of the Atlantic, the final result is now emerging that his own country has turned against his unique method of making policy and ultimately, against the man himself. I think that when President Bush steps down in 2008, it will probably be with some relief and I'm pretty sure this wasn't his original plan.

There has however, always been a desire amongst the British and American populations to see their respective leaders in political and social agreement with each other and each to be highly regarded by both nations. It was last seen in the Thatcher/Reagan and Blair/Clinton eras respectively where there was a genuine sense of mutual affection between the leaders, in stark contrast to the awkward handshake scenes regularly played out in the cringingly staged photo-opportunities between the various heads of state in Europe. However, I don't currently foresee a Brown/Bush alliance happening at any point in the future, there's just no chemistry, and neither has enough time left to forge one.

The current 'cash for honours' debacle is providing the latest hot topic in British politics. In England, it's alleged that a number of British businessmen, who were seeking peerages or knighthoods, had made multi-million pound loans to the Labour Party in exchange for a personal title, come the Honours List giveaway at New Year, and apparently with no real requirement that the loans ever be repaid. Of course, if the United Kingdom had scrapped the pitiful and outdated honours system years ago, we wouldn't be witnessing the current scenario where a Prime Minister might pay the ultimate price for glory with a spell behind bars alongside the arrogant crackpots who can't bear to live without the words 'Sir' or 'Lord' before their names.

There are no 'honours' to be bought in the American political system but cash is always king in the USA. It is suggested that the backers of the American golden boy, John F. Kennedy, during his titanic election battle against Richard Nixon in 1960, ensured that money-filled suitcases were exchanging hands behind the scenes right up until the final vote count. JFK's father Joseph Kennedy Sr., on the eve of voting day, asked his son how many votes he would require to win the Presidency. When asked why he needed to know, Kennedy Sr. allegedly replied that while he was prepared to finance a victory, he certainly didn't want to waste money paying for a landslide. The use of his own wealth to ensure his son sat in The White House was clearly a business proposition to him and not just a family photo album investment. (Until the shambles of the Bush/Gore election vote-count, the Kennedy/Nixon battle was the narrowest margin of victory ever seen in the USA, Kennedy winning by 0.2%, the difference being a mere 100,000 votes) However, no country can claim to be a democracy when the party with the biggest money-clip wins the election. There is good reason in both countries why the inordinately large sums of money that are used to promote the political parties, should be completely removed from the entire system of political campaigning. You never know, if you limit the funding, you might get a level playing-field.

There is a different perspective in the way the political systems operate in the UK and the USA. The ancient method employed in politics of 'you scratch my back and I'll scratch yours' is used in both countries but in absolutely different ways. There has always been a more clandestine approach in London where 'favours' are the political currency and God forbid that filthy lucre should ever be seen to soil 'these hands of trust'. In America, the enormous cash donations given to political figures, whether via charitable organisations or as direct gifts, is done quite candidly. I suppose that this is just the way it's always been, the British MPs scurrying nervously to darkened corners of men-only clubs while the Americans put the cash right out on the front doorstep.

Unlike in the UK, there are a number of political power families in the USA. They exist and survive to retain, protect and promote the tradition for which they have become famed and empowered. In the twentieth century we saw Joseph Kennedy Sr. build a patriarchal power base at the Kennedy Compound, one that was publicly spearheaded by his sons John and Robert and one whose legacy still continues today. Even during the extraordinary feats of legal escapology amongst the various members of the Kennedy clan, the family has maintained its lofty high-society perch, an institution of almost royal regard and still an untouchable profile in the American mind. The real reason behind the death of Marilyn Monroe still remains a mystery today, her alleged sexual partnering of both Kennedy sons and Kennedy Sr. fuelling speculation that she was becoming dangerous to their fiefdom and therefore deemed surplus to requirement. At this stratospheric level of power and authority, it would seem that these families become impervious to anything that the outside world can throw at them.

The Bush family has now become the new supreme empire. George Bush Sr. laid the foundations to build his own compound, successfully installing his son as President just eight years after he himself had stepped down and then began working tirelessly on maintaining governance with his younger son, Jeb. I've always been impressed by Jeb Bush. As well as being eloquent and charming, he is physically handsome and shows a high degree of charismatic intellect. I vividly remember a news story shown on television in England that concentrated on the subsequent arrests made in Miami after the September 11th massacre. I don't fully remember the crux of the story, save that the police had chased a car suspected of being involved in the 9/11 plot. I do remember however, the news conference given by the then Governor of Florida, Jeb Bush, who dealt with the baying newshounds in a manner of pure elegance. He explained in articulate and coherent English, everything that had happened during this particular incident and afterwards took questions from the screaming reporters without any trace of anger and without seeming remotely harassed. He then proceeded to conduct an identical news conference for the Hispanic press, this time in perfect Spanish. I was suitably impressed.

But whether you live in Europe or in the USA, generally speaking, the best candidates never venture into politics and time and time again, the wrong people often seem to end up running the show. Those who want to take part in politics are usually the ones in need of some perception of power to bolster their own inadequacies. The real truth is that heading up a country is much the same as running a business. You need to balance the books and keep the people happy at the same time, it's not easy. In the UK, the financial rewards in politics are so relatively small that any smart businessman or businesswoman who might make a worthy candidate as Prime Minister or even as an MP, wouldn't waste his or her time even thinking about it. In world politics generally, it is the financial wealth and power behind the campaign that wins the day rather than the prudence in the choice of candidate. Put simply, the true visionaries that have historically built the great nations of this world, are no longer the nominees for the job.

Chapter 25

Social & Economic Problems

One of the many reasons enticing new immigrants to the United States, is its social and cultural diversity along with the fact that anyone who has a mind to do so, can achieve any secretly harboured ambitions no matter how diverse or radical. The sky is the proverbial limit. However, when you have a country with arguably the most multi-cultural, multi-racial and multi-religious society in the entire world, there will always be problems in the mixing of these values. We're no different from animals in the sense that as a race, we don't get on particularly well with each other if we look or sound different, in much the same way that one breed of dog will inevitably attack another breed of dog because it looks or sounds different. It's just the way it is.

I've gradually begun to understand that I'm not a great fan of the human race. I believe that spontaneous acts of kindness, manners and courtesy and the simple message sent by a genuine smile are the foundations of any society. But the truth is that most people are not intrinsically 'nice'. Our main focus it would seem, whether in our suicidal attempts to get twelve feet ahead on the road, our neighbourly arguments over the size of a boundary hedge or in the way we shove past fellow shoppers through a closing door without a look back in our wake, is to effectively get one over on someone else and score a win at their expense. As a race, we are so fundamentally involved with our own little armour-plated world that we stop caring or even thinking about anyone else. We stop doing things that are just plain 'nice'. It could be the overbearing father who can only focus on his son on the football field and forgets completely about the essential enjoyment of the game itself for all the other participants and spectators, or perhaps it's the horrendous mother who gives unsolicited parenting advice to other mothers whilst she remains oblivious to her own offspring running riot. Whatever scenario we choose, this is invariably the type of behaviour seen amongst similar members of the same race, class and culture. It is therefore easy to see why there are more inter-racial and inter-cultural clashes when we mix it up a little.

When looking at the breakdown of these multiple religions, races and cultures I've mentioned, it becomes a bit clearer. In 2005, the American Census Bureau published the following figures regarding the breakdown of the US population:

Total population of the United States: 298,444,220.

- White American: 74.7% (215.3 million)
  (This figure includes those originating from European, North African, Middle Eastern, Central Asian & Hispanic countries)
- African American: 12.1% (34.9 million)
- Asian American: 4.3%   (12.5 million)
- American Indian: 0.8%   (2.4 million)
- Hawaiian Islander: 0.1%   (0.4 million)
- Two or more races: 1.9%   (5.6 million)
- Others: 6.1%   (17.3 million)

Of the entire population, 14.5% or about 41.9 million people declared themselves to be Hispanic. As previously stated, I would expect this number to increase exponentially as the Hispanic race typically reproduces at a far greater rate than the average American level of 2.1 children per family.

Approximately 90% of the American people declared a religious faith with only 10% citing no religion at all. The majority of the

American population follows Catholicism and the second major religion is stated as Baptist.

Compare these statistics to the figures reported in the 2001 Census in Great Britain:

Total population of the United Kingdom: 60,609,153.

White:	92%	(55.8 million)
Black or Black British:	2.0%	(1.2 million)
Asian or Asian British:	4.0%	(2.4 million)
Chinese:	0.4%	(0.2 million)
Mixed Race:	1.2%	(0.7 million)
Others:	0.4%	(0.2 million)

The Church of England was stated as the main religion in the UK, and also the selected denomination of 47% of the entire poll. Catholicism came in second with 16% and another 6% chose either Muslim, Protestant, Jewish, Sikh, Hindu or other minority faiths. An enormous figure of 37% of the population declared themselves to be completely non-religious. From a personal standpoint and also given that the Church of England is a quite undemanding church, I would guess that in reality, the non-religious sector probably forms more than 65% of the entire population – people are not always completely truthful when filling out questionnaires.

From the figures shown above and bearing in mind that religious and racial disagreements have historically been the cause of most conflicts and wars, it is therefore easier in some ways to understand why the mix of religion and ethnicity in the UK has been somewhat less of a problem than we have seen and continue to see in the USA. There are less racial and religious conflicts in the UK, the media mainly choosing to focus on the odd occasion when a Union Flag is burnt by extremists on the streets of Birmingham or the photo opportunities during minority demonstrations at some of the London embassy buildings. But while as a nation, we appear content to suffer the slings and arrows of foreign extremists who can't live peacefully, I can't help recalling one particular expression. Although it's been in use for over 500 years and is possibly overused, it is one that I still believe has some pertinence, "When in Rome, do as the Romans do". It's really simple. In England, we've seen the immigrant clustering that culturally divides and identifies ethnic areas of the country. Areas in Birmingham, Southall, Brixton and Manchester have almost uniquely immigrant, non-British native populations. The same also happens in the USA – there are even some towns that have mainly Iraqi residents. Clustering isn't new. In the USA, the middle-classes have long had an overwhelming desire to be members of a club or a society that houses other members who are exactly like each other, all protected within their own gated compound, whether it's a retirement community or a country club. It's one of those things that happens all over the globe but its rate of occurrence in America is far greater than in any other country I've visited. But while the world continues to label people, while we continue to cluster in isolation to each other and while the minorities continue to demand individual attention because they believe that they are so different, we will continue to live in a society that fails to live in harmonious agreement or disagreement.

In 1950s Great Britain, as our government imported new immigrants to do the jobs that the British natives no longer wished to be involved in, we also began to see the steady decline of the nation's manufacturing industries over the next three decades. The reputation that we once had as a player in the textiles, engineering, electronics and vehicle manufacturing markets has all but disappeared. The stranglehold that the unions had on government and industry in the 1970s, effectively killed the car-makers in England. After the demise of marques like Austin, Rover, Morris, MG, and Triumph, the only brands that now remain are the smaller niche companies like TVR, Morgan,

Land Rover, Rolls-Royce and Aston Martin, although the last three of these companies are now in foreign hands.

When Margaret Thatcher came to power, standing up to and subsequently defeating the unions, a change had already begun to happen in the way that we sought new markets to provide jobs to replace those that had been lost by a unionised Great Britain. Over the last thousand years, Great Britain has had a history of conquering and therefore controlling many parts of the world, the Commonwealth a far-reaching and respected institution. We had never before had to think about the absurd notion of becoming a service-orientated country but as the British Empire slowly crumbled and faded away, that is exactly what was necessary by the late 1970s and in fact once we had grasped the theory, it seemed that we were actually quite good at it.

It would seem now, that the USA is facing a similar prospect. Service industries are quickly replacing manufacturing and there is a steep and at times, reluctant learning curve to grasp and adopt this new type of business, in the same way that the UK had initially suffered in adapting to its new market transformation. Cars, oil, electronics and textiles will not be the future industries in the USA. Year after year, Chrysler, Ford and General Motors all fail to provide the quality, reliability and profits that have become synonymous with the brands from Japan, Korea, China and Taiwan. It is impossible for American manufacturers to compete on price as the cost of making the product will always be substantially higher than the labour and material costs in the Asian markets. The same is also true for the production of electronics and domestic and professional appliances.

Although farming in the USA rightly remains protected by government subsidy, this once oil-rich nation is not quite as fuel-wealthy as it once was. An intriguing fact comes to mind that whilst the UK, with its still flourishing oil production rigs in the North Sea, continues to export more oil than is imported, the USA is such an outstanding burner of fuel that its oil imports now far outweigh its oil exports. If that was a quite unimaginable situation fifty years ago, the picture will become even more depressing in the next half century. While the American population continues to complain about the price of petrol which is incredibly cheap at around a third of the price paid in Europe, it still continues to burn the stuff at a higher rate per capita each year than any other country. (In fact, I often wonder where the world would be in terms of power, physically or otherwise, if oil hadn't been accidentally discovered in the desert by the first King of Saudi Arabia, *Saud ibn Abd al-Aziz ibn Abd al-Rahman Al Saud*, when he was desperately searching for water back in the 1930s.)

It is the same with domestic appliances. GE was once a company that would feature heavily in American stores but now the Japanese or Korean equivalent sells for less and offers better reliability. Granted, Maytag, Kenmore, Sub-Zero and Whirlpool still hold immense sway in the market but even these brands are now under threat from the likes of LG and Samsung with Bosch, Miele and Gaggenau the European choice of the middle classes.

Zenith and RCA are now consigned to history when compared to the audio-visual market-share held by the Japanese brands of Sony, Samsung, Toshiba, Panasonic and JVC. Best Buy and Circuit City are no longer stocking American brands as their main sellers because most of its stock is now imported from Asia or Europe. It would be somewhat futile and even hypocritical in telling the nation to "Buy American" if you're preaching this whilst driving your Toyota Camry (best selling car in the USA) or while watching the news on your Samsung Plasma (best selling TV manufacturer in the USA). The likelihood is that you can't even voice or text this message of protest on your dreaded cell phone as it's likely made by LG, Sony or Nokia.

Chapter 26

Politically Incorrect

The term 'Politically Correct' was first coined in the USA in a 1793 court case although its satirical use began more recently in the early 1970s. Its definition however, is generally neither political nor correct, more concerned with forcing people to abandon opinion or individuality and conform to blandness. As I may have already mentioned in this book, I am a huge fan of HBO's Mr. Bill Maher. He looks vaguely similar to U2's Bono, he's extremely non-PC, probably receives hate-mail and death threats on a daily basis but for me, he's a genuine breath of fresh air. He is able to conduct his business as an unshackled American commentator and opinionist without being gagged or constrained by the normal rigid network controls, because he makes Home Box Office the home for his soap-box, HBO being a subscription channel. This is a great example of something he said recently, regarding the current problem in Iraq: "Why can't we just admit that we fucked up the script? We thought we could cut out the cancer, spread a little freedom dust and assumed that inside every Iraqi, there's an American trying to get out." He pretty much says what he likes and I pretty much like what he says.

The politically correct society in which we live, whether in Britain or America, means that we are governed by new sets of rules which undermine everything we say or do. Without wishing to promote the idea of physical punishment to children, it would seem that an innocuous reprimand can now result in the easy reporting by neighbours or friends, of apparent child abuse. Some people resent the idea of any type of corporal punishment in schools and some like me, who went all through school under the abject fear of the headmaster's cane and therefore ensured that its sting was avoided at all cost, believe that if there is no threat then there is no boundary to keep within.

We live in a Western society that is quick to blame everything but the source of the problem. I don't believe that schools are primarily to blame for kids that turn out to be menaces to society. I also don't believe we can blame the surroundings into which we are born, whether wealthy or poor. I believe that we are genetically coded to be good or bad and there are some people who really shouldn't have the right to reproduce in the first place, such is the lamentable state of their own gene pool together with their deplorable methods of parenting. How is it that the worst candidates for parenthood are the ones that have the most children? Some children are born with so many advantages and some are born with none but we rarely become bad, we're normally just born that way. It's not an XYY chromosome thing either, it's just a fact of life. Some kids need a smack on the behind, some just don't. Tantrumous children are not pleasant and shouldn't need to be accommodated, particularly in public places. It isn't acceptable to spend ten transatlantic hours on a plane in the close proximity of an uncontrolled six-year-old hooligan while the demented parents continue to ignore the situation just as it is unacceptable for any teacher in any school to be forced to suffer at the hands of a maniacal pre-teenage pupil who threatens his very existence. If you allow children to do just as they please when they are infants then it is reasonably safe to assume that they will continue in the same vein for the rest of their lives.

"Happy Christmas", I shouted to a distant neighbour. "Happy Holidays", he yelled back. What is it about this new politically correct method of 'dumbing down' a traditional greeting? I was duly informed that I shouldn't use a religious term, regardless of its innocuousness, for fear of insulting the other religious faiths. But surely the word 'holiday' is merely a conjunction of the words 'holy' and 'day' so its use, is in itself a bit presumptuous. Although the original meaning of Christmas has gradually been eroded all over the world, in Britain and in America, the word itself is now becoming verboten. The term which is quickly gaining popularity though, is 'Happy Hanukkah'. I'd never heard this expression in England but over here it is used tirelessly, even amongst non-Jews and while the traditional Christmas tree (or Holiday tree) is not yet extinct, the nine-candled menorah is a regular and increasingly popular feature at Christmas time. It's easy to see how religious disagreement and political correctness can completely ruin what is essentially, a festivity aimed more at children than anyone else.

In America, it's all about fear factor. Not the television show of course, but the fact that everything in life is designed to scare you into taking evasive action or a warning to make you avoid making a mistake, whether it's to do with health insurance, hurricane shutters, termite infestation or just the fear of being sued by your neighbour. Each time I rent a movie from Blockbuster or NetFlix, I slide the disc into the tray and wait for the first message or disclaimer from the studio responsible for making the film. Whether it's Sony Pictures, Warner Bros. or whoever, the movie is always preceded with a statement that informs you in no uncertain terms that the opinions or views that may be expressed in the film are not indicative of those that are held by the studio. Apparently, it seems vitally important that you should know this before you watch the movie and not afterwards lest you decide to hit the eject button before the credits start rolling. This is pretty amusing, given that the big Hollywood studios of the 1930s and 1940s tended to have a maverick approach to everything they put out. They dared to be daring and they put out precisely what they wanted to say, mostly from the personal standpoint of the studio president, notwithstanding the politically correct but quite insane era of McCarthyism in the USA. Today's bland corporate studios cannot bear to think that they might be responsible for something different or something new, instead interpreting this kind of radical publicity as merely bad publicity.

And it's not enough that the studio is disassociating itself with the product that the company nurtured and financed, because no sooner has their ridiculous disclaimer disappeared from your screen, the next warning is from the FBI threatening you with a $250,000 fine or even jail time if you dare to copy the DVD. At this point you're wondering if it's still OK to discuss the movie afterwards or maybe now there's a gag order or copyright on content debate. So how do you feel? You've paid your four bucks to Blockbuster and now you're terrified to watch the movie in case you get another ticking-off.

I said previously that I would avoid personal opinion as much as possible in this book. However, the latter content of this chapter is mostly based on my own personal viewpoint and may be substantially different to those views and opinions held by some readers, but whilst the politically correct brigade hasn't yet managed to abolish freedom of speech, I will maintain this as my opinion even if it conflicts with others.

Chapter 27

What's In A Name?

There used to be an element of romance attached to air-travel. The black and white photographs that British Airways used recently, evoking memories of a bygone age of elegance and sophistication are really now images that should be confined to the golden but distant memories of the now defunct airlines BEA, BOAC, PAN-AM and TWA. Gone are the gentlemen passengers resplendent in their worsted suits and fedora hats and the 1950s ladies in their finest twin-sets, coiffed hair and perennial strings of pearls, replaced now by travellers in sweat suits, baseball caps and Nike trainers. You can't blame the passengers of today; flying is no longer an eagerly anticipated pleasure, more a battleground of strained human emotions and utter desensitisation.

The shockwave from the events of 9/11 changed air travel in America almost overnight. From a time when a passenger could literally walk from the car park directly to the gate without meeting any form of security whatsoever, air travel has now changed to a situation where every passenger is literally stripped down to bare essential clothing in order to pass through a rigid set of security checks. The TSA (Transportation Security Administration) now enjoys stratospheric new levels of power in the USA which depending on the airport of departure, will manage to both intimidate the passengers and as an added bonus, strip them of their dignity too. The removal of belts often precedes sudden and immediate trouser descent and the surrender of shoes reveals a variety of socks that should have been replaced years ago. The callous confiscation of toothpaste or perfume, exceeding the miniscule 3oz limit, has re-energised the ruthless zealousness of the ladies and gentlemen from the dreaded TSA. I should however balance this accusation by saying that not all US airports maintain the same approach. The TSA people at San Diego are one of the most helpful and friendly teams I've come across whereas any departure from Miami will see the passenger reduced from human to cattle status.

But putting aside all of the above and condemning my rose-tinted view to the "do you remember when" archives, there is something about American air travel that still offers a romanticism that really does make me smile whenever I'm at an airport and it is truly unique to the USA. I first noticed this while waiting to board a flight in Los Angeles. For those of us who arrive at the departure gate with time in hand, it's inevitable that we innocently survey our surroundings to relieve the boredom. It was whilst sitting and waiting to board a flight to Houston that I noticed the destination cities shown above the other gates and almost every one of them immediately put a song in my head. Whether it was San Francisco, New York, or my own favourite in California which immediately sparks the line, *"Do you know the way to San José?"*, I could always relate one song or another to most of the gate destinations. Even seeing a flight boarding for Atlanta, I couldn't help humming Gladys Knight's immortal *"Midnight Train to Georgia"*. It's unique to American place names because I can't quite imagine any songs that would work as well in the UK. *'I left my heart in Eastbourne'* or *'Blackpool, Blackpool, so good they named it twice'* and even *'24 hours from Grimsby'* just doesn't cut it. The USA just has superior place names to the UK and they always work well in a song lyric.

American auto manufacturers are historically renowned for coming up with some of the most exotic names for their new cars. Some of the model names that were introduced in the 1950s and 1960s are now making a comeback mainly because it has clearly been difficult to improve on some of the original ideas. The Beach Boys song *'Fun, Fun, Fun' ('til her daddy takes her T-bird away)* immortalised Ford's stunning 1950s Thunderbird convertible, and the car company decided that when it introduced a new version of the car in 2001, not only was the retro styling a celebration of the original design, the name Thunderbird was to be given a new lease of life, fifty years after it was originally introduced.

There seems to be a preference now among the US car makers to give their bigger models a selection of names that clearly have an affinity with long-distance travel and exploration. Mercury's Mountaineer, Lincoln's Navigator, Cadillac's Escalade, Buick's Rendezvous and Chrysler's Voyager are typical examples while Ford seems to be on its own outdoor mission with the naming of its larger SUVs, the models Explorer, Expedition and Escape, effortlessly conjuring visions of mountains, lakes and the great outdoors. It's equally sad though that the smaller cars they're producing have all been given the indistinctive monikers that have been deliberately thought up to suffice all world markets and languages; Fusion, Focus, Edge and Flex, blandness personified. But in Ford's defence, they've cleverly decided to retain the Mustang brand-name which has served the company well since it was first introduced in April 1964. The car has been a monumental American success story and such was the speed that the cars were leaving the showrooms during that first launch year, that one mischievous New York eatery put a sign in its window, declaring, "Our hotcakes are selling like Mustangs."

Without any doubt, the names given to some of the American cars of the last fifty years are not only exotic but they've also become legendary in their own right. Chevrolet's classic Corvette Stingray and Bel Air convertibles, Buick's Skylark and Electra, Lincoln's Continental, Cadillac's Eldorado and DeVille, and Pontiac's Trans Am and Firebird are all irresistible names that evoke memories of a golden and bygone era. Even the late and great Enzo Ferrari couldn't resist the urge when naming the Carozerria Scaglietti-designed Maranello racer which was aimed at the affluent American west coast customers. The rare and beautiful Ferrari California Spyder, forever immortalised in the film, *'Ferris Bueller's Day Off'*, has become an almost priceless automotive work of art.

I have decided that names are important to Americans. Without doubt, their place names are more romantic and definitely much sexier than the British equivalents, although there would appear to be a town called Richmond in just about every US state. But the names that Americans give to their kids however, are equally impressive. Our own Victoria & David Beckham seem to have followed the American style when choosing names for their children. Their first, Brooklyn was allegedly given his name based on the town of conception, the assumption here that it was in Brooklyn, New York. I'd guess that the boy may be eternally thankful not to have been conceived in Peckham, South London. But if we forget about the Beckham children for a moment (Brooklyn, Romeo and Cruz) and concentrate on American celebrities, we can see that there are some superb examples from some extremely vivid imaginations.

While Zowie Bowie was never enamoured with the name given to him by his English father, now just preferring to be called Joe, the American entertainer and magician Penn Jillette, gave his own kids names that he and they might all live to regret, in Zolten and Moxie CrimeFighter. The Jolie-Pitt children have pretty exotic names in Shiloh, Maddox and Zahara while the recent Best Actor Oscar winner Forest Whittaker, has thought up some truly beautiful names for his four children, Autumn, Sonnet, Ocean and True. Even the Anglo-German partnership of the British singer Seal (great name, great talent) and supermodel Heidi Klum has produced a truly international title for their child, Johan Riley Fyodor Taiwo Samuel although I would guess that the boy will soon adopt the name Joe as his preference later on, just like Mr. Bowie Jr.

My absolute favourite set of first and middle names are those given to their children by Arlyn & John Phoenix. Summer Joy,

214

Rainbow Joan of Arc, Leaf Joaquin, Liberty Mariposa and the late River Jude are without doubt, a proud celebration of the Californian hippie generation. It's just slightly incongruous that the children's father John, changed his surname to Phoenix in 1972, his inherited name at birth being Bottom.

But as the use of more exotic Christian names increases, it is becoming increasingly fashionable to use surnames as first or Christian names. Riley, Ripley, Cameron, Kennedy, Harrison, Mackenzie, Sterling, Hunter, Cole and Crawford immediately spring to mind but as with anything that is new or different, I suppose these names will in time become as normal and accepted as Skyler, Ariel, Summer, Paris and Chelsea. Well, maybe not. In the meantime, I was recently surprised to hear that Mohammed has overtaken George in the list of the most popular names for boys in the UK, lying in 22nd place, not far behind Alfie, Charlie, William and Harry.

I am especially fond of some of the names seen on the TV production credits that flash past at the end of the programmes. I saw one recently, R. Brian DiPirro, an acclaimed and successful television producer. I'm fairly certain that the USA is unique in this practice of having the primary Christian name downgraded to an initial but the name Brian isn't the most exotic in the world so I was always interested to know what the 'R' could possibly stand for and this Christian name reversal when combined with an Italian surname becomes even more odd.

In fact, there is a distinct desire amongst the middle classes in the USA to 'big up' their names. It often begins with the father giving his son an identical first name to his own and thus the father becomes Senior and the boy becomes Junior. (The heavyweight boxing champion George Foreman took this a little too far when deciding to name all five of his sons, George). Then the son in turn also has a complete brain blockage on what name to give his future child and can only repeat his father's actions of donating his own to his newborn. Hence we get into a numbering system where Junior and Senior just will not suffice. The golfer

Davis Love III is clearly a victim of this system and his own son has also followed in the Love tradition; yes he is Davis Love IV although I understand Mom and Dad call him Dru.

These families, which are generally either wealthy, powerful or famous or as in many cases, all of the above, are becoming almost molecular 'royal families' in their own right. Their name numbering system is not dissimilar to the method applied by the Kings and Queens of England and France, with our prevailing British monarch holding the Elizabeth II title (obviously a little new at this game) but with King Louis XVIII holding the record in the now defunct French monarchy. But while George Foreman's kids are moving through the numbering system at a rate of knots, already at George Foreman VI in just a couple of decades, it took a little longer in the French royal family. Louis I was crowned way back in 814AD and exactly 1000 years would pass before the 18th and final Louis would eventually become king in 1814.

Chapter 28

Born In The USA

There are many things that are relatively unique to America and can therefore rightfully boast the title, 'Born in the USA'. None of the subjects in this section warrant their own chapter and the examples I've chosen are multifarious, unconnected and just a miniscule sample of American uniqueness but I think it's worth mentioning some of them in passing.

The bugs, reptiles and critters found in the USA, make this country seem like one big national park. The more humid states have the most exotic species whereas the mountain states are home to pretty much every type of bear along with numerous species of wild cat including the Jaguar, Cougar and the rare Florida Panther. Beware of snakes in Florida though, most of them – mainly the black varieties are harmless but some of the more colourful ones like the Coral Snake and the Diamondback Rattlesnake can be deadly. The south-east of the USA also has a thriving population of racoons which although fairly anonymous during the day, these creatures wreak nocturnal havoc so it is important to tie down your garbage at night as the racoons will have it spilled out everywhere by morning.

In Florida, where there was once a fear of alligator extinction, it is now estimated that there are approximately 1.5 million of them in that state alone. That's one for every ten inhabitants. Don't be surprised to see one lurching across the fairway at your local golf course although they likely won't attack you unless you get too close. The bright green Iguanas on the other hand are my favourite reptiles here, although surprisingly, they aren't native to the USA. Many Florida residents see them as a nuisance as these friendly and luminescent lizards have a habit of adopting the nearest swimming pool as their personal lavatory.

Florida has an ardent tradition of maintaining and protecting wildlife habitats. The Manatee, sometimes referred to as the sea cow, is the endangered mammal that Florida strenuously attempts to preserve. Dolphins are also suffering in this state as the increased use of boats and other recreational sea craft causes physical damage, often resulting in unnecessary fatalities amongst these incredible creatures. Turtles are heavily protected and if you are driving in Florida and see one that's strayed onto the road, it is customary to stop and move the creature to a place of safety. Such is the concern regarding natural habitat, it is said that The Florida Fish & Wildlife Conservation Commission is the single most powerful agency in the state, with more rights of access to your home than the FBI, CIA or Homeland Security.

The sub-tropical areas of the USA are not only home to reptiles, exotic birds and tree-dwellers, but the bug-life is also a whole new eye opener for most people. Although you'd be best advised to avoid stepping into a fire-ant nest as the ensuing pain from the bites is unbelievably painful, the termites that are found in these areas are a real danger to your home and its structure. An inordinate amount of wood has historically been used in the construction of homes in the south-east and for the termites, this is a veritable banquet once it becomes moist. Anywhere in the house where there is a build-up of moisture will attract the termite. It is so important to keep dampness out. Avoid plants and bushes growing too close to the house and any woodpiles and debris should be kept well away from the building. There are stories of termites literally eating houses down to the foundations and the annual cost of the damage caused by these innocuous little flyers is estimated to be close to $2billion in the USA alone. It is also a little known fact that the combined weight of all the termites in the world far exceeds the total weight of all humans.

If nothing else amazes you about this country, you cannot but stand in awe at the speed of construction in the USA. The thousands of miles of roads that link every part of the nation and which are often driven relentlessly through mountains and valleys are to be completely marvelled at. The superstructures and skyscrapers that stand in testimony to this pioneering nation alongside the extraordinary feats of engineering like the Hoover Dam on the Nevada and Arizona border and the Golden Gate Bridge spanning the bay of San Francisco, are truly magnificent man-made monuments. Without doubt though, my own personal favourite is the breathtaking Mount Rushmore National Memorial in the Black Hills of South Dakota which depicts the faces of the four American Presidents, Washington, Jefferson, Roosevelt and Lincoln, carved imperiously into the mountainside. The monument, which took fourteen years to build was realised by the extraordinary sculptor, Gutzon Borglum. Each face is over sixty feet in height and it is universally agreed to be one of the greatest sculpting achievements of all time.

To be honest, it came as some surprise to me to find that Yellowstone National Park is actually the world's very first national park. With an area covering over two million acres mostly in the state of Wyoming but also partly in Montana,

Yellowstone is bigger than the states of Delaware and Rhode Island put together. It was an enormous achievement from the efforts of the explorer Ferdinand Hayden and the countless others before him to eventually persuade Congress to remove the territory from a planned government land auction and in 1872, President Ulysses S. Grant finally signed the bill that made Yellowstone National Park a protected national trust which flourishes to this day.

In the USA, there's a duplicitous ploy used to entice and encourage shoppers to spend more. This is commonly known as the Mail-In Rebate. It doesn't exist in the UK but it's worth explaining how it works. Let's say that you buy an item for $500 and attached to this is a mail-in rebate offer of $50 value. You are then required to send in a completed rebate form to a processing centre, along with the bar-code cut from the packaging and a copy of the receipt. The time taken for the rebate company to send back a cheque for the $50 often takes up to six months and in many cases, the cheque never arrives at all. These shameless organisations work on the theory that the consumer will either fill out the form incorrectly, forget to enclose barcodes or even forget about submitting the rebate in the first instance. In the interim, if you've remembered to do everything correctly, you will likely have forgotten about the rebate and if you haven't chased up the cheque in the given timeframe, the elapsed period of time will render the refund invalid. The other insidious method that these companies use to further avoid payment, is to give the cheque an appearance of junk mail so in many instances, the recipient will probably discard the cheque to the wastebasket. Make sure you don't inadvertently throw away a valid cheque and at all times, keep copies of the entire submission. It's a deliberate ploy to avoid giving the customer a reduced price when the reduction should have been applied at the checkout and for that reason, the mail-in rebate is anti-customer and should be abolished.

Although American employers generally give far less paid vacation time when compared to their English counterparts, the number of federal or public holidays slightly exceeds the total given in England. The lists below illustrate the dates and names of the public holidays, or bank holidays as we know them at home, in the USA and in England respectively:

Federal or Public Holidays in the USA:

January 1st:	New Year's Day
Third Monday in January:	Martin Luther King Day
Third Monday in February:	Washington's Birthday
Last Monday in May:	Memorial Day
July 4th:	Independence Day
First Monday in September:	Labor Day
Second Monday in October:	Columbus Day
November 11th:	Veterans Day
Fourth Thursday in November:	Thanksgiving Day
December 25th:	Christmas Day

National or Bank Holidays in England:

January 1st:	New Year's Day
April 6th:	Good Friday
April 9th:	Easter Monday
May 7th:	May Day
May 28th:	Spring Bank Holiday
August 27th:	Summer Bank Holiday
December 25th:	Christmas Day
December 26th:	Boxing Day

Boxing Day has always intrigued my American friends, the assumption being that it is the day to relegate to the trash, all of the boxes and paper that engulfs the family home once all of the presents have been opened on Christmas Day. It's also probably fair to say that many English people are equally unaware of the true meaning of the term. As a boy, I presumed it referred to the multitude of sports that played out on television sets on the day after Christmas, boxing included on that list. There are several versions of the meaning of this holiday, mostly dwelling on the idea that wealthy 17th Century employers and landowners gave out boxes containing money and food to the servants and employees of the company or estate but most of these theories are wide of the mark. So for anyone who doesn't know, here is the definitive origin of Boxing Day as I understand it. Dating back to the Middle Ages and starting sometime around 600AD, the village church would have an 'alms box' installed in the rear section of the building, effectively an early version of a charity box. This box would have a slit in the top through which coins would be donated by the congregation throughout the year, up to and including Christmas Day. On the day after Christmas, the boxes would finally be opened up and the money distributed amongst the poorest people in the village, thereby coining the term, Boxing Day.

Invariably, it seems that the majority of American federal or public holidays have more relevance to the celebration of an important event or achievement than those awarded in England, which mostly masquerade as an excuse to take a day off from work. But whilst saluting the reasoning and therefore empathising with most of the US national holidays, my small brain still has a minor problem in trying to comprehend Thanksgiving. I suppose my own slightly warped view of Thanksgiving in the US appears to be a celebration of the European and therefore immigrant Pilgrims saying to the Native American Indians, "Thanks for giving us all your land!", and in my time here, I haven't seen an awful lot of evidence that disproves this theory. The other strange thing is that it's absolutely traditional to eat turkey on Thanksgiving Day in the USA (don't try offering a substitute for this dry old bird as it will be wholeheartedly rejected by one and all) even though it's fact that turkeys weren't indigenous to Plymouth Beach when the Mayflower first landed in 1620. It's more likely that the surviving Pilgrims shared a meal with the Wampanoag Indians of either duck, chicken or venison although it is believed that cranberry sauce was probably on the menu at that first Thanksgiving Dinner one year later in 1621. However, it is true that more than three centuries on, roast turkey was the first food to be eaten on the moon as Messrs. Armstrong and Aldrin celebrated a belated Thanksgiving during that first Apollo landing, even if it was vacuum-packed in a tin-foil container.

Independence Day is different. It's a very odd thing because I have celebrated the 4th July with many Americans on many occasions and been shown enormous hospitality. However, given that I am English and Independence Day celebrates the date that England finally ceded control of America, I think the irony is probably lost on most of my American friends of the enormous hurdles I had to jump to be able to live in a country that might have been part of the British Commonwealth were it not for the taxation greed of the 17th century British government and its monarchy. It's not something to dwell on because the festivities of the 4th July are a true celebration of freedom and independence in the USA and Americans welcome one and all with open arms. It really is a day to cheer a country and its people who have achieved so much, so quickly.

Dwelling for a moment on times of celebration, one of the first things that hit me when I spent my first Christmas in the USA was the effort put into the decorating and lighting of the exteriors of American homes during the Christmas period. I had never seen anything quite so breathtaking as the millions of coloured lights and decorations that adorned just about every house in the neighbourhood. The attention to detail, the time, effort and expense involved is just enormous and it couldn't fail to bring a smile to the face of even the most miserable Scrooge. There are bound to be some who will say that the Americans are a little overboard in their neon-enhanced acts of festivity and others who might even see this Yuletide expression as a little over-zealous but for me, these people just love a celebration, and so do I. Bring it on.

There is no secret that car rental companies make most of their profit from selling insurance to the unwitting customer. But in the USA, if you have your own auto insurance, you can use your personal policy to cover the rental car, therefore avoiding a high rental bill. You can't do it in England but you should do it here as this will save you around 60% of the total cost. On the negative side of car rental in America, I am amazed at the amount of items that the customer is instructed to initial on the rental form. If every customer exercised his right to have each of these sections on the form, read and explained to him, bearing in mind that the legalese is in miniscule and unreadable text, it would take around four hours to process each customer. What I'm saying to the car rental companies, is that if you don't expect the customers to understand what you are asking them to sign, then don't ask them to do it just to ensure your own backside is covered for any circumstance that might put you at risk.

Staying with cars for a moment, the automobile retail industry in the USA has what I call, a dirty little secret. I have only recently discovered this wonderful but clandestine nugget, and in fact it happened quite by chance and although I don't know if this is unique to the USA, I do know that this practice doesn't happen in the UK. I had been looking for a family utility vehicle and decided that a particular model from a Japanese manufacturer would probably be suitable. Having visited the dealer, I was appraised of the situation regarding models and prices but as I wasn't yet ready to make a decision, I returned home to study the vehicle details online. It was at this point that I discovered a little department hidden deep inside the dealer's website called

'Internet Sales'. I discovered that this two-man sales team, working in the same dealership, was selling the same car that I had looked at only an hour previously, for $8000 less than the sticker price shown on the vehicle on the forecourt. When I called my salesman to ask why he hadn't told me of this price differential, he informed me that he was trained to sell vehicles solely on the sticker price and wasn't allowed to refer me to the Internet Sales area. So, provided that you're not trading in a vehicle, (the trade-in price will also be wholesale and therefore substantially less attractive) then you can benefit immensely from making initial contact with the dealership via their website email. I should make one caveat at this point that not all car manufacturers admit to this practice. However, one particular German company who claims never to discount its vehicles, did in fact offer me a lower price through the internet so I truly believe that any car is available at substantially lower prices if you are prepared to do your homework.

Another method of buying a brand new vehicle at a vastly reduced price is to buy the car after the month of June. In the UK, the model year starts in January so a car registered on the 1st January, 2007 is a 2007 model. Likewise, it is still a 2007 model even if it is registered on 31st December, 2007. But in the USA, around halfway through the year, the manufacturers begin delivering the next year's model and even if the model itself hasn't seen any visual or mechanical change over the previous year's version, the older model will be substantially discounted. For example, a local Porsche dealer (a company that has rigorously avoided any discounts on any of their models) is currently offering $10,000 off the price of all brand new '07 Caymans and Boxsters, the cars standing side by side next to the full-price 2008 versions. But the fact remained that they were all brand new vehicles and seemingly identical. The moral of the story is that if you're looking for a new car and you want a great deal, then buy it later in the year, and preferably via the Internet Sales Department.

No matter how long I live here in America, I will never get used to calling my garden a yard. For me, a garden evokes a vision of colour and beauty whereas a yard conjures up a dusty concrete area where you might park up a fleet of concrete mixer trucks. However, the word 'garden' is rarely used here except in reference to herbs or vegetables and 'yard' is the accepted term for your rear-facing piece of paradise. When we first moved to America, we settled initially in Florida but the maintenance of lawns in this state is however, a completely different matter. In England, we seem to take great pride in cutting our own grass, having perfect striped lawns like the tennis courts at Wimbledon. It's a British thing that just has to be done and generally speaking, we do all the work ourselves. So once we arrived in Florida, I bought all the equipment, the lawn tractor, the push mower, the strimmer, the blower, the hedge trimmer, the chainsaw and after my first attempt, there I was, five hours later, ten pints of sweat lighter and feeling pretty ill. There seemed to be only one thing left to do and that was to photograph everything that we'd bought and put it all on eBay. Basically, I hadn't cottoned onto the fact that no smart-thinking person over here cuts their own lawns, so now we have a lawn-man who charges $120 a month while I can put my feet up and try and find an English soccer channel, hidden somewhere between all the American sports networks.

I have briefly commented earlier in this book on the danger of litigation in America. It is worth saying also that the law practiced in this country is somewhat different to our own legal system even though it is apparently based on English Law. Notwithstanding the various differences that occur state to state, there are a number of legal aspects that really are cause for concern, as an outsider looking in. However, this is the way it's always been in the USA so it may just be that we are such very different nations in so many ways that causes this concern. Different strokes for different folks.

The Motion to Suppress Evidence immediately suggests to me that American law is heavily weighted in favour of the guilty. In layman's terms, it means that a request is made to a judge to exclude evidence at a trial or hearing when one party believes the evidence has been obtained unlawfully. Surely if it is evidence which is relevant or fact, then it should be available to both defence and prosecution, no matter how it is obtained? To me, it is just another method used to ensure that the guilty are set free.

The practice of jury selection in America is very different to the methods employed in England. The term 'voir dire' which is derived from a Latin/French term, describes the American pre-trial process whereby both sides effectively interview candidates from a large pool of potential jurors, to select a jury which best suits the defence and the prosecution alike. Both sides have a set limit of 'peremptory challenges' whereby the defence and prosecution can exclude a potential juror without the need to give reason for doing so. Jurors can be ruled unsuitable on grounds of race or religion or for political or emotional bias, for or against the defendant. In England, there would need to be a significant reason to object to any juror, the main objection being that the juror was acquainted with or related to the defendant. In the USA, the right to take jury selection to such extremes begs the question, whether either the prosecution or the defence should have the opportunity to choose a jury that best serves their case. Because in some ways it could be seen as effectively manipulating the result before the trial has even begun.

The interference of the justice system doesn't stop with jury selection. The electronic and video surveillance monitoring of a trial, gives either legal team the opportunity to externally track the trial progress, often resulting in victory for the side with the better financial resources. The insertion of television cameras and microphones into American courtrooms, whilst providing popular television entertainment during the trials of celebrities like O.J. Simpson and Michael Jackson, have turned the American legal system into a bit of a circus. It's also pretty clear that the lawyers who defend these cases, relish their new found celebrity status and the dream of the stratospheric wealth which will follow once the trial has ended.

Finally, and absolutely unique to America, a witness in an American court who feels that his or her testimony may effectively self-incriminate on other possible charges, can choose not to answer questions from either the prosecution or the defence lawyers during questioning. This practice is known as 'Pleading the 5th Amendment' or 'Taking the 5th'. In movies, we often see a witness repeat this response over and over to a barrage of questions from the lawyer and the reason for this is that as soon as the witness answers one single question, the right to remain silent is irrevocably lost.

In the UK, we have grown accustomed to seeing speed cameras at the side of the road, constantly photographing our careless use of the accelerator and automatically sending us a fine whilst also adding a number of penalty points to our licenses. Although the cameras are not yet universally in place in the USA, the police are now targeting more fervently than ever, those motorists who disobey the speed limit. The interesting thing for me, having been caught once for speeding in the USA, is that there is a unique and novel way of avoiding penalty points added to your license, something which is impossible to do in England. In Florida (I don't know if this is countrywide), you have the opportunity, once a year and up to a maximum of five times in your lifetime, to attend an online Driver Improvement School. If you pass, which takes only a couple of hours in front of your PC, you will avoid any points added to your driving license although you will still have to pay the fine and also for the cost of the DIS. Effectively, this means that the driver can maintain lower insurance rates and the police keep more cars on the road and have a larger pool of speedy drivers from which to extract speeding fines, such is the reliance now on income derived from traffic violations.

I was once burgled at my home in England. When the police arrived, who to be honest, cared less whether they found the intruder or not, they quietly advised me that if I were to have discovered the culprit during the crime and I'd assaulted him, I would myself have been arrested. In order to avoid being arrested, were I to be the victim of a burglary in the future, I was advised to do a little 'damage' to myself in order that the altercation might appear to the police as self-defence. When I enquired what sort of 'damage' I should do to myself, I was told that a torn shirt and one modest cut with fresh blood should be sufficient. (It was interesting that after the police had taken notes, tested for prints and decided there was nothing further to do, I subsequently located one of my carving knives that the burglar had dumped in a trash can outside my house) The big difference in the USA is that an American's home truly is his castle, and I absolutely salute the idea of having the right to protect yourself in your own home without fear of subsequent prosecution. It's just plain silly to think that you can't do so in England.

OK, staying for one final moment on all things legal, there is one thing that the Americans do which blows nicely into the faces of the Civil Liberties groups and that is the local newspaper publication of photographs of wanted felons with copious offers of rewards attached. These full page notices are updated in subsequent editions with any results marked 'solved' or 'pending' printed bold on the pictures. The local papers also publish whole pages listing the paedophiles and sex offenders in the area. They publish the names, addresses and photos of the convicted men and women. I've never known if this provokes any sort of violence towards the offenders but it certainly makes them unable to cover up their guilt or hide what they are likely to try and repeat again and again, as is often the case in this type of hideous crime.

Although many cash-strapped customers are now turning to the less expensive areas in the world, like South Africa and some of the Eastern European countries, there is no doubt that the USA is the birthplace of cosmetic surgery. From botox to liposuction, from breast augmentation to rhinoplasty and from labia reduction to vaginal tightening, the world is your oyster here in America. Ten years ago, it would be uncommon to meet a woman who had undergone breast augmentation surgery. It is now becoming the norm in America, particularly in California, to see the bowling ball shaped curves that thrust perilously forward from a woman's chest in cartoon-like fashion. But here's the funny thing. When women ponder the size of implant that might be best for them, 425, 450 or 500cc, (325cc is my personal recommendation) it seems to be discussed in the same vernacular that adolescent boys might brag about car engine sizes. Although breast augmentation has provided enormous benefits for the many women who have endured the emotional and physical scarring caused by mastectomy, the majority of women who choose this surgery for solely cosmetic reasons, don't seem to understand that most men actually prefer natural curves and not ballooning bosoms that have no real possibility of delicate or passionate handling. And although some of the other types of surgical procedures do provide enormous benefits to patients who have suffered disfiguring injuries and scarring and also for those born with unfortunate physical defects, I have yet to see a normal person whose looks are improved, post-surgery. Tighter yes, and often with a permanent grin too, but rarely does the result prove to be a natural looking one.

We all know the song *'New York, New York'* and the line that states, *'so good they named it twice'*, but when I asked my wife if she knew why they named it twice, she admitted that she'd never really understood the line. For those people who don't know the background, it's worth explaining a couple of things about this unique city. New York of course, isn't named twice, it's just that New York City is in the state of New York and therefore the mailing address would be New York, NY. Simple explanation. There is of course, one other anomaly. When you mail a letter to someone in Manhattan, after you've written the street address, you must then add NY, NY. The reason for this is that The Borough of Brooklyn is in Kings County, The Borough of Queens is in Queens County, The Bronx is in Bronx County, Staten Island is in Richmond County and Manhattan is in New York County. For some reason, letters to Manhattan are addressed to the County and not to the Borough as with the other four Boroughs. However, for those who have never been to New York, it is also worth clarifying what and where New York is, in simple tourist terms.

New York City is actually made up of five boroughs, Staten Island, Brooklyn, Queens, The Bronx and Manhattan but something I only recently realised is that New York City is actually a set of islands, except for The Bronx which is the only part of the city connected to the United States mainland. The Bronx gets its name from the original owners of the farmland that made up most of the area. Their farm was called Broncks Farm and so the family were referred to colloquially, as The Bronx, which subsequently became the borough's name.

But anyone who is travelling to New York as a tourist, is likely going to Manhattan, the part of New York which is generally accepted as the city of New York. This is where you'll find Central Park, Broadway, Fifth Avenue, Times Square, Wall Street, Madison Square Garden and the stunning skyscraper panorama that defines the very essence of how people remember and picture the city of New York. Manhattan also houses not only the biggest, but also the most beautiful train station ever built, in Grand Central Terminus or as it's more commonly known, Grand Central Station. A visit there should not be hurried as the surrounding architecture, sculpture and art is quite breathtaking. Situated on Vanderbilt Avenue, this masterpiece was built by the legendary Vanderbilt family in 1903 and the opulence of the concourse still maintains a wonderfully decadent feeling and dining there in the now famous Oyster Bar, is a real treat.

There are obvious similarities between New York and London in the fact that they both house the main financial centres of their countries and they are equally regarded as the best cities for tourism, shopping and shows, in the USA and UK respectively. But although there are towns in the state of New York with London-originated names, Camden, Kensington, Waterloo, St. James and most surprisingly, Hyde Park, it is also interesting to note that in both cities of London and New York you'll find neighbourhoods known as Chelsea and Soho. But one area that is common only to New York, is the exquisitely named TriBeCa area. This part of Manhattan, which is now a hip and fashionable, arts and entertainment destination for tourists looking for something a little different, is so named for it's actual location; quite simply, it is the **Tri**angle **Be**low **Ca**nal Street.

I have always viewed New York as one of the biggest and busiest cities in the world but I was surprised to discover that while New York has the highest population of any American city at around 8 million inhabitants covering all five of its boroughs, it is still remarkable to me that this figure is only around half the total population of London. (Although London does accommodate 25% of the entire UK population) It was also surprising to note that London's Heathrow Airport is the busiest international airport in the world, annually serving over 60 million world travellers, while New York's JFK Airport lies in 18th spot with just 20 million international passengers. Strange, but quite true.

With the knowledge that the USA is so diverse in culture, people, wildlife and landscape from east to west and from north to south, it is hardly surprising that this country also experiences just about every weather condition known to man. Natural hazards & disasters are almost a weekly news item. In the south-east, the hurricane season starts on 1st June and continues through to 30th November, a full six months of nail-biting. The season in 2005 which was one of the busiest and most devastating on record, saw 27 named tropical storms, fifteen of which officially developed into hurricanes, including the now legendary and deadly hurricane sisters, Wilma, Rita and Katrina. Wilma was the most intense hurricane ever recorded in the Atlantic, Rita was the most intense hurricane ever recorded in the Gulf of Mexico and Katrina was the most deadly and costliest of all hurricanes on record, causing over $80 billion of damage and killing almost 2,000 people in its path. It is also agreed that Katrina was the worst natural disaster ever seen in the USA.

Many of the horrific events in New Orleans that followed in the wake of Hurricane Katrina wouldn't have happened if the levee system, which should have protected this sub-sea-level city, had been designed and built to a level that might have withstood a Category-5 hurricane. The devastation was not entirely as a result of the fragile construction of the city's homes and historic buildings. In fact, more damage was caused by the sudden deluge of millions of gallons of sea water surging into the huge bowl that is New Orleans. It should also be noted that the actual damage caused by a hurricane is not normally as significant as the isolated areas of immense destruction caused by the tornadoes that circulate at the edge of the hurricane itself.

Whilst the east coast and the south-eastern regions are annually subjected to hurricanes and tropical storms, no area of America is spared some form of catastrophic weather condition. In 2007, the town of Greensburg in Kansas, witnessed a 205mph EF5 tornado, (Enhanced Fujita Scale 0-5), probably the strongest twister on record and one which resulted in ten fatalities and the destruction of 95% of the town. In 1999, Oklahoma suffered tornado damage exceeding $1 billion for the first time in American history in what is now referred to as The Oklahoma Tornado Outbreak. The 66 tornadoes of this 72 hour period wreaked havoc across the state, killing 48 and injuring nearly 700. It destroyed over 2,000 homes and damaged another 6,500.

On the west coast, Californians live with the constant reminder that having a home sitting on a fault line which runs 800 miles from the top to the bottom of the state means that there is always the potential threat of disaster from an earthquake. The San Andreas Fault is effectively the meeting of two land masses that are sliding by each other under the influence and control of tectonic plate movement, one headed NW and the other headed SE. It's not a new phenomenon, in fact it's the method that has shaped the world for the last 100 billion years but it does concern Californians that if the 'big one' does come, then their particular piece of paradise might suddenly become a floating island in the Pacific, although I'm assured that this isn't something that's going to happen any time soon. However, the San Andreas Fault is responsible for many of the extraordinary earthquakes that have occurred in California, including the legendary San Francisco Earthquake of 1906 which killed 3,000 people. More recently in 2004, the earthquake that hit 6.0 on the Richter Scale in the Californian town of Parkfield was the sixth one that had been experienced there since the first in 1857, each previous quake approximately 22 years apart. Even as recently as June 2005, California witnessed six earthquakes in a two week span that measured up to 7.2 on the Richter Scale. These tremors were as far north as Crescent City on the very north-western tip of the state and as far south as Anza just above San Diego.

It doesn't matter where you are in the USA, there will always be the threat of hurricanes on the east coast, twisters in the central and mid-western areas and earthquakes on the west coast. But the new concern is now focused on the predicted tsunamis that threaten New York and Washington and the entire Eastern Seaboard from as far away as the Canary Islands in Spain and the potential destruction of Los Angeles and San Francisco from a future Pacific tsunami. We know it's going to happen at some point but like the 159 people killed on Hawaii in 1946 during what is now called the April Fools Day Tsunami, many east and west coast dwellers prefer to ignore it or treat it as something that won't ever happen. But then again, no-one expected that a tsunami would arrive in Thailand the day after Christmas in 2004 and kill 300,000 people in its deadly and relentless onslaught.

I thought I was being teased recently when a friend from Tennessee informed me that moonshine is still alive and kicking in some areas of the USA. However, this is absolutely true and there are still many 'dry counties' in the southern states particularly in the more mountainous regions. Moonshine in the USA was the name given to alcohol that was brewed and sold illegally during the Prohibition years from 1920 to 1933, (an era sometimes referred to as the Dry Movement) when the production, sale and distribution of alcohol was made illegal in this country. Makeshift distilleries would be hidden in the woods or in barns and the liquor would be produced at night, under the 'shine of the moon', with the resulting product sold off in recycled milk or medicine bottles. Oddly enough, the term 'moonshine' is believed to have originated centuries ago when illegal brandy was brought into the Britain by smugglers via the coast of southern England, the pirates dismissing their illegal bounty as *"nothing but the shine of the moon"*, a mere irrelevance, a small trifle. But in the USA, the clandestine practice of taking empty milk bottles to the local grocery store in exchange for 'shine, still goes on in the dry counties where the sale of alcohol continues to remain illegal.

The tradition of tipping in the USA is not limited to restaurants and the percentages given here are generally higher than at home. In the UK, we work on the idea of giving somewhere between 8% and 15% in restaurants but we rarely tip in a bar or in a pub. In America, it falls anywhere between 15-30% in restaurants, depending on the service and all bar service requires at least a dollar to be left on the counter. I was in Las Vegas once with a couple of colleagues attending a television-production exhibition and quite by coincidence, a good friend of mine was also there during that same week and he had just tied the knot with his fiancé. We decided to treat the newly married couple to dinner at the Stratosphere, the casino-hotel that towers high over the Las Vegas Strip. After the meal, I had signed a $420 restaurant bill, rounding it up to $500 to include service, representing approximately 19% in gratuity. I was then abruptly asked by the restaurant's Maitre d' if there had been a problem with the meal. When I replied that on the contrary, it had been a pleasant evening, I was told in no uncertain terms that the tip should be at least 25% and actually, 30% was recommended. He was so forthright and I was so shocked that I ended up giving the required amount, lest I be strong-armed into the kitchen to wash the dishes with my friend and his new bride.

For many years, Americans have been unfairly accused of laziness when it comes to the use of the motor vehicle. The more ambulatory and pedestrianised Europeans have always vilified the USA in their overindulgence when it comes to fuel usage. However, in defence of our Atlantic neighbours, I must point out that in most parts of rural and even suburban America, it is incredibly difficult to get anywhere or do anything without using a vehicle. In England, as in much of Europe, we're often able to walk to the local shops or pubs without the need of a car but in large areas of America, it is almost impossible. Even in Florida, the occasions are rare that you can stroll to the supermarket or to a local restaurant without suffering heat exhaustion or heart failure. Added to this, there is a profound lack of public transport in most areas of the USA. They do not share the enormous choice of national transport services that we enjoy in Europe, of local buses, trains and even underground links so I think we need to do our research before we preach to our American friends. However, transport for the elderly is essential and largely ignored in this country. Only recently, I read about a 94-year-old man, his licence still valid for another three years, who had inadvertently driven his car through the doors of his local bank. He had been trying to park in a handicapped space but his foot had slipped off the brake and onto the accelerator, with the result that his car finally came crashing to rest in the bank's lobby area. Apparently, he had gone to the bank to make a withdrawal and had ended up making a fairly sizeable deposit instead. But the main concern for me is that many very elderly people in the USA are forced to continue driving way beyond the age and the ability that might be considered safe but these people are made to do so, simply because they have no choice but to continue to travel in their cars. The situation can be remedied but the older generation who helped make this country the empire that it is today, are largely ignored in their plight.

In the same way that English politicians can commit all manner of crimes, misdemeanours or indiscretions and return untarnished to greater power, it is also indicative of American society that no matter how far you fall, there is always a way back into the American heart. Martha Stewart exploded into the lives of the American middle classes, an untouchable and perfect hostess who advised and led the entire country on presentation, cuisine, interior decor, housework and everything else from napkin folding to Christmas tree decoration and in effect, she pretty much created a rule book on how to live the American Dream. But this powerful billionaire businesswoman allegedly made the mistake of selling stocks in a company, armed with the knowledge that those stocks were about to take a tumble. It's called insider dealing to the rest of us. She was tried, found guilty and sent to prison and everyone thought that this might be the end of the line for Martha Stewart. However, having done her 'porridge', she has re-emerged from jail, slightly soiled but with a definite grubbiness that has resulted in a new found sex appeal. Prior to her stint in the slammer, I viewed her as this perfect maternal icon, a high priestess of American etiquette that bathed in a whiter than white and almost virgin light but now she seems to have that 'been there, done that' naughty twinkle in her eye. Whatever, I think she looks better for the experience and I should now confess that I really rather like her and what's more, America now seems to love her more than ever.

The practice of unsolicited telephone calls at all times of the day and night in the USA, continues apace. If I thought it was bad in England, then I should have known it might be worse here. At first, I began by gently trying to get rid of the caller but now, as soon as I realise the reason for the intrusion, I immediately terminate the conversation without even a goodbye. There are ways to filter telephone calls by using the government sponsored www.donotcall.gov website but even subscription to this will not rid you of all intruders to your evening. Sometimes, the blocks that are applied to your line to avoid nuisance calls can often result in the barring of incoming international calls and for some reason, there seems to be no way to stop the local Police Benevolence Society from calling, insisting that you make a pledge to their association, so beware.

America is responsible for creating the greatest public marketplace the world has ever seen in that remarkable success story, eBay. It may be true that the man responsible for this company was born in France of Iranian extract, but without doubt, eBay was absolutely born in the USA and is therefore uniquely American. Like all great ideas, there was a simple notion inside Pierre Omidyar's head that whatever it is that you no longer require, or whatever it is that you desperately need, someone, somewhere, wants to buy it from you or sell it to you. It has resulted in the one of the most phenomenal and profitable, international companies the world has ever seen.

Just before my family moved to America, we realised that the cost of shipping everything from our home in Britain to the USA, would be significant, if not astronomical. At the time, my brother alerted me to the potential of using eBay to offload our 'baggage'. It was with some trepidation then, that I set up my eBay account and began listing every single item in our home. To be frank, it was a monumental and at times, absolutely daunting task. From sofas to silverware, from dining tables to table lamps and from brass beds to grandfather clocks, it took three months to finally list and auction all of our worldly possessions but we eventually sold everything in the house, including our cars. In fact, when we arrived on American soil, we had little more than half a dozen suitcases to our name and I don't think I'd ever felt so cleansed and free of all constraints. Anyone who is changing country will need eBay. It's a perfect time in your life to completely de-clutter and start again. And remember, your junk is someone else's pride and joy.

Regardless of the fact that the game of golf was invented and nurtured in Scotland, I am sorry to inform the weather-beaten die-hards of British golf that the real game is now played in America. The USA not only has the best golf courses in world, bar none, they also have the most varied selection on offer in every possible climate condition and more importantly, they have the best customer approach too. I've played on many courses in England, Ireland and Scotland (oddly, never Wales) and although some of the Irish courses are hard to better and many English courses have tried to follow the standards set in the States, I am still confused as to why anyone would want to play on the majority of Scottish courses. This is not an anti-Scottish section as I'm grateful to them for coming up with the game in the first place. It's just that when you look at a world-famous and legendary course like Carnoustie for example, which even at the height of summer, still carries the look of a bleak winter scene, it is difficult to tell where the fairways end and the greens begin, more akin to a piece of farmland. The game in Scotland still seems to be based on the idea that golf should be hard work for the player and that whilst you toil on an unforgiving course, it is mandatory that the accompanying scenery should remain grim and miserable, contemptuous of your very presence.

But having succumbed to the absolute pleasure of playing golf in America, I'm not sure I would want to play again in Great Britain. I'm not saying that there aren't any decent clubs there, of course there are, it's just that I'm not of the opinion that a pastime should be painful. While English clubs continue to frown on their very existence, let alone anyone should dare to use one on a course, I am now accustomed to riding in a buggy where I can store all my bits and pieces and from where I can idly watch the beauty of the surroundings from the comfort of a padded seat. I like not having to carry or drag round a set of clubs and other necessary paraphernalia and I like the breeze in my face from whizzing down the fairway in my E-Z-GO. I also like the fact that everything about the American courses is manicured. The grass is green, the water is blue, the greens are perfect and the landscape is immaculate. Golf should be pleasure, not pain. But more importantly than anything else, when you pull into a golf club in the USA, they are actually pleased to see you. You are a welcome contributor and participant to their club and they are glad to have you play there. This is generally the opposite of the sometimes hostile reaction at most English clubs. Let's be honest here, the backward-thinking old fogies that run the UK establishments, mostly in a pitifully non-businesslike and loss-making fashion, don't really want you to even think about venturing into their private kingdoms in the first place.

The truth is, if you want to play golf and have fun while you do it, America is the best place in the world for it. There are just too many outstanding courses in this country to even start to think about listing them, private and public. Of the more famous courses, Pebble Beach, Kiawah Island, Torrey Pines, Sawgrass, Bay Hill, Myrtle Beach and the infamous Augusta National spring to mind, all available for the public to play on except the latter, which really doesn't welcome anyone at all, save for its own brethren. Added to the availability of outstanding courses all over the USA, you can also choose to play in any weather condition that suits your game and never have to suffer the inadequacies of temporary tees and greens as is often seen for six months of each year in Britain.

As a final note on golf, the terms 'bogey' 'par', 'birdie' and 'eagle' are used in identical fashion in both the UK and the USA, but the rare and beautiful 'albatross' doesn't appear to have made the trip across the Atlantic. For some odd reason, an albatross here is referred to as a 'double-eagle', an anomaly I can't quite fathom. This uniquely American term, meaning that a hole has been completed in three strokes under par, has the same definition as an albatross has in the UK. But to my mind, if an eagle universally describes a hole played at two shots under par, then surely a double-eagle would suggest that the hole was completed four strokes under? However, for me it's probably a moot point as I've never yet had the opportunity to shout "Albatross", my score-card littered more with double-bogeys than double-eagles.

I believe that the word 'icon' might have been singularly invented for the USA. America is full of them and new ones seem to be created every day. John Lennon once said *"Before Elvis there was nothing"* and in iconic terms as well as in originality, he was right. As Elvis Presley became an icon for the American music industry, his image and recordings quickly became commodities to be traded on, even decades after his death. Hollywood is the icon of the film industry and Hollywood icons are the film stars that it produces. Billions of dollars have been subsequently earned from the iconic images of long since departed silver-screen legends, Marilyn Monroe and James Dean. In America, even the nation's currency, the mighty dollar bill is an icon of success and prosperity. The Nike brand, another pioneering success story of 20th century America is now solely recognisable by the simple and effective use of the Nike 'tick' while the McDonalds golden arch (yellow M) is equally iconic. However, there is one image which is universally accepted as portraying the very essence of America, the legendary Coca-Cola logo. This beverage, which was originally a recipe that combined coca leaves and kola nuts, has become one of the most recognisable brands anywhere in the world. In fact, the logo was created in 1885 by the company's then bookkeeper, Frank Mason Robinson who was blessed with impeccable, almost calligraphic handwriting and who also preferred the Spencerian font, popular at the time in 'the professions'. It is a tribute to his design and vision that the Coca-Cola logo has remained unchanged more than 120 years on.

When considering what might immediately come to mind, should we think of icons that typify the British psyche, the same old ancient and clichéd pictures of Big Ben, Buckingham Palace, Harrods, London taxis, double-decker buses and the inimitable red tunics and black busbies of the Queen's Guard are the images that habitually spring to mind. The odd thing is that all of these iconic symbols are really only representative of London itself and not of the whole of Great Britain. The focus on London rather than Britain as a whole, reminds me of the story of an American tourist who, whilst completing her immigration card on a flight to London's Heathrow Airport, discreetly asked a stewardess, "Is it London, England or England, London?"

Finally, given the fact that this country is really a set of fifty countries that in relative terms, all fall under the same flag, it is intriguing to me how each state has such wildly differing rules and laws. In England, we all live under one set of rules and because of that, it is easier to abide by the law and consequently the bureaucracy is kept at a sensible level. In America, not only do the taxes vary from state to state as I've already mentioned, but the laws that govern your very existence also differ wildly, depending where you live. As an example, some states maintain the death penalty as a punishment for murder, while in others it is against the law to set a mousetrap without a license. In Alabama, it's illegal to play dominoes on Sundays while in parts of Connecticut, it is against the law for a man to kiss his wife on the Sabbath. English is not a legal language in Illinois, but American is. In some states, the mistreatment of a man's mother-in-law isn't grounds for divorce while in one Arizona town, it is illegal to drive a car in reverse. You can be fined for flirting in New York, sleeping with your shoes on in North Dakota and only the missionary position is deemed legal in Florida. The fact that none of these laws are ever really enforced is not an issue but in my mind, they show wonderful extremes of silliness and provide great entertainment at no-one's personal expense and I like that.

However, it would be grossly unfair to omit mention of some of the more obscure and absurd laws in Great Britain before closing this chapter. Whilst the placing of a postage stamp in an upside down position on an envelope is effectively an act of treason in Britain, it is also against the law for a Member of Parliament to wear a suit of armour in the House of Commons. It may be illegal in England for a woman to be topless in public but it isn't if she happens to be working in a tropical fish shop in Liverpool. But my own personal favourite, which I discovered around twenty years ago, is the fact that in the English town of Chester, it is apparently still legal to shoot a Welshman using a bow and arrow, provided that the act occurs within the city walls and it's after midnight and before sunrise, all of which might be cold comfort to any Welsh inhabitants of Chester.

Chapter 29

The Little Things In Life

There are bound to be many things that the British migrant will yearn for, once settled in the USA. Initially, there is so much that is new and so much to get done that the things we miss most in life, will not be immediately apparent. From the outset, this period will feel like an extended vacation but after a while, we'll experience emotional recollections of home and these might be memories of a walk in the local park or even something as simple as a favourite chocolate bar. Conversely, there are just as many things that are easy to forget, be it the misery of supermarket shopping, the relentless grey skies, our ridiculously high-priced homes or even the fact that we are forced to suffer an unelected Scottish Prime Minister.

All of the things that we start to miss are often of minor importance but some of them can prove to be extremely precious to our greater sanity. When we first arrived in America, my own selfish mind was more concerned about being able to find PG Tips teabags, Heinz salad cream, Branston pickle and Cadbury's chocolate but I needn't have worried as all of these items are mostly available in the British section of the local supermarket. I also realised how much importance I had previously placed on the great satellite orbiting Earth that effortlessly delivered Sky Sports to my television at home in England, until I discovered that pretty much everything I wanted to see was available on cable in the USA.

But other memories are less tangible and therefore more difficult and sometimes even, impossible to replace. A lot depends on whereabouts you settle in America but for me, the English seasons are now a dim and distant memory. I sometimes even miss moaning about the weather. I miss early spring and late autumn walks in the local woods with the dogs, wrapped up against the cold, marvelling at the ice crystals that dangle on the fences and then arriving home with cherry coloured cheeks to a roaring log fire and a cup of tea with McVitie's chocolate biscuits. Of course I know this sounds a little Blyton-esque in description but it's truly an image I remember and one for which I occasionally yearn.

There are moments when I wish I could stroll down to the local village and buy a Cornish pasty or sausage roll from one of England's ever-present high street bakeries. I also wish I could buy the Sunday papers on the way so I could waste away the remainder of the day, struggling with the seemingly endless sections devoted to news, fashion, money, lifestyle and sports.

I frequently want to switch the television on and hear a BBC newsreader's voice, giving me the latest world news without the associated fear-mongering, characteristic of most American news anchors. I want to hear unbiased and non-partisan reporting and I want to know the facts and not just opinion. Well, that's my opinion anyway.

I miss the different coloured British banknotes that make it easy for everyone to see the value of the bill they're handing over. I even miss seeing the Queen's face on my money although I don't know if Charles will ever have the same effect. In fact, I miss Prince Charles and I miss the tabloid newspapers that continue to mock someone who actually thinks outside the box, somewhat of an achievement given the circumstances of a royal existence.

Everyday things are taken for granted when living in the UK. Whether we go to the library or make a trip to the pub, often we will walk. The simple pleasure of walking to the shops is an everyday experience for many in England. It doesn't happen much in America. It seems that every trip is by car.

While communication should remain the bedrock of any society, most Americans would probably agree that even basic communication in the States is not as easy as it once was. I suppose there is some comfort in that I can understand most accents in England, with the possible exception of those from Dudley or Wolverhampton but I have to listen intently to translate what is being imparted to me on the other end of the telephone in America. I even have to make a selection between English and Spanish, prior to moving forward with the call.

I don't miss *Benny Hill* or *Hyacinth Bucket* but the Americans love talking about them as being our greatest comedy exports. Of course I did once enjoy John Inman and Mollie Sugden in *Are You Being Served?* but that was when we had two-channel television so absolutely anything was acceptable at that time. I find it hard to join in with my American friends' unbridled enjoyment of our worst sit-coms, at times nodding in agreement that these programmes are veritable comedic masterpieces, just to avoid offending anyone here. However, I do miss the outstanding brilliance of programmes like *Fawlty Towers* and *Blackadder* but because of the profound Englishness of this genre of comedy, Americans generally don't get how intensely clever and funny these types of programmes are. The dialogue between Rowan Atkinson's *Captain Blackadder* and Stephen Fry's *Captain Darling* is some of the best I've ever seen performed. But as with all things in film and television, the impeccable performance is founded on brilliantly original scripts.

Humour is a key ingredient in any form of communication and the humour found in America is in many ways, similar and different to our own brand of comedy. A fart sound will always be funny in any language, but no matter how much indulgence there is at lavatory level, there is still a requirement to stretch the mind a little further. But there are many types of American humour that I absolutely enjoy. The sophisticated and often politically incorrect humour from the likes of Jerry Seinfeld, Bill Cosby and Bill Maher always brings a smile to my face, even if the latter's recent assertion that *"England is a second rate country"* is just a little wide of the mark. The hilarious and self-deprecating styles of comedians and satirists like Jackie Mason are a breath of fresh air too and bearing in mind that the Jewish race has an image historically more associated with finance than with comedy, I've often wondered if Jewish people are so funny because of, or in spite of their religion.

In many ways and at many times, I wish I was less selfish and that my glasses weren't so rose-tinted about all things English but the truth is, I'm human and like the rest of my race, I will always retain an emotion and an ideal based on where I was born, how I was raised and what has been taught to me. It's easy to avoid understanding the many and varied cultures that aren't bound by our own parameters of what we believe to be the rules of life. It's too easy to throw disdain at a faith or belief that doesn't exist in harmony next to the ones that we ourselves choose to follow and it's ignorant to adopt an attitude that only looks at the broader strokes of how every civilisation survives and thrives so differently to our own. Truth be told though, my time living in America has made me more acutely aware of my own roots in England. But if before moving to America, I had thought there would be nothing that would shock me or that there would be situations or ideals that I couldn't agree with, then I would have been a complete fool to have come to America in the first place.

So whether you believe that Jesus will be our eventual saviour or that Polygamy is an okay way of life, or whether every man should have the right to bear arms and that the only legal immigrants are the current tenants of this world and all others are ne'er-do-wells who should be repelled at any cost, there is no doubt in my mind that the USA is a country of such exciting diverseness and opportunity that no matter what your race or creed, there is something here for everyone. No matter how many idiosyncrasies you find in the USA, the one thing that I discovered almost immediately when I first came to the USA is that from a personal standpoint, I like America and more importantly, I like Americans. Plainly speaking, they treat me as one of their own and it's something I appreciate more than anything else about living here.

But is it still possible to define The American Dream and is it such a very different idealistic way of life than it was forty, even fifty years ago? Does it even really still exist? Could the term 'The American Dream' itself be oxymoronic and is this overused expression that depicts a perfect life existence, more applicable to other countries? Perhaps Italy, Switzerland, France or even England? While it's now a subject for debate, I still believe that America has the greater potential to persist with that fabled ideal in the future.

When looking at the phenomenal success of this country and its happy band of colourful inhabitants, from the time that the Pilgrims first landed in 1620 through to the early 1960s, then there is little that equals the incredible achievements of this unique nation. But if you look at the uncomfortably negative aspects of American life today; increased pollution, lack of universal healthcare, inflated economy, increased obesity, manufacturing decline and ultimately, the slow deterioration of the general quality of life during the last forty years, then my real worry is how this trend may radically affect America and its inhabitants during the next twenty years.

However, even when taking into consideration any of the doubts raised in this final chapter, I would never want to deter anyone from their desire to taste something different, to try something new or simply to explore the challenge and excitement of a different way of living within a completely new set of rules. The reality is, I still remain living in a country that will never feel like home, in fact couldn't ever feel like home, and my lifestyle will always retain the feeling of a somewhat fabricated existence. But I still choose to continue living here, partly because of a better quality of life than can be found in Britain and partly because there is a magical notion in my head that there is always something new to be learned and discovered here.

Since we moved to the USA, the subject of vacations is rarely raised. We've been to different states for a few days at a time, but more out of curiosity than any real need to de-stress. In England, the next trip abroad was a perennial subject; no sooner would we return from a vacation than we'd be planning the next one, such was the constant desire to get away. The fact is, the only way to really enjoy living in England is to be wealthy enough to leave often.

But changing the country in which we live is so much more radical than the adoption of a vacation spot as a year-round Nirvana. It's not a step to take lightly and if it doesn't work out, it will be an incredibly expensive mistake and any regrets or blame, may linger for years after. There are many things to consider, whether the ability to work and financially and practically survive in such different surroundings or even the emotional struggle that may follow once a 6000 mile barrier is placed between you and your family in Great Britain. Remember, when you go away on vacation, your family knows you'll be back in a couple of weeks but when you emigrate, it may be years before you see each other again. Some families have extremely close relationships and those personal ties may cause so much emotional upset that it might ultimately stop you from moving forward at all. In our case, my immediate family members thought long and hard on whether or not we should move to the USA and the decision-making process endured tearful and distressing moments on more than one occasion.

There is one other extremely important point to remember. When you have finally made the move to live in another country, it is highly likely that you'll have an immediate yearning to return home, possibly even after just a couple of months. This will happen primarily because of the things that you miss but also because you will find it initially difficult to adapt to your new

250

surroundings. Many people are made painfully aware of how reliant they've become on the support of friends, neighbours or family members and the shock of that loss is sometimes too much to bear. Therefore, it is vitally important to allow at least a couple of years in your new country before giving up and heading home. I was given this advice by others who had emigrated before me and it is probably the one thing above all else, that has helped us adapt to life in America.

At the start of this book, I stated that if I had known what pitfalls and hurdles lay ahead of me or if I had realised how difficult and time-consuming the whole immigration process would be, then I doubt I would have bothered emigrating in the first place. However, hindsight is not always a valuable commodity and sometimes it's better to push on regardless of the difficulties you may face and in spite of any negativity you may encounter. Fortunately for my family, the long, arduous and often emotional transition of moving from England to settle in the USA, worked out immensely well and fifteen years after I had first stepped foot on American soil, the childhood daydreams of an eight-year-old English boy who yearned to live in his televised vision of The American Dream, were finally realised.

About The Author.

Nick Robson was born in 1961, in the East End of London, England. After a brief spell as a recording artist with RCA Records in the late 1970s, he then spent the next 25 years working in the film & television industry in London's Soho district. In 2005, he moved with his family to the United States where he still continues to write music and literature. He is married with one daughter and one step-daughter.

To contact the author, please email any comments or questions to
nickrobson@btinternet.com